Dedicated to My Family:
Tehya, Ian, and Peter McIntosh

PRESENCE OF THE
INFINITE

PRESENCE OF THE

INFINITE

THE SPIRITUAL EXPERIENCE OF
BEAUTY, TRUTH, AND GOODNESS

STEVE McINTOSH

This publication has been generously supported by
The Kern Foundation

QUEST
BOOKS

Theosophical Publishing House
Wheaton, Illinois * Chennai, India

Quest Books
Theosophical Publishing House
PO Box 270
Wheaton, IL 60187-0270

www.questbooks.com

Cover image: Lynn Watson/Shutterstock.com
Cover design by Rolf Busch
Typesetting by Datapage

Library of Congress Cataloging-in-Publication Data

McIntosh, Steve.
The presence of the infinite: the spiritual experience of beauty, truth, and goodness / Steve McIntosh—First Quest edition.
        pages   cm
Includes bibliographical references and index.
ISBN 978-0-8356-0941-8
1. United States—Religion. 2. Spirituality—United States. 3. Experience (Religion).
4. Leadership—Religious aspects. I. Title.
BL2525.M4224 2015
204—dc23   2015006728

Printed in the United States of America

5   4   3   *   15   16   17   18   19   20

CONTENTS

CONTENTS

CONTENTS

ACKNOWLEDGMENTS

I wish to offer my heartfelt thanks to my friend and neighbor Jeff Salzman, who provided invaluable encouragement and guidance in the writing of this book. Further, I need to acknowledge progressive German theologian Hans Küng, whose wisdom served as a guiding light for the birth of these ideas. I also wish to acknowledge my friends Brian McLaren, Morgan McKenna, Bruce Sanguine, Ross Hostetter, Mary Hostetter, and Wayne Gunther, who helped nurture these ideas as a group. And special thanks to my friends and readers Jeff Wattles, Lindsay Moore, Michael Zimmerman, and Tom Thresher. I am also grateful to my endorsers and friends John Mackey, Craig Hamilton, Terry Patten, Andrew Cohen, and Carter Phipps. Also special thanks to Tony Schwartz, whose insightful method facilitated my creative process. Thanks to my friend and content editor Byron Belitsos and to my able line editor Will Marsh. Also thanks to my agent John White and my publishers Sharron Dorr and Richard Smoley. Finally, I must express eternal gratitude to my wife Tehya McIntosh, without whom my writing would be impossible.

INTRODUCTION

This book is about spiritual experience, which can be understood as an encounter with the presence of the infinite within our finite universe of time and space. While the human experience of spirit takes many forms and can be conceived of in a wide variety of ways, I have found that this idea of spirit as the "presence of the infinite" sheds a considerable amount of light on this complex subject. Gaining a deeper understanding of spiritual experience is important because as we come to better appreciate what spiritual experience is and how it works, this enhances our ability to have such experiences more abundantly and to use them more effectively for our personal growth and for our service to others.

My foundational premise, based on my own experience and the reported experience of millions of others in both ancient and modern contexts, is that spirit by whatever name is real and that it is possible for humans to make authentic contact with it. The question of what spirit is in itself, of course, is subject to debate. But the idea that spiritual experience is—actually and literally—an experience of that which is infinite or transcendent may find agreement among many who are open-minded about the possibility of some kind of spiritual reality.

All humans crave spiritual experience (properly understood), whether they know it or not. Indeed, an encounter with transcendence is an end in itself. Such experiences can be thrilling and delightful; they can be illuminating and inspiring; they can be heartwarming and comforting; and they can even be awesome and terrifying. But as we will explore, what all authentic spiritual experiences have in common is this connection to a *quality of being* that is best described as *infinite*. Within the context of spiritual experience, the idea of the infinite includes not only a *mathematical infinity of quantity*—boundless, endless, unlimited, immeasurable, and eternal—but

1

also a *metaphysical infinity of quality*—unified, whole, complete, perfect, self-sufficient, and largely beyond definition or conception. Yet even though the infinite is largely transconceptual and elusive, it can be directly experienced by humans.

For those who have experienced spirit personally and directly there can be little doubt about the authenticity of this reality. And even those who claim not to be acquainted with spiritual experience have nonetheless had such experiences, whether they are labeled "spiritual" or not. Everyone who has felt the power of truth, the kindness of goodness, or the loveliness of beauty has had an experience of spirit. The only reason such common yet profound experiences are not universally identified as spiritual is that our collective understanding of spiritual experience remains underdeveloped. However, recent advances in the philosophy of consciousness are now making it possible to understand this important subject with new depth and clarity.

Spiritual experience is important not only because it is an intrinsically valuable end in itself, bringing joy, happiness, and a greater sense of wellbeing. Spiritual experience is also important because it causes us to grow. The experience of spirit evolves our consciousness, develops our character, and makes us more real. Our experiences of spirit, however, are not only personally beneficial; they can also benefit others by inspiring us to share our gifts and bring spiritual experience into the lives of our fellows.

In fact, history reveals that increasing the quantity and quality of spiritual experience in a given social context results in cultural evolution. In other words, spiritual experience, broadly understood, is what causes consciousness to evolve. And when consciousness evolves among a critical mass of people, their larger culture also evolves in the process. Our personal encounters with a transcendent or infinite dimension of reality can therefore have indirect political implications. Accordingly, as I will argue, deepening our understanding of what spiritual experience is and how it can be fostered in ourselves and others is one of the most direct ways we can make the world a better place.

Much has been written about spiritual experience in academic, religious, and even popular contexts. But as of the time of this writing the most famous and influential book on spiritual experience remains *The Varieties of Religious Experience* by American psychologist and philosopher William James. First published in 1902, *Varieties* is remarkably prescient of many of the developments and controversies that would subsequently appear within spiritual and religious culture during the last century. And while progress has been made by both scholars and spiritual visionaries since James first penned his cogent insights over a hundred years ago, most of the literature in the field continues to be framed in terms of James's focus on mysticism. But as we will see, while mystical experiences are certainly a significant kind of spiritual experience, other kinds of spiritual experience can be had more frequently and used more effectively to develop our characters and bear spiritual fruit.

How I Came to Write This Book

Although I was not raised in any religious tradition, throughout my life I have consistently pursued the experience of spirit, and have found it in many places. As a young man I began finding it in California's wilderness—in the fleeting rays of sunset on the mountaintop and in the delicate mist of the waterfall. I found it in the depths of psychedelic journeys and in the stillness of meditation and prayer. I even discovered it in the light that shone out from the pages of revelatory texts. Then as I grew older, spirit came to me through intimate relationships— in the gleam in my beloved's eye and the gentle touch of her love. My beautiful sons were also messengers of spirit; their fresh innocence and zest for life caused love to blossom inside me anew. To this day, this feeling of fatherly love connects me with spirit more deeply than anything else, bringing me into direct communion with the Creator of the universe itself. Yet I continue to cultivate the experience of spirit in all its many sources—even in the writing of this book.

Over the years my ability to experience spirit has grown through a series of distinct awakenings. Beginning in adolescence and continuing periodically throughout my life, there have been times when I felt touched by grace. These pivotal moments of awakening produced a strong sense of having been reborn into a new life of fresh possibilities and expanded potential. And through these experiences I have found my calling as a writer of spiritual philosophy.

As a teenager growing up in Los Angeles in the 1970s, I was attracted to the counterculture and became involved with some of the alternative forms of progressive spirituality that were gaining popularity at the time. Even at that young age I felt strongly identified with progressive spiritual culture and knew that this would be an important theme in my life. However, I also knew that to become an effective agent of this emerging form of post-traditional spirituality, I needed to acquire real-world experience and establishment credentials. This led me to business school and law school in the 1980s, where I developed writing and thinking skills while continuing to practice my spirituality in relative isolation.

During this same period, as the countercultural momentum of the sixties and seventies faded, progressive spirituality went underground, so to speak. But then beginning in the 1990s there was a palpable quickening in alternative spiritual culture across America. At first, it seemed to me and many others to be the cultural awakening we had been anticipating since the 1970s. I thus felt a strong call to make a contribution to this exciting new development. So I left my job as a corporate executive and started a company whose explicit mission was to design and manufacture "cultural artifacts of the spiritual renaissance." I named the company Now & Zen, with the ambition of intuiting and expressing the tenets of the art movement that I felt would inevitably accompany the emergence of this new spiritual culture.

Yet, as the millennium approached I became increasingly disillusioned with New Age culture due to its seeming inability to provide spiritual leadership for the larger society. Despite its popularity, the magical thinking that pervaded much of progressive spirituality prevented it from being taken seriously by the mainstream. It thus eventually became clear that the spiritual renaissance my friends and I had hoped for would not be achieved by progressive spirituality alone.

My dissatisfaction with progressive spirituality caused me to look for alternative sources of potential cultural uplift, which led to my involvement with the emerging integral philosophy movement. And for more than a decade now, integral philosophy has been the primary focus of my working life, resulting in my 2007 book, *Integral Consciousness*, and my 2012 book, *Evolution's Purpose*. While this integral or evolutionary perspective has emerged largely out of progressive spirituality, as I will show, this new way of seeing transcends the limitations of progressive spiritual culture and illuminates the way forward into a more mature and sophisticated form of spiritual understanding known as *evolutionary spirituality*. This evolutionary approach to the reality of spirit enhances existing forms of spiritual practice, while also introducing new methods and techniques for experiencing spirit. Indeed, as I hope will become clear, evolutionary spirituality holds the potential to provide more effective forms of spiritual leadership for our society overall.

THE RISE OF EVOLUTIONARY SPIRITUALITY

Evolutionary spirituality is being born out of the growing realization that the scientific and historical story of our origins actually presents a profound spiritual teaching about the purpose of the universe and our place within it. Evolutionary spirituality, however, is not a religion or belief system. Rather, it represents a new level of cultural agreement that can include and uplift many of the existing forms of spirituality found in contemporary culture. In other words, evolutionary spirituality aspires to create a widely agreeable public form of spirituality that can provide a greater sense of solidarity and cohesion for those living in the developed world, while simultaneously retaining pluralism and making abundant room for a diversity of convictions about what is ultimately real. In short, evolutionary spirituality endeavors to transcend and include what is currently on offer in the spiritual marketplace of ideas through a new approach to spiritual teaching and practice.

Evolutionary spirituality, as I understand it, transcends previous forms of spirituality through two crucial insights that serve as its foundation. The first insight comes from an enhanced recognition of the spiritual nature and behavior of the intrinsic values of beauty, truth, and goodness. And the second insight involves what is coming to be known as the "spiritual teachings" of evolution itself. As I argue in chapter 2, the scientific truths of cosmological and biological evolution, together with the historical truths of humanity's cultural evolution, reveal a truth so comprehensive and significant as to have spiritual implications of its own. Properly interpreted, the evolutionary unfolding of nature and history, as well as the evolution of human consciousness itself, represents a kind of revelation that serves as a useful criterion for evaluation—a reliable standard of measurement—for practically all spiritual truth claims.

Moreover, through the practice of evolutionary spirituality we become agents of evolution—emissaries of the future—whose mission is the improvement of the human condition. And the experience and creation of that which is spiritually real—that which is beautiful, true, and good—is ultimately how we make things genuinely better. In other words, we become direct participants in evolution's unfolding—the process by which something *more* keeps coming from something *less*— as we work to increasingly perfect ourselves and our world. Thus, those who are on an evolutionary spiritual path recognize that their purpose in life is to participate in the gradual perfection of the evolving universe of nature, culture, and self.

Integral Philosophy and the Evolution of Worldviews

As mentioned above, evolutionary spirituality itself is arising as part of a larger cultural emergence known as the integral or evolutionary worldview, which is founded on the insights and discoveries of integral philosophy. This philosophy has gradually emerged through the efforts of a line of distinguished thinkers that includes G. W. F. Hegel, Henri Bergson, Alfred North Whitehead, Pierre Teilhard de Chardin, Sri Aurobindo, Jean Gebser, Ken Wilber, Holmes Rolston, and many others. Although these founders of integral philosophy differ on numerous points, they have all endeavored to discern the spiritual meaning of evolution overall.

While this book is more cultural analysis and theological reflection than philosophy per se, integral philosophy informs the arguments and conclusions presented. So although prior familiarity with integral philosophy is not required, one fundamental integral concept needs to be introduced here at the beginning. This key concept concerns the evolution of worldviews—the sequential emergence of values-based stages of human cultural development.[1]

Integral philosophy's view of cultural evolution sees history as unfolding according to a clearly identifiable *developmental logic*, or cross-cultural pattern, that underlies the growth of human society. This developmental logic is not understood as a "deterministic law of history" or as implying a strictly unidirectional course of cultural development, but it does reveal a recurring theme in humanity's narrative story. The unfolding of this theme or pattern has produced a sequential series of cultural stages or levels that form a dialectical structure within human history. The most obvious and widely accepted example of this stage structure can be recognized in the distinct, historically significant worldviews most frequently referred to as *modernism* and *traditionalism*.

Regarding the worldview of traditionalism, history makes clear that prior to the Enlightenment the majority of the world's population was divided among the great religious civilizations. These are the worldviews identified as Christianity, Islam, Buddhism, Hinduism, Confucianism, and others. While there were, of course, major differences between these civilizations, there were also many remarkable similarities. And these similarities allow us to classify these diverse religious worldviews together under the general heading of the *traditional* stage of development. Contemporary traditionalists value family life, lawful authority, self-sacrifice, and the sanctity of their beliefs. Although every traditional worldview has been significantly impacted and modified by the developments of modernity, this stage of cultural development continues to define reality for billions of people alive today. Even in the developed world, the traditional worldview provides the cultural center of gravity for significant minorities who give more credence to scripture than to science.

Regarding the worldview of modernism, history also makes clear that beginning in the seventeenth century a radically new, reason-based worldview emerged, which can now be identified as the *modernist* stage of cultural evolution. Like the traditional worldviews that preceded it, modernism is a complex structure of value agreements that frame a well-defined view of nature, history, and what it means to live a good life. Modernist values include personal achievement, financial prosperity, individual liberty, democratic government, scientific reasoning, and higher education. The values of the modernist stage are distinct from and in many ways antithetical to the values of the traditional stage. And the ongoing tension between the enduring traditional level and the spectacularly successful modernist level reveals the structure of these dialectically related stages of historical development.

Although there are many ways to divide up the course of human history and a variety of competing stage theories, few will disagree that traditionalism and modernism are authentic stages of cultural development. Like practically all forms of evolution, cultural evolution unfolds by discrete, emergent steps rather than along a seamless continuum of growth.

To paraphrase developmental psychologist Jean Piaget, there is no development that lacks a structure, and the development of human civilization is no exception. I am introducing these worldview structures here at the beginning because I will be using the words *traditional* and *modernist* as defined terms to describe these stages of cultural evolution. And to this list I must add one additional defined term: the controversial concept of *postmodernism.*

While the word *postmodern* has been used in a narrower sense to describe art movements or critical forms of academic discourse, integral philosophy uses this term more broadly as a general description of the distinct cultural worldview that has emerged beyond modernism in many parts of the developed world. Those who identify with this progressive postmodern worldview, sometimes called the "cultural creatives," ascribe to a well-defined set of values that contrasts with both traditionalism and modernism. And the clear identification of this worldview that has now emerged beyond mainstream modernity is a crucial element of integral philosophy. So even though the term *postmodern* has baggage, the other potential terms are even more problematic. *Postmodernism* has accordingly become the preferred defined term for this worldview within the intellectual community of integral philosophy, and it is thus the word I will use in this book to describe this relatively new countercultural worldview.

While postmodernism includes a wide diversity of outlooks and beliefs, it does cohere as a recognizable worldview structure, showing many similarities to the historically significant worldviews that have preceded it. Like modernism and traditionalism, the postmodern worldview provides people with a sense of identity and thus creates strong loyalties to its perspectives. And following the pattern of the rise of previous worldviews, postmodern values stand in antithesis to the values of the existing culture from which they arose. Postmodernists are generally united by their reverence for the natural environment, by their concern for social justice, and by their desire for self-actualization, or spiritual growth.

With the rise of postmodern values comes a rejection of the stale materialistic values of modernism and the chauvinistic and oppressive values of traditionalism.

However, as with the rise of modernism and traditionalism, the emergence of the postmodern worldview has also brought new problems and pathologies. Postmodernists can be prone to narcissism, value relativism, a return to magical or mythical thinking, and intense forms of antimodernism that threaten to undermine the social foundations upon which postmodern culture itself ultimately depends.

A rough overview of the characteristics of these three major developmental stages is provided in chart 1. But notwithstanding this simplified chart, it is important to emphasize that these worldview structures are exceedingly subtle and complex. And it is possible for the same person to make meaning using more than one worldview, depending on the circumstances.

In America, the three major worldviews of traditionalism, modernism, and postmodernism each vie for the allegiance of the population, with modernists in the majority with approximately 50 percent, followed by traditionalists with approximately 30 percent and postmodernists with perhaps as much as 20 percent, as shown in figure 1. These demographic estimates have been arrived at through extensive research on both the psychology of individuals and the sociology of large groups.[2] Yet we don't need social science to confirm these cultural realities. America's "culture war" is evident on practically every evening's news broadcasts.

According to integral philosophy, these stages of cultural evolution naturally emerge over the course of history as people work to improve their social conditions. And when people try to improve their conditions they often end up improving their definition of improvement itself, which results in the appearance of new systems of values and new frames of reality. Yet integral philosophy also recognizes additional cultural and psychological lines of development besides values and worldviews, such as cognitive or emotional lines of development, which are not directly tied

Stages of Worldview Development

Historical Timeline: →

Earlier "Pretraditional" worldviews ←	Traditional Worldview	Modernist Worldview	Postmodern Worldview	Future → "Post-postmodern" Wordviews
	Faith in a higher order, black and white sense of morality, self-sacrifice for the sake of the group	Birth of reason, progress through science and technology, rise of democracy	Birth of environmentalism, multiculturalism, and a new spiritual sensitivity	
Cultural Contributions	• Sense of duty • Honors traditions • Strong faith • Focus on family • Law and order	• Science and technology • Meritocracy • Middle class • Belief in progress	• Environmental priority • Race and gender equality • Worldcentric morality	
Examples in Culture	• Traditional religions • Patriotism • Conservativism • Military organizations	• Corporations • Modern science • Mainstream media • Professional sports	• Progressive culture • Critical academia • Environmental movement	
Types of Organization	• Feudalism • Dictatorships • Bureaucracy	• Democracy • Corporations • Strategic alliances	• Democratic socialism • Consensus committees	
Exemplary Leaders	• Winston Churchill • Pope Francis • Rick Warren • Confucius	• Thomas Jefferson • Charles Darwin • Thomas Edison • John F. Kennedy	• Mohandas Gandhi • Martin L. King, Jr. • John Muir • John Lennon	
Potential Pathologies	• Rigid intolerance • Dogmatism • Fundamentalism • Chauvinism • Denial of science	• Materialism • Nihilism • Unscrupulousness • Selfishness • Exploitiveness	• Value relativism • Narcissism • Denies hierarchy • Dislikes modernism and traditionalism	

Chart 1. Stages of cultural evolution

to a person's worldview. So again, this understanding of the trajectory of cultural evolution is not a unilinear conception.

Admittedly, using a vertical scale of values development to describe American culture is certainly controversial, and claims that postmodern values are somehow more developed or evolved than the values of previous stages may be especially difficult for some readers to accept. Integral philosophy, however, does not claim that later-appearing stages

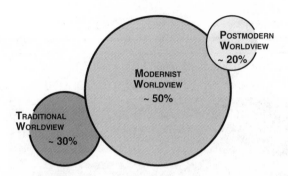

Figure 1. Estimate of each worldview stage's percentage of the
American population

of development are absolutely better in every way. It is thus important
to emphasize (1) that each of these historically significant worldviews is
evolutionarily appropriate for a specific set of life conditions, (2) that the
accomplishments of earlier levels are prerequisite for the achievements
of later appearing levels, (3) that the core values of every worldview have
a crucial and ongoing role to play within our larger culture, and (4) that
every one of these perspectives deserves consideration and respect.

Understanding the dynamics of the *cultural ecosystem* formed by
these stages of development is a primary focus of integral philosophy.
We will return to a consideration of these cultural structures in the context of examining their respective forms of spirituality in chapter 1.

Where I Stand and What I Assume on the Part of the Reader

As mentioned above, I was not raised in a religious family and I have
never subscribed to any organized religion, but I have been on a personal
spiritual path since adolescence. As a result of this background, my spiritual convictions are eclectic; I eschew exclusivism and try to appreciate
spiritual truth wherever I find it. And throughout my life I have found it
abundantly in the wisdom of Christianity, Buddhism, Hinduism, Judaism,

and Taoism, and in indigenous forms of spirituality as well. Further, I have found spiritual truth in nontraditional sources and unaffiliated teachings and even in spontaneous realizations that seemed to come from the very source of my self.

Moreover, I have also found significant spiritual truth in science. Indeed, the stupendous discoveries of the physical sciences serve as an important foundation for evolutionary spirituality, which recognizes that the structure, function, and order of nature is a spiritual teaching in itself. As discussed at the end of chapter 4, evolutionary spirituality seeks to develop a unified understanding of physics and metaphysics through which science and spirituality may become harmonized and increasingly seen as complementary.

Although I will not be contending here for any particular belief system or religion, I am an enthusiastic advocate of evolutionary spirituality. Yet, as we will see, this emerging new form of spirituality endeavors to encompass and integrate the truth teachings of a wide variety of spiritual paths, as well as the truths of science, as noted. Evolutionary spirituality is therefore committed to respectful pluralism and is always willing to discover and include new forms of spiritual truth, whatever their source.

Given that this book is about spiritual experience, it is important to affirm that I believe in God and am coming to know God day by day. But my loyalties are to a postmythic God best understood within a panentheistic theological frame of reference. The term *panentheism* refers to a family of spiritual views that recognize the divine as both immanent and transcendent. According to the *Stanford Encyclopedia of Philosophy*, "Panentheism considers God and the world to be inter-related with the world being in God and God being in the world. It offers an increasingly popular alternative to both traditional theism and pantheism."[3] Although I understand the ultimate source of my spiritual experience primarily as a loving Creator, I have also come to increasingly appreciate the nondual character of ultimate reality. And while these contrasting conceptions of ultimacy may seem to be pointing in different directions, chapter 7 focuses on how the dialectical tension that exists between these two existential forms of spiritual experience (nondual and theistic) may become increasingly synthesized.

Sincerity and transparency are important values for me. But this book is not about me, so I trust this brief disclosure of where I stand will be adequate for our purposes. However, although I want my personal convictions to be transparent, I will not assume any such beliefs on the part of the reader. Yet neither will I assume that readers need to be convinced that spirit by whatever name is real. My previous book *Evolution's Purpose* presented arguments for the tenets of evolutionary spirituality designed to persuade skeptics and even atheists. In the present book, however, I will not argue at that level. In this exploration of spiritual experience I will proceed under the premise that there is a transcendent dimension of reality with which humans can make authentic contact. In fact, it seems clear that the countless people who claim to have had spiritual experiences down through the ages are not entirely mistaken about the reality of such experiences and are otherwise not deluded or deceived.

In the end, there is no denying that *something* is ultimately real. Some conceive of ultimacy merely in terms of themselves, acknowledging nothing bigger or more important than their own well-being. Others understand the ultimate as the God of history, as described by the Abrahamic religions. Still others hold that matter and energy are all there really is and thus conceive of ultimacy as simply the quantitative total of physical reality. Conversely, as we will explore in chapters 5 and 6, those who identify with progressive or alternative forms of spirituality tend to understand the ultimate through a wide variety of different teachings. Some interpret ultimate reality in terms of emptiness or nonduality. Others conceive of it as an impersonal force or creative current. And still others within progressive spiritual culture continue to use the word *God* to refer to the ultimate, even as they understand God in ways that differ from the teachings of traditional religions.

As a result of our culture's divergent and competing convictions about ultimate reality, there is a growing need to improve our comprehension of what the experience of spirit actually is. And through an enlarged understanding of such experience, we may also come to appreciate better the referent of the experience itself. Yet even for those who remain skeptical that humans can know anything ultimate whatsoever, I trust this discussion will be interesting nonetheless.

OVERVIEW OF THE CHAPTERS

Spiritual experience cannot be understood in a vacuum. It is almost always received in the context of some form of spiritual teaching and practice. And almost all spiritual teachings are organized around a specific concept of ultimate reality. Therefore, gaining a deeper understanding of spiritual experience requires us to engage the "hermeneutic circle" of teachings, practices, and the idea of experience itself. Teachings illuminate practice, practice results in experience, and experience in turn refines and develops teachings and practices.

So we begin in chapter 1 by briefly considering the major forms of spiritual teaching currently on offer in contemporary culture. This is followed by chapter 2's discussion of the emerging teachings and practices of evolutionary spirituality, as I understand them. Chapter 2's overview of evolutionary spirituality is necessary because the book's larger goal of strengthening our grasp on spiritual experience is actually made possible through the insights of this new form of spiritual understanding. Then in chapter 3 we begin to examine spiritual experience itself by reviewing the various ways that spiritual experience has been previously conceptualized by both religious and academic commentators. Chapter 3 also considers what the differing perspectives of neuroscience and natural theology have to say about spiritual experience.

Chapter 4 then gets to the heart of the matter by exploring how evolutionary spirituality can expand our comprehension of the spiritual experience that can be found within the intrinsic values of beauty, truth, and goodness. This focus on the beautiful, the true, and the good is intended to bring out the spiritual essence of these qualities so that they can be experienced more abundantly and used more effectively to improve both our lives and the world around us.

In chapters 5, 6, and 7 we turn to the question of what is ultimately real. Chapter 5 identifies an existential polarity within the human experience of spirit itself. In chapter 6, we use the enlarged understanding of ultimate reality that is disclosed by this polarity to constructively critique some of progressive spirituality's most advanced teachings, which leads to chapter 7's exploration of the potential *synthesis* of nondual and theistic teachings of truth that is implied by the existence of this dialectical polarity. As we will see, the achievement of such a spiritual synthesis can pave the way for the cultural advance that is the promise of evolutionary spirituality.

The book concludes with chapter 8, which explores the potential of a new method for evolving consciousness through spiritual experience. The potential for such a method follows from the insight that human evolution can be fostered most effectively through the experience and creation of spiritual realities. As we explore in this final chapter, this new approach promises to solve some of our most pressing social problems by increasing the scope of what people are able to value.

Admittedly, reading this book may be challenging. In the course of writing it I have tried to steer between two poles. On the one hand I have attempted to say something new and meaningful about a very deep subject that has occupied the attention of some of humanity's best minds. And on the other hand I have tried to serve the audience through a discussion that I hope is highly readable, relatively accessible, and interesting throughout. Keeping these challenges in mind, I invite you, dear reader, to go slowly and skip ahead whenever you feel like it.

This exploration of spiritual experience is ultimately intended to increase your ability to recognize, evaluate, and use teachings of spiritual truth from a wide variety of sources. As I hope to show, in its most intrinsic or essential expressions, truth itself is a spiritual experience. So no matter how you may understand spiritual truth here at the beginning, my promise is that by the end your grasp on spiritual truth will be strengthened. I am certainly not claiming to know what is spiritually true in any final or ultimate way, but I do contend that there is real truth and that humans can discover it increasingly as our consciousness evolves. Thus, to the extent that you find some truth in this discussion, I trust you will also find it useful and therefore good, and perhaps even occasionally beautiful.

Chapter One

SPIRITUALITY IN AMERICA:
IN SEARCH OF LEADERSHIP

As I argued in the introduction, and as I hope to show throughout this book, spiritual experience is very important for human life. When spiritual experience is conceived of broadly to include not just mystical states, but also more common experiences of beauty, truth, and goodness, we may begin to see how important such experiences are for the well-being and happiness of each person. And beyond the personal benefits that such experiences bring to individuals, when spiritual experience becomes integrated and infused within a culture the overall vitality and progress of that culture are enhanced.

As discussed in this chapter, spiritual experience cannot be fully appreciated or understood apart from the cultural context in which it occurs. While it is certainly possible to have powerful spiritual experiences without previously accepting or even considering any kind of spirituality, spirit is most often experienced within the framework of some form of spiritual teaching and practice.

Moreover, as explored in chapter 4, getting the most out of our spiritual experiences requires that we share them with others. Stated otherwise, the potential for personal growth inherent in our experiences of spirit is only fully brought out when we share or express such experiences in a way that gives others an authentic spiritual experience of their own. And the effective sharing of spiritual experience usually requires the existence of agreements—cultural agreements framed by the various forms of spirituality on offer in our larger society. Therefore, we will begin the project of gaining a deeper understanding of spiritual experience with an analysis of the teachings and practices that are almost always associated with such experience.

In chapters 5, 6, and 7 we will closely examine the relationship between spiritual experience and specific teachings of spiritual truth. But in this chapter we focus on spirituality in general, and this involves a cultural analysis. The task of making sense of the diverse landscape of spiritual culture is greatly facilitated by the integral or evolutionary perspective, which is particularly adept at such analysis because it views culture through a developmental lens. The evolutionary perspective shows how the evolution of culture is bound up with the evolution of consciousness, and this understanding sheds considerable light on the different forms of spirituality that now exist in the developed world.

As explained in the introduction, consciousness and culture coevolve. And history shows that as consciousness evolves, the human ability to recognize and experience what is real and true evolves along with it. Therefore, because the ability to experience spirit grows and deepens as consciousness evolves, and because the evolution of consciousness is bound up with the evolution of culture, our exploration of spiritual experience begins by examining the existing types of spiritual and religious culture that currently serve as the frames or channels of such experience.

As also discussed in the introduction, the coevolution of human consciousness and culture unfolds through specific stages or levels of development, and in the developed world the most active and relevant cultural stages are recognized by integral philosophy as *traditionalism*, *modernism*, and *postmodernism*. This chapter accordingly focuses on the distinct kinds of spirituality that originate within each of these respective cultural worldviews. As justified in the section after next, I will use defined terms for each of these major forms of spirituality, labeling them *religious spirituality*, *secular spirituality* (or *aspirituality*), and *progressive spirituality*.

Although these distinct types of culture can be found throughout the world, our analysis will concentrate on their contemporary expressions in the United States. Narrowing the focus to the current state of spiritual evolution in America, both in this chapter and throughout the book, will prevent the discussion from becoming overly complex or otherwise bogged down. And limiting the analysis to American culture will also ensure that the discussion does not stray beyond the scope of my own knowledge and experience.

As we consider the major types of spirituality in America, it is important to recognize what each of these contending forms of culture is trying to do. Although they each have a variety of goals, at the most fundamental level they are each attempting to provide cultural and spiritual *leadership* for our civilization. Put differently, the three major forms of spirituality examined in this chapter—religious, secular, and progressive—are each attempting to define what is real and thus what is ultimately true and worthwhile. By defining what is real, true, and good, these forms of spirituality provide leadership for those who follow them. That is, these respective forms of spiritual culture lead by providing their followers with a sense of common identity and by illuminating the values that result in growth and happiness. They also provide leadership by identifying the problems that need solving and the things that need to be improved, thereby setting the direction and supplying the motivation for further cultural evolution.

I thus believe the best way to understand these major kinds of spirituality at a cultural level is to examine the spiritual leadership each is attempting to supply. This focus on spiritual leadership sheds light not only on these existing types of spirituality, but also on evolutionary spirituality, which is now beginning to emerge. Spiritual leadership will thus be an important theme in this book. The relevance that the idea of leadership has for our analysis of spiritual experience will become increasingly evident as the discussion proceeds.

As we will see, evolutionary spirituality includes the best of what has come before, while also going beyond uncritical acceptance or simple relativism. It does this by carefully integrating and synthesizing the achievements of the major forms of spirituality that have preceded it in history. And as with the other forms of spirituality we will consider in this chapter, evolutionary spirituality is likewise attempting to provide spiritual leadership for our society. Evolutionary spirituality's approach to spiritual leadership does not involve trying to persuade people to believe in the same religion or follow the same spiritual path, but it does involve identifying the elements of spirituality that most of us already share.

Providing spiritual leadership by framing a higher-level agreement about the reality of spirit, however, will not be achieved through vague platitudes or by simply identifying common principles so general or abstract that they avoid every possible objection. In order to represent an authentic evolutionary advance, the substance of such a new cultural agreement about spiritual reality must carry forward the best while simultaneously pruning away the worst of each of the preexisting forms of spiritual culture that it seeks to include in its transcendence. Because evolutionary spirituality is emerging primarily out of progressive spirituality, a clear understanding of progressive spirituality is necessary to appreciate both where evolutionary spirituality has come from and what it is trying to transcend. Progressive spirituality itself, however, can be adequately understood only in the context of its current cultural competitors: religious spirituality and secular spirituality.

Keeping these considerations in mind, this chapter explores what it means to provide spiritual leadership on a cultural level. This is followed by an initial description of the three major kinds of spirituality. Then, after describing the broad contours of the contemporary milieu, we next explore the respective limitations and shortcomings of these three major forms of spirituality—limitations that ultimately render each of them incapable of leading our society forward into a new era of solidarity and cooperation. The chapter concludes by considering the potential cultural and political benefits that could result from the provision of more effective forms of spiritual leadership.

What Is Spiritual Leadership?

Those who are already committed to an established religion or a well-defined type of spiritual culture often tacitly assume that more effective spiritual leadership for our society will necessarily involve the ascendency (or rediscovery) of their particular form of belief. Yet most existing forms of American spirituality have been around for a long time and show no signs that they will eventually rise to become the majority outlook, despite their best hopes.

Meanwhile, a significant percentage of Americans, including the majority of America's youth, continue to describe themselves as "spiritual but not religious." While a portion of those who identify themselves this way certainly have affinities with progressive or alternative forms of spirituality, the size of this spiritual but not religious demographic segment is much larger than the current audience of progressive spirituality alone, leading to the conclusion that the majority of those who describe themselves as "spiritual" have not yet found a specific form of spirituality they can identify with or fully participate in. Though most of those in the spiritual but not religious demographic category may understand their spirituality as a personal and even private matter, they nevertheless have definite needs for spiritual leadership, even if they are not always aware of these needs.

Spiritual leadership, of course, can mean many things. The most obvious and visible examples of spiritual leadership can be seen in the figureheads of the world's major religions, such as the Pope or the Dalai Lama. But spiritual leadership can also be demonstrated through heroic political action, as seen in the case of Mahatma Gandhi, Martin Luther King Jr., and Nelson Mandela. Spiritual leadership can also be seen in lives dedicated to selfless service, such as the work of Mother Teresa. And it can be recognized in those who lead sacred causes, such as America's environmental sage John Muir.

Spiritual leadership can also be found in the arts. As a recent example, Jamaican reggae artist Bob Marley has provided spiritual inspiration for millions, especially in the third world. Some of the late music by the Beatles might also be cited as an example of spiritual leadership through music. In fact, spiritual leadership can be recognized in practically any act or communication that produces the experience of spirit in others. And under this definition, just about any meaningful expression of beauty, truth, or goodness could be recognized as a form of spiritual leadership.

In terms of explicit spiritual teaching, however, spiritual leadership in the developed world is most often provided through authors and teachers whose books, lectures, and workshops speak to people's inner needs and produce cultural solidarity around such teachings. Examples of this kind of leadership can be found within every established cultural worldview. For instance, in traditional Christian culture, Pastor Rick Warren's book *The Purpose Driven Life* has sold over thirty million copies. Within secular culture, Oxford professor Richard Dawkins's book *The God Delusion* has sold over two million copies. And within progressive spiritual culture, enlightenment teacher Eckhart Tolle's book *The Power of Now* has sold close to four million copies.

While these popular authors certainly know their subjects, much of their thinking finds its origin in the work of other less popular but more distinguished writers. For example, Warren is standing on the shoulders of C. S. Lewis, Dawkins is following Bertrand Russell, and Tolle has clearly relied on the teachings of D. T. Suzuki and Ramana Maharshi in his writing. So although a good deal of spiritual leadership has been provided to America's masses by the authors of the bestselling books mentioned above, it is important to acknowledge that the most significant kinds of spiritual leadership are not always the most popular.

The subject of spiritual leadership could obviously fill an entire book of its own, and we will be returning to this topic frequently as the discussion unfolds. But by citing the work of these popular authors and considering the common needs that these "thought leaders" are fulfilling for their readers, we may get an initial idea of the function of spiritual leadership and the goods it delivers. And this sets the stage for our brief examination of each major type of spirituality currently on offer within American culture.

MAJOR TYPES OF SPIRITUALITY: WHAT'S ON OFFER IN THE SPIRITUAL MARKETPLACE

As mentioned above, this chapter charts the landscape of spirituality in America using three broad and general categories of spirituality: *religious spirituality*, which includes most of America's organized religions; *secular spirituality*, which includes atheists, scientific naturalists, and other active nonbelievers; and *progressive spirituality*, which includes the wide variety of nontraditional beliefs and practices that make up the contemporary social environment of alternative spiritual culture in the United States.

Sociologist of religion Robert Wuthnow defines spirituality as "all the beliefs and activities by which individuals attempt to relate their lives to . . . a transcendent reality."[1] However, while this definition can be read to include both progressive spirituality and traditional forms of religion, it does not include secular ideas of the real, which explicitly deny or rule out any "transcendent" features of reality. Yet, as I argue below, secular ideas of the real, which claim that the only reality is physical reality, are inescapably metaphysical and thus function as a form of spirituality even though this term is never used. I thus ask the reader to allow me to stretch the meaning of the word *spirituality* in this context to include all the forms of culture that are contending to define what is ultimately true, real, and worthwhile.

Religious Spirituality

This category comprises America's organized and historically established religions, including Christianity, Judaism, and Islam. It also includes

25

traditional forms of Buddhism, Hinduism, and other faiths that provide a cultural or ethnic connection to the ancestral heritage of their members. While organized forms of religion can also be found in the category I am identifying as progressive spirituality, the distinguishing characteristic of these religious types of spirituality is their connection to historically established forms of religion. Mormonism, for example, fits squarely in this category because it functions much like other long-established organized religions. By contrast, even though the Unitarian Universalist Church and the Unity Church are both forms of organized religion, they are far less conservative and traditional than Mormonism and are probably best classified in the progressive category. There is obviously some overlap among all three categories.

At its best, religious spirituality inspires believers to bear spiritual fruits in their lives, such as heartfelt devotion, faithful love, committed loyalty, contrite humility, and selfless service to one's family and community. And all religious forms of spirituality provide moral guidance and a sense of peace for their members, as well as an orienting belief system and creation story. Through their participation in a common story or system of belief, those who ascribe to a given form of religious spirituality feel a strong sense of membership and fellowship within a community of like-minded religionists.

Beyond the fulfillment of social needs, however, most forms of religious spirituality also connect their members with ancient wisdom, venerable scriptures, and the insights of the great saints and sages of history. It is in this way that religious forms of spirituality provide intergenerational continuity and an important connection with humanity's past. These institutions also include charming rituals and ceremonies, inspiring music, instruction in religious practices, and professional ministers charged with caring for the individual spiritual needs of members. Further, many followers of religious spirituality gather weekly within beautiful buildings. Some of America's most inspirational architecture is found in churches, synagogues, and other traditional religious structures.

Although organized religion has been maligned by many secular and progressive commentators, and although its membership is in general decline in America, religious forms of spirituality continue to fulfill a vibrant and indispensible role in American society, especially for the elderly and many minority groups. Despite its overall and ongoing gradual decline, religious spirituality remains the largest by far of the three categories I am describing. A 2012 Pew poll showed that 79 percent of Americans identified with an organized faith group, but less than 40 percent attend on a weekly basis. Although this category of spirituality includes many modernists and even some postmodernists among its members, most of those who do attend regularly have a cultural center of gravity that generally corresponds with a traditional worldview, as first described in the introduction.

Secular Spirituality

While atheism can be traced all the way back to some forms of ancient Greek philosophy, secular spirituality generally begins with the Enlightenment. When it first emerged, secular spirituality often took the form of Deism, which is nominally theistic. But today, almost every form of belief found within this category denies the reality of God along with all other supernatural notions. Contemporary secular spirituality takes form as atheism, secular humanism, existentialism, Marxism, and scientism, as well as what is coming to be known as "religious naturalism."

Atheist talk-show host Bill Maher once quipped, "Atheism is a religion like abstinence is a sex position." And I certainly agree that atheism is not a "religion." But given that we still know very little about the origins of the universe and the nature of the human mind—given that so much remains to be discovered—atheists' certainty that the universe is merely physical and that nothing transcendent exists is clearly a belief system in its own right. Further, in addition to its metaphysical commitments to exclusive physicalism, secularism can also be recognized as a kind of spirituality in the way that most forms of secular discourse about "what's really true" seem to be chiefly concerned with expressing opposition to other forms of spirituality.

By claiming to offer a more rational explanation of reality than the religious worldviews they oppose, secular teachings are clearly holding themselves out as an alternative form of spirituality.

Secular spirituality does deliver forms of truth that can be recognized as spiritual. This can be seen in the reverence secularists show for the truths they celebrate. For example, the elegance of physics, the wonder of biology, and the perfection of mathematics are all forms of spiritual truth that secularists accept. And their heartfelt commitment to these forms of truth shows how they are clearly sensitive to spiritual experience, despite their denial of spiritual reality. The late cosmologist Carl Sagan, for instance, provides an excellent example of an inspiring spiritual teacher who worked within the confines of secular spirituality.

One of the biggest strengths of secular spirituality is its critical-thinking practices and its healthy skepticism. Its hardheaded rejection of myth and superstition and its fidelity to reason and science have helped to define the way forward for many of those who have become disillusioned with traditional religion and who seek to identify with the modernist worldview. And while secular spirituality cannot be conflated with science, it does clearly demonstrate how scientific truth can be used as a basis for an extrascientific frame of reality that does the work of spirituality.

The goal of secular spirituality is often conceived of in terms of the heroic triumph of the autonomous individual. The ideas of Friedrich Nietzsche have been particularly influential in this regard. Nietzsche held that humanity betrays itself by submitting its freedom to the fictitious demands of an imaginary god. Personal "self-actualization" is accordingly achieved by rejecting the traditional God so that humans can become ever more godlike themselves, taking responsibility for their own unfettered autonomy. In practical terms, secular spirituality understands self-actualization through the goal of becoming a thoroughly rational agent who is not duped by superstition or myth. Beyond material success or other forms of achievement recognized by mainstream sensibilities, becoming a self-actualized secularist means being a "grown-up." This tacit goal of secular spirituality is well identified by the eminent philosopher Charles Taylor, who observes, "An unbeliever has the courage to take up an adult stance and face reality."[2]

Contemporary secular spirituality benefits from the leadership of many prominent public intellectuals, receiving cultural support from much of mainstream academia. It also finds subtle but significant support within prominent forms of American media such as the *New York Times* and the *Charlie Rose* television program. At its best, secular spirituality is fiercely heroic in its commitment to what it sees as the truth. And like the other types of spirituality we are examining, its aim is the betterment of humanity. Secular spirituality has indeed advanced profound and enduring truths, and it has helped establish important practices such as rational discernment and an insistence on evidence. So despite its frequent belittling of other kinds of spirituality, it nevertheless deserves our interest and respect.

The demographic makeup of secular spirituality, as understood through the worldview structures of cultural evolution described in the introduction, is mostly modernist. Some active nonbelievers have a postmodern center of gravity, and a few of the most "orthodox atheists" are essentially fundamentalists themselves who closely resemble the traditionalists they despise. But the vast majority of those who can be identified within the category of secular spirituality subscribe to the modernist worldview.

Secular spirituality, however, is only a subset of modernism overall. Recall that modernism provides the worldview for approximately 50 percent of Americans, and the majority of American modernists continue to believe in God in some form. So even though secular spirituality is growing, and polls on the issue are said to be unreliable, a reasonable estimate is that atheism, together with other related forms of secular spirituality, holds the allegiance of about 10 to 15 percent of the American population, as shown in figure 1.1 below (which builds on figure 1 from

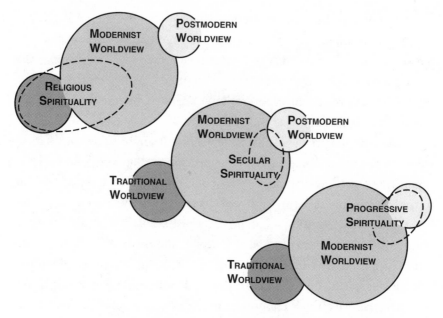

Figure 1.1. Estimated distribution of the types of spirituality within America's major worldviews

the introduction). But despite its relatively small numbers, although it is not always obvious, secular spirituality effectively dominates the culture of education in general and the culture of science in particular. It thus exerts a significant influence on American culture overall through the use of this powerbase.

Progressive Spirituality

Although each of the broad categories of spirituality we are examining includes a wide variety of forms, progressive spirituality is by far the most diverse. While some of its roots can be traced back to the Emersonian transcendentalism of the nineteenth century, progressive spirituality only became a significant cultural force (and a sizable market) in the 1970s as the youth culture of the 1960s became assimilated by portions of the larger society.

Progressive spirituality's wide diversity is explained by the fact that welcoming pluralism is one of its central values. Those attracted to progressive spiritual culture are typically not interested in just one religion; they are interested in spirituality in general. And this spirit of experimentation has led to significant cross-pollination among the various belief systems embraced by this culture. As a result of this trend, progressive spirituality's numerous sects have often been merged or otherwise blended over the last forty years.

The most popular forms of progressive spirituality have their roots within the Eastern traditions of Buddhism and Hinduism. But progressive spirituality also includes alternative forms of belief that originate in the West, such as the New Thought movement, Theosophy, ecospirituality, and many other forms of spirituality that can be grouped under the heading of "New Age." This cultural category also includes numerous psychological approaches to spirit, especially Jungian and transpersonal psychology. And the rise of New Age psychology has resulted in a plethora of self-help programs, life coaches, and visionary personal-success strategies. Also represented in progressive spirituality are pretraditional forms such as shamanism and paganism. Progressive versions of Christianity and Judaism can also be found within this alternative spiritual milieu, but these groups are relatively small, partially due to their association with the old establishment.

The primary factor that binds these various forms of spirituality together is that they are all practiced and interpreted within a postmodern cultural frame. That is, although progressive spirituality includes forms of religion from every stage of cultural development, the values and mores of this culture are supplied by the postmodern worldview, as first described in the introduction. Again, these values include egalitarianism, feminism, multiculturalism, social justice, and a strong orientation toward nature and the environment. And perhaps most importantly, the postmodern worldview is largely defined by its opposition to the globalizing culture of modernism. Antimodernism is thus the hallmark of postmodernism in practically all its forms.

It is important to emphasize that many of the strengths of progressive spirituality stem from its association with postmodern values. And, as explored below, like the other major types of spirituality we are considering, its weaknesses are tied directly to its strengths. Progressive spirituality is open, welcoming, tolerant, and highly eclectic. Through the rise of this alternative spiritual culture, forms of mysticism and esoteric spirituality that were once hidden or obscure are now celebrated and widely practiced. By "letting a thousand flowers bloom," progressive spirituality has effectively revitalized spirituality within a significant demographic segment of the developed world. Prior to the rise of progressive spirituality, many Western intellectuals assumed that religion was in an irreversible decline and would soon die out. But the appearance of the now large and vibrant movement for alternative forms of spirituality testifies to the ongoing vitality of the religious impulse and to humanity's unquenchable thirst for spiritual truth.

Perhaps progressive spirituality's biggest strength is that most of its forms promote themselves more as methods or paths for spiritual growth than as exclusive creeds or systems of belief. Progressive spirituality has accordingly gained a significant advantage over other types of spirituality through its emphasis on practice and its focus on the direct experience of spirit.

Just as secular spirituality represents only a portion of the larger worldview of modernism, progressive spirituality is likewise only a subset of the larger postmodern worldview (although it also includes many modernists). While the research of some sociologists suggests that postmodernism overall accounts for approximately 20 percent of the US population, there is no hard data on the size of the progressive spiritual demographic itself. If progressive spirituality is defined broadly to include everyone who has read a self-help book or has an affinity for yoga, then we might say that practically all American postmodernists embrace some form of progressive spirituality. But if the definition is confined to those who actually orient their lives around their spiritual practices, the extent of this demographic is probably about the same size as secular spirituality, comprising approximately 10 to 15 percent of the American population overall, as shown in figure 1.1.

Also, like secular spirituality, progressive spirituality is much more influential in American society than its relatively small population might suggest. Practitioners of progressive spirituality are typically well educated and often financially well off, which results in a strong economic demand for progressive spiritual books, workshops, and conferences. And even though progressive spirituality remains largely countercultural, it has nevertheless enjoyed the support of the elite entertainment establishment, as exemplified by celebrities such as Oprah Winfrey and Madonna, who have shown enthusiasm for many alternative forms of spirituality.

This concludes the initial description of the three major forms of spirituality within American culture. This survey, however, would not be complete without a critique. That is, in order to appreciate why a truer and more inclusive form of spirituality is needed, we must sympathetically examine the shortcomings of each of the existing types of spirituality being considered.

SHORTCOMINGS OF EACH TYPE OF SPIRITUALITY: WHY THEY CANNOT LEAD

My purpose in appraising the shortcomings of each major kind of spirituality is to help identify how we can do better. So although I will mention the worst versions of each type, my critique will focus on the *best* examples of each type in order to understand why even the most evolved expressions of these contemporary cultural forms are unlikely to develop teachings or practices that can deliver more inclusive spiritual leadership. But before beginning, let me reiterate that each of the major types of spirituality we are discussing stand for very important truths, and each has enduring strengths, as described above. Again, in order to succeed in developing a more inclusive and effective type of spirituality, we will need to preserve and carry forward many of these important truths and put them to use in our attempt to reach a higher-level understanding of spiritual reality.

Further, it must be acknowledged that every form of spiritual truth we can know as humans will always be attached to partial and somewhat erroneous belief systems. Such systems of belief, however, cannot be dispensed with; even the most nondoctrinal forms of spirituality still make necessary use of beliefs of one kind or another. Yet even as we acknowledge that serviceable forms of spirituality will always be "true but partial," from an evolutionary perspective we can see that it is these very partialities that provide opportunities for our further development. In other words, it is precisely the shortcomings of these major types of spirituality that help define the way forward—their problems provide our points of departure. An important strength of evolutionary spirituality is thus found in its ability to push off against what is evidently partial in its efforts to grow into something larger and higher.

Shortcomings of Religious Spirituality

Turning first to the problems of religious spirituality, it is easy to see the shortcomings of the weakest examples of this cultural form. In America, the least evolved traditionalists are Christian fundamentalists who are wedded to outworn historical perspectives. Fundamentalists are distinguished by their insistence on biblical literalism, which often places them in opposition to the development of human knowledge and morality, leaving them in an anti-intellectual cultural backwater. Yet even in the face of these challenges, fundamentalist churches are nevertheless serving the spiritual needs of millions of Americans and generally doing good at the community level.

Notwithstanding the anti-intellectual fundamentalism with which religious spirituality is often associated, this cultural category also includes intellectually sophisticated academic theologians, such as Philip Clayton and John Haught, who are fully engaged with science and contemporary philosophical debates. But although religious spirituality's brightest intellectuals are mostly open-minded liberal modernists, they nevertheless remain tied to their respective religious institutions. And this loyalty to historical forms of religion gives them an inherently conservative orientation. Most of the academic leaders of religious spirituality tend to have a difficult time recognizing the validity of promising new spiritual developments because such new shoots of spiritual truth are not yet recognized by mainstream academia. As a result of this conservative bias, most of religious spirituality's intellectuals remain out of touch with the leading cultural edge of America's spiritual evolution.

Even as religious spirituality continues to evolve within its own sphere through the work of dedicated teachers, ministers, and intellectuals, short of some radical reform or rebirth, its ancient institutions will remain incapable of providing a widely agreeable form of spirituality for American society overall. So while traditional Christianity and Judaism are here to stay, they are not capable of supplying the spiritual leadership we need at this time in history.

Shortcomings of Secular Spirituality

Religious spirituality may be backward, but secular spirituality is even more limited in its leadership potential. The most deficient forms of secular spiritual discourse in America can be found in the work of "militant atheists" such as Jerry Coyne and P. Z. Myers, who roundly condemn both religious and progressive spirituality using a snide and superior tone that belittles all believers. These despisers of spirit characterize belief in

God—the God of Lincoln, John Muir, and Martin Luther King—as equivalent to belief in the tooth fairy. While they may be entertaining to some, in pursuit of their ostensible mission of overcoming myth and superstition they end up corroding the moral foundations of our society.

On the positive side of secular spirituality we find the important work of academic "religious naturalists" such as Stuart Kauffman, Terrence Deacon, and Bron Taylor. Although these authors are physicalists who identify with the culture of scientific materialism and reject both religious and progressive spirituality, they have nevertheless found ways to recognize an "enchanted" dimension of nature. For example, in his book *Reinventing the Sacred*, Kauffman identifies the ceaseless creativity of the universe as a source of awe and reverence that can provide a kind of spiritual social solidarity that remains scientifically respectable. Similarly, in his book *Dark Green Religion*, Bron Taylor argues that reverence for the earth and the purely immanent sacredness of life can serve as the foundation for a new movement that fulfills the social functions of religion without the accompanying metaphysical baggage. Because of their faith that answers to existential questions can indeed be found in the truths of science, the work of religious naturalists such as these is important for the development of more inclusive forms of spiritual leadership. And as we will explore in the next chapter, the truths of science provide an important foundation for evolutionary spirituality.

In appraising the shortcomings of secular spirituality, it must also be acknowledged that secular spiritual writers are positioned at an important fulcrum of history. Many are honestly engaged in the indispensible work of evolving premodern consciousness into modernist consciousness. As a result of the success of these efforts, contemporary secular spirituality is growing and is even fashionable, as seen in the popularity of authors such as Sam Harris and the late Christopher Hitchens. The substance of secular spirituality's message, however, is formed largely in reaction to the perceived myths of traditional religious teachings. The leaders of secular spirituality thus end up defining themselves primarily by what they are not. But authentic spiritual leadership requires more than the dismantling of falsehoods.

Secular spirituality will undoubtedly continue to grow and articulate its fierce commitment to what it sees as true. But there is really no way it will ever become the leading authority on ultimate reality in America. Because teachers of secular spirituality want to reduce consciousness to the physical activity of the brain, because they fail to recognize the validity of any spiritual teaching but their own, and because they are unwilling to accept the authentic reality of spiritual experience, they will never be able to supply the unifying spiritual leadership that America needs.

Shortcomings of Progressive Spirituality

Finally, turning to the shortcomings of progressive spirituality, the weakest versions of this cultural form are found in abundant examples of New Age magical thinking and ill-informed pseudoscience. Indeed, much of progressive spirituality is childish and untethered from common sense. And it sometimes seems that within this culture, the crazier a teaching sounds the more popular it becomes. Even progressive spiritual teachings that do make sense are often marred by intense commercialism. But despite the presence of hucksters and charlatans, even the more tawdry and lowbrow elements of this kind of spirituality nevertheless fulfill at least some of the spiritual needs of a significant segment of American society.

On the more noble side of progressive spirituality we find inspirational teachings that deliver genuine spiritual wisdom. As examples, Zen Buddhist monk Thich Nhat Hanh and popular author Barbara Marx Hubbard both teach forms of spirituality that are insightful, inclusive, and usable by ordinary people in their quest for spiritual growth.

Yet even the best of progressive spirituality is still unequipped to provide spiritual leadership for a significantly larger demographic segment than it presently reaches. In keeping with their postmodern worldview, most leading teachers of progressive spirituality are generally too countercultural or otherwise too antimodernist to appeal to the majority of Americans. Despite its ongoing growth and gradually increasing legitimacy, most of progressive spirituality remains disconnected from academic philosophy and current science. Even the expressions of progressive spirituality that are not at odds with science remain inevitably associated with the more magical or otherwise off-putting elements of New Age culture. And because progressive spirituality's unwavering commitment to pluralism prevents it from purging these elements or otherwise effectively distinguishing the good from the bad, it will continue to fail to be taken seriously within academia and mainstream intellectual discourse. This failing leads to the conclusion that contemporary progressive spirituality will be unable to appreciably expand its spiritual leadership beyond its current audience.

Advocates of progressive spirituality anticipate a great awakening in which a significant segment of American society will consciously adopt the cultural agreements of progressive spirituality. But they have been expecting such a shift since at least the 1980s, and the fact that it has not happened by now is a clear sign that something new and different is needed.

Evolutionary spirituality is thus attempting to transcend progressive spirituality in a variety of ways, one of which involves critiquing its shortcomings. So we will return to this important task of pushing off against the limitations of progressive spirituality in chapter 5, where we will carefully distinguish the most evolved forms of progressive spirituality from the distinct and newly emerging teachings of evolutionary spirituality.

Concluding this initial examination of the contemporary spiritual marketplace of ideas, it must be emphasized that while the existence of distinct religious and spiritual groups within American culture is obvious even to the most casual observer, defining or delimiting such groups is fraught with difficulties. Almost anything that can be said or concluded about a given cultural group can be easily disputed with abundant counterexamples and exceptions. However, as will become clear in the chapters ahead, evolutionary spirituality's promise of providing a more effective form of spiritual leadership for our society can be brought about only through a higher-level integration that includes the best of each of these existing forms of spirituality. Therefore, charting the landscape of these types, even if in a very broad and general way, is prerequisite to the task of attempting to transcend and include them in a higher form of synthesis. So in anticipation of this potential synthesis, this chapter concludes by considering the potential benefits that could be brought about by more effective forms of spiritual leadership.

POTENTIAL BENEFITS OF SPIRITUAL LEADERSHIP: A MORE UNIFIED CULTURE

Returning to where we started in this chapter, I am optimistic that a new kind of unifying spiritual agreement is looming on the horizon of American history. Again, this new form of cultural solidarity will not consist of a monolithic belief system or a singular spiritual path; respectful pluralism and religious freedom will clearly remain. But such a new spiritual agreement could nevertheless help us overcome many of the problems of our contemporary culture war and provide a more welcoming place for spiritual experience in American public life.

Exactly what such a new agreement would look like and how it could gain currency in America's fragmented culture is the primary focus of the rest of this book. Yet even before examining the contours of such a potential agreement, we know that even if it swept the nation and became wildly successful, it would not erase or otherwise replace the major types of spirituality examined above. These religious, secular, and progressive forms of spirituality will each likely endure throughout this century and beyond. However, as it gains acceptance in the culture, because of its transcendent yet inclusive nature this newly emerging agreement of evolutionary spirituality will appeal to many of those who remain loyal to one of these existing forms of spirituality, as well as to those who are ready to adopt this new form as their primary spiritual path. Simply put, in order to provide the more effective spiritual leadership we need, this new agreement must be agreeable to a wide diversity of truth seekers.

And this is indeed the promise of evolutionary spirituality: that it can act as a supplement to existing forms of spirituality, effectively recruiting culturally significant numbers of people to agree with its teaching while they still retain most of their existing spiritual loyalties, and can at the same time provide a distinct new form of spiritual culture in its own right. Such a transcendent yet inclusive new form of spirituality is certainly a tall order, and by the end of this book readers can conclude for themselves whether or not evolutionary spirituality is actually capable of achieving these kinds of results. But even as we are now only beginning to consider the possibility of the rise of an emergent new form of spiritual understanding, it is worth imagining in advance the potential benefits that such an agreement could provide.

The most direct and immediate benefits of greater spiritual solidarity in America would be political. At the domestic level of politics, increasing accord around values and matters of ultimate concern would reduce polarization and gridlock by disempowering ideological extremists and decreasing the intensity of the culture war. This would in turn pave the way for the formation of more effective forms of political will and a stronger collective determination to address problems such as climate change and the growing disparity between rich and poor.

At the international level of politics, greater spiritual solidarity among Americans could result in America becoming more effective in its global leadership, even while it becomes less hegemonic and less concerned with its narrowly perceived national interests. As this century unfolds, even as America's global economic leadership fades its cultural and spiritual leadership can increase. And assuming a more benign role in world affairs may actually bolster patriotism among Americans while simultaneously giving them a larger sense of their global citizenship.

Beyond the political benefits that may accrue from such a new form of inclusive spiritual agreement, other potential cultural and economic benefits can also be anticipated. As one example, by enlarging our culture's understanding of ultimate reality, evolutionary spirituality can strengthen value commitments. Remember that each of these existing kinds of spirituality serves to frame reality for its adherents. And by framing reality, these cultural forms thereby ground or justify the values of their adherents. For instance, philosophers and social theorists from each camp have sought to justify their definition of morality by grounding it in the reality frame of their chosen form of spirituality. Morality has thus been justified alternatively either in religious authority or in the rational subject or in the intersubjective agreements of free people. Given this need to ground values in some kind of reality-defining worldview, one of the promises of evolutionary spirituality is that by expanding and improving our understanding of what is ultimately real, it can serve as a stronger justification for our values by grounding them in the purpose of the evolving universe itself.

In this way, by developing a more evolved understanding of spiritual reality, American culture could become both *more traditional and less traditional*—more in touch with the wisdom of our heritage yet less ethnocentric and xenophobic. Similarly, such a new agreement could help us become both *more modernist and less modernist*—wealthier and better connected yet less concerned with the acquisition of status and material possessions. And greater spiritual solidarity among Americans could also lead to our society becoming simultaneously *more postmodern and less postmodern*—more determined to work for social justice and protect the environment yet less hostile toward America's history and its role as the world's leading modernist nation.

Finally, and perhaps most importantly, a greater sense of spiritual consensus within American culture could improve the overall quality of our collective spiritual experience, which would inevitably produce better art and music, a more inspiring educational system, a more sophisticated intellectual life, and a more moral society wherein greater fairness and compassion could prevail among our citizens. In short, a more evolved understanding of spirit could lead directly to a higher level of civilization—a sustainable society that works better for everyone.

In chapters 4, 7, and 8 we will see how evolutionary spirituality may actually be able to accomplish its optimistic and ambitious goals. But before going further, we need to gain a more specific understanding of what evolutionary spirituality actually is and why it has the promising potential that I am claiming for it.

Chapter Two

THE SPIRITUAL TEACHINGS
OF EVOLUTION

Ever since Darwin, the theory of evolution has been used as an effective weapon against traditional religious teachings. By providing an entirely natural and apparently purposeless account of humanity's origins, evolutionary science is often assumed to have made all spiritual or supernatural explanations of the source of reality superfluous and thus ultimately invalid. So it may at first appear incongruous to claim that the story of evolution presents a spiritual teaching of its own. However, as we explore in this chapter, the spiritual quality of evolution's ceaseless process of becoming can be recognized in its ongoing creation of value. As I will argue, evolution is definitely going somewhere—*evolution has a purpose*. And this purpose, properly interpreted, is to make things better. As I hope to show, despite abundant pathologies, inevitable setbacks, and even occasional regressions, evolution is gradually moving in the direction of greater beauty, truth, and goodness—*evolution is progressive*.

For the scientifically minded, these claims may seem unwarranted or unsupported by evidence, but the arguments and interpretations that justify these conclusions do not rely on any supernatural explanations or spiritual authorities. The essential tenets of evolutionary spirituality summarized in this chapter are based either on the evidence of science or on experiential realities familiar to all of us.

Our exploration of evolution's spiritual teachings begins with the recognition of how almost everything in the universe is evolving. Evolution is not just a matter of changes in biological species; the unfolding development of the universe encompasses the cosmological evolution of matter, the biological evolution of life, the cultural evolution of human history, and, most importantly, the evolution of consciousness itself. This overarching understanding of evolution as a universal phenomenon shows how evolution is not just something that is happening *within* the universe; a more accurate appraisal recognizes that the universe *is* evolution happening—the finite universe *is* a process of becoming in time.

Now that we are coming to better see and understand this process of becoming in the cosmos overall—in matter, in life, in human history, and ultimately within each of us—we can begin to use this knowledge to uncover some of the universe's most intimate spiritual secrets. Realizing that the universe is what it does—that the universe is evolution—leads to the foundational proposition of evolutionary spirituality as I understand it: *our evolving universe provides the gift of experience through which free-will creatures may participate in the gradual perfection of the finite cosmos.* While this dense theological conclusion may at first seem rather lofty or overly idealistic, it begins to make perfect sense once the spiritual teachings of evolution are learned, practiced, and directly experienced.

My last book, *Evolution's Purpose*, presents a detailed and extended argument for the idea that evolution is a spiritual teaching. Aimed at an educated mainstream audience, the book carefully builds on what the sciences of cosmology and biology have revealed. It also employs arguments from academic philosophy and theology to reach the conclusion that the purpose of evolution is to grow toward ever-widening realizations of beauty, truth, and goodness. By simplifying these arguments and recounting them in condensed form, this chapter provides an overview of my interpretation of the spiritual teachings of evolution. While this condensed context prevents me from arguing every point to the satisfaction of potential critics or skeptics, I will endeavor to cover the fundamentals of this emerging perspective on the nature of spiritual reality. Then with these basic premises in mind, the chapters that follow further explore how evolutionary spirituality can expand our understanding of spiritual experience and illuminate the way forward into a new era of social solidarity and progress for our culture.

As a preview of this chapter, first we explore how the nested sequence of *evolutionary emergence* provides a structural demonstration of evolution's continuous generation of qualitative novelties—entities with entirely new properties that exhibit increasingly more complex behaviors. This emergent structure of interactive levels of development clearly shows how evolution creates real value as it unfolds. Next comes a discussion of the *evolutionary impulse*, which begins in biological life as the urge to survive and reproduce and develops further in humans to include the desire for self-actualization and spiritual growth. This discussion leads to an initial introduction to the intrinsic values of *beauty, truth, and goodness*, which provide the primary focus of human desire and the overall directional heading of evolution's progressive advance. Then we take a closer look at the controversial idea that evolution is a *purposeful and progressive* phenomenon, followed by a discussion of how this newly emerging interpretation of evolution points to a *panentheistic theology* that recognizes spirit as both *immanent in* and *transcendent of* the finite universe. This initial discussion of panentheism will be revisited in later chapters where we consider how the enlarged understanding of spiritual experience revealed by evolutionary spirituality can expand our conception of what is ultimately real.

This overview of my interpretation of the fundamental tenets of the spiritual teachings of evolution is followed by a discussion of the *practice of evolutionary spirituality*, which examines how these newly understood truths can be lived out and used for our personal growth and in our service to others. The chapter concludes with a brief discussion of the current state of evolutionary spirituality's nascent emergence in American culture.

Although I am contributing to its emergence, evolutionary spirituality does not originate with me. This new form of spirituality has gradually developed over the last two hundred years or so through the work of numerous distinguished visionaries who have each sought to understand the larger meaning of our evolving universe. Even before Darwin, many could see that the universe was in the process of becoming and knew intuitively that hidden within this fact was a very deep truth.

As mentioned in the introduction, evolutionary spirituality has arisen primarily through the insights of integral philosophy. The beginnings of this line of spiritual philosophy can be traced to the work of the German idealists Fichte, Schelling, and Hegel in the early nineteenth century. Then, after Darwin's revelation of the natural development of life, the important task of interpreting evolution's spiritual significance was taken up again in the twentieth century by eminent philosophers such as Henri Bergson, Alfred North Whitehead, and Pierre Teilhard de Chardin. Then, beginning in the 1990s, largely through the work of American philosopher Ken Wilber, integral philosophy was expanded to include the insights of systems science, developmental psychology, and postmodern philosophy. As a result of this new synthesis of evolutionary ideas, over the last two decades integral philosophy has taken root within progressive culture. While still relatively small, the integral movement is now a vibrant intellectual community with participants on almost every continent. And since 2000, integral philosophy and the evolutionary spirituality it discloses have been the primary focus of my working life. However, it is important to add that while I am indebted to Ken Wilber's work, my interpretation of integral philosophy differs from his. These differences are described in *Integral Consciousness* and developed further in chapters 6 and 7 of the present book.

LESSONS FROM THE STRUCTURE OF EVOLUTIONARY EMERGENCE

Over the last three hundred years or so, human knowledge has been most dramatically and reliably expanded by the stupendous accomplishments of physical science. Science has revealed the previously unseen realms of the microscopic and the macroscopic, and it has shed light on many of the mysteries of the human body, leading to scientific medicine, which has improved the human condition immensely. Despite the environmental damage caused by the impact of our scientific civilization, very few of us would be willing to go back to living in a prescientific world. And among all the amazing discoveries of science, the most significant by far is its discovery of evolution.

The Three Big Bangs

Scientists have now confirmed that evolution began just 13.8 billion years ago with the white-hot flash of the big bang. Then, from the simple hydrogen debris resulting from the explosion of this first foundational emergence, a series of additional emergences followed, each one building on the accomplishments of its predecessors. This marvelous sequence of complexifying emergence within matter can now be clearly seen in the periodic table of elements, which provides a kind of fossil record of the evolution of the prebiotic universe.

Then 3.6 billion years ago on this planet (and likely at other times and other places throughout the universe) a kind of *second big bang* occurred. This second big bang, arguably even more astonishing than the first, could never have been predicted as a possibility. Yet somehow, out of dead matter, life emerged. With the emergence of life came the appearance of an entirely new domain of evolution—a self-reproducing, entropy-defying, quasipurposive new form of reality—a "river that runs uphill."

Evolution, however, did not reach its conclusion in life alone. We are now coming to understand what can best be described as a *third big bang*. At some point within the last two hundred thousand years, another completely unpredictable emergence occurred that produced yet another new realm of evolution: a domain of development in which the products of evolution have come to control the process of evolution itself.

And this, of course, is the evolutionary domain in which human consciousness and culture have partially transcended their biological origins and embarked on a path of development that has led to our global civilization.

As eminent philosopher Holmes Rolston observes in his 2010 book *Three Big Bangs*, the evolutionary development of our universe discloses an interdependent structure of emergent levels, a sequence of steps that have continuously built upon themselves, leading to increasingly complex and accomplished forms of organization and eventually to conscious organisms capable of discovering the process of their own origination.

From an external perspective, the scientific and historical story of evolution is by far the largest truth we can know with relative certainty. And a truth this big inevitably spans the spectrum from mundane physical facts to profound, life-changing revelations about the nature of ultimate reality. In other words, as we realize that evolution is what the universe actually is, we may come to appreciate why this newly achieved, comprehensive understanding of the cosmos actually represents an authentic spiritual teaching in its own right.

The Entire Structural Sequence of Emergence Is Alive within Us

One of the elements of this evolutionary story that grounds it in experience, making it useful as a spiritual teaching and not just an inert scientific theory, is that we contain practically every major level of evolutionary emergence within our own bodies. The steps of emergence from the universe's simplest beginnings to our current stage of biological development are all present and active in our human organisms. From the hydrogen atoms of the big bang in our water molecules through the periodic table of elements in our bones, we embody practically every level of cosmological evolution. We also embody practically all the steps of biological development that have led to the partial transcendence of the biosphere itself. For example, we carry the evolutionary accomplishments of the eukaryotes in our cells, the vertebrates in our backbones, and the mammals in our neocortexes. These historical emergences are not just events of the distant past; their achievements are being used here and now within us. Each one of these distinct forms of emergence is thus making an ongoing and vital contribution to the leading edge of evolution in the present.

Just as we embody and use the structures of cosmological and biological emergence in our bodies, we are likewise using practically all the stages of humanity's cultural development that have contributed to our current states of consciousness. Building on the field of developmental psychology, integral philosophy has shown how the accomplishments of each stage of human history continue to make an ongoing contribution to the evolution of consciousness within humanity overall. This can be seen in the development of children, who roughly recapitulate humanity's historical stages of evolution as they grow, moving from magical consciousness to mythical consciousness to more rational forms of consciousness as they mature, and potentially beyond that to higher stages in adulthood.[1] These stages of humanity's psychosocial evolution thus form a kind of "internal mental ecosystem" wherein the accomplishments of each stage depend on the value achievements of previous stages. For example, healthy modernist consciousness depends on the values of fair play and abiding by the law, values that arise within the traditional stage of development and serve as a foundation for successful modernism.

This nested sequence of emergence is how evolution works at every level—something more keeps coming from something less. Yet the "more" almost always takes up and uses the achievements of the earlier, less developed level from which it emerges. This evolutionary technique of transcendence through inclusion is what allows evolution to make ongoing progress toward more complex forms of organization and greater degrees of awareness.

The way we each embody the emergent structure of evolution confirms that the evolution of consciousness and culture is real evolution. The development of human history is not merely analogous to other forms of evolution; it is actually a continuation of this universal process in and through us. Although the evolution of human civilization cannot be conflated with biological evolution, it is real evolution nonetheless because it participates in the chain of transcendence and inclusion leading all the way back to the big bang. Stated differently, the evident structure of evolutionary emergence confirms that humanity's ongoing cultural development relies on the previous accomplishments of the biosphere in bringing forth the human body, just as the biosphere in turn relies on the previous accomplishments of the evolving cosmos that brought forth planet Earth. This structural sequence of use and dependence across all the levels of emergence that have given rise to our global civilization ties all forms of evolution together as a unified cosmic process. Evolution's emergent structure, however, reveals more than a linear sequence of transcendence and inclusion. As Wilber has shown in his four-quadrant model of evolution, emergence unfolds simultaneously in both individual and collective dimensions, and not only externally and physically, but also within the interiors of consciousness and culture.[2]

THE EVOLUTIONARY IMPULSE

The fact that every modern human is a living demonstration of the entire history of evolution in microcosm—both physically and mentally—points to another essential feature of evolutionary spirituality as I understand it. This involves recognition of the spiritual significance of our sense of purpose, our internal urge to improve our conditions and pursue happiness for ourselves, for those we love, and even for all of humanity. This urge is known as the *evolutionary impulse,* and the practice of feeling and cultivating it is an indispensible element of evolutionary spirituality.

Feeling into our evolutionary impulse is important because it provides a direct experiential connection to the purpose of evolution overall. That is, according to evolutionary spirituality, the impulse that compels us to develop our potential and work for a better world is the same impulse that has been driving evolution from the beginning. As anthropologist Terrence Deacon has written, "To be human is to know what it feels like to be evolution happening."[3]

Although the idea that evolution is a purposeful, teleological phenomenon is rejected by scientific materialists, purpose is actually a centerpiece of evolutionary emergence. Indeed, it is purpose itself that is actually emerging through evolution. The momentous emergence of purpose is what distinguishes life from nonlife. All life forms, no matter how primitive, embody the purpose (or quasipurpose) to survive and reproduce, and this inherent "will to live" is what makes evolution by natural selection possible. Similarly at the human level, it is the momentous emergence of our free-will purpose that sets us apart from other forms of life. Animals may have a rudimentary sense of purpose, but humans have a higher level of self-reflective purpose. And this is what gives us the ability to evolve our culture, distinguishing us from other animals.

As I argue at length in *Evolution's Purpose*, the rising flow of creativity that has given birth to our universe is coursing within us at this very moment. And because we have a direct phenomenological experience of this creative urge to evolve, we know for ourselves that this rising flow is inherently teleological and purposive. Thus, just as we embody evolution's structure in our bodies and our minds, we also embody evolution's purpose in our sense of duty and desire—our deep-seated drive to strive for something higher and better. When at their best, our evolutionary impulses provide a personal disclosure of the larger purpose of the evolving universe. So to discover evolution's teleological purpose we need only look within ourselves. Our purposes are its purposes.

This central insight serves as the foundation of evolutionary spirituality's natural theology of intrinsic value. This "natural spirituality" is discovered through an examination of the values and qualities that attract our attention and engage our personal purposes. In other words, our evolutionary impulses are generally attracted and magnetized toward improvement, however we may define it. And for at least the last fifty thousand years, humans have been working to improve their life conditions. Yet our ability to improve things is constrained by our definition of what counts as improvement. Stated differently, our capacity to make things better is largely determined by our culturally conditioned notions of what is relatively more valuable and what could potentially be better.

As first described in the introduction, this capacity to envision a better way has itself evolved through the sequential emergence of values-based stages of consciousness and culture. These historical stages of development, identified by integral philosophy as the pretraditional, traditional, modernist, postmodern, and post-postmodern worldviews, frame and define what is beautiful, true, and good for a given group of people at a given time in history. Each of these worldviews has achieved an evolutionary advance over its predecessors primarily by improving its definition of what counts as improvement itself. For example, the emergence of the modernist worldview during the Enlightenment made it possible to improve society in entirely new ways as a result of modernism's more powerful set of values. The new truths of science and the new political ideals of democracy made it possible to evolve beyond the religious myths and feudal governments of the Middle Ages.

Each emergent worldview brings forth an enlarged set of values, which can be understood as a "new octave" or a "wider bandwidth" of beauty, truth, and goodness. As humanity develops clearer views of reality and more inclusive forms of morality through the advance of science, philosophy, and spirituality, this expands what we are able to value, and this in turn expands our capacity to improve our life conditions. It is in this way that the evolutionary impulse itself evolves through us.

Beauty, Truth, and Goodness—An Introduction

Another fundamental tenet of evolutionary spirituality is that the beautiful, the true, and the good represent the most intrinsic forms of value humans can experience and create. As described above, this triad of values is restated within each stage of humanity's cultural evolution. Although notions of love and freedom are also often conceived of as belonging to the set of the most intrinsic values, there is something very special about the triad of beauty, truth, and goodness. Philosophers have argued since antiquity that beauty, truth, and goodness function as the primary values from which all forms of quality can be ultimately derived, just as the three primary colors combine to produce practically all the colors visible to humans. These values represent the capstone qualities at the heart of the aesthetic, rational, and moral dimensions of human experience. Figure 2.1 shows some of the many subvalues that can be derived from or otherwise related back to these primary values.

Now, in *Evolution's Purpose* I took forty-five pages to make the careful philosophical arguments that justify the proposition that beauty, truth, and goodness are the most intrinsic values. Although I will not repeat

Figure 2.1. Primary values and some of their derivatives

those arguments here, we will be revisiting the subject of these primary values throughout the rest of this book, especially in chapter 4. I am introducing the idea here in this brief overview of the tenets of evolutionary spirituality because a basic understanding of the spiritual teachings of evolution requires familiarity with the role these values play in evolution overall. In fact, evolutionary spirituality could also be called "beauty, truth, and goodness spirituality" because the experience and creation of these intrinsic values are really its essence.

The concept of a tripartite system of primary values from which all forms of quality can be derived represents more than a convenient rubric or a contrived heuristic framework. These three values taken together form a kind of dynamic system providing a profound window into the nature of spiritual reality. As we will see, these primary values are a *conceptual cathedral* in which the polarized perspectives of science and spirit become harmonized.

Through my practice of evolutionary spirituality I have come to see how this triad of intrinsic values serves as a "great attractor" for the evolution of human consciousness and culture. These values exert a kind of gravity on human consciousness, pulling it forward into ever-widening conceptions of a better way. As noted above, our civilization has evolved primarily because humans are continuously driven to improve their conditions. While the perceived needs of animals become satisfied when their biological requirements are fulfilled, human needs can never be fully satisfied. As soon as one set of problems is solved, we awaken to a higher level of needs. Yet this human quest for endless improvement is itself constrained by a given culture's values-based worldview. Again, what counts as "better" depends on the value horizon of one's cultural perspective. Indeed, the value frame of every worldview is constructed by its unique definition of what is beautiful, true, and good. So although humans have been attempting to improve their conditions since the dawn of history, humanity's most dramatic improvements have come from the emergence of new sets of values focused on ameliorating new sets of problems.

And it is primarily through this ongoing process of the emergence of increasingly inclusive value frames that humanity's consciousness and culture has transcended our biological origins and moved forward into a new domain of evolutionary development.

The fact that humanity's evolution is pulled forward by our ongoing quest for ever-deepening forms of intrinsic value was well understood by Alfred North Whitehead, one of the founders of integral philosophy and a strong proponent of the centrality of beauty, truth, and goodness. Whitehead actually defined evolution as *an increase in the capacity to experience what is intrinsically valuable.*[4] This is one of my favorite ideas in all philosophy. I think Whitehead's consciousness-centric definition of evolution goes to the heart of what evolution is all about—the gradual perfection of the universe. And this perfecting process is achieved both internally and externally through the experience and creation of the three most intrinsic values, which are ends in themselves. As discussed further in chapter 4, our ability to intuit the direction of further transcendence, as disclosed by these primary values, instructs us regarding how our conditions can be continuously improved. And it is through this process that human evolution progresses.

Evolutionary spirituality's recognition of the central significance of goodness, truth, and beauty does not represent a return to premodern notions of static Platonic forms or other historical conceptions of transcendent-value realism. The insight that values themselves evolve helps us see how they are neither simply objective nor purely subjective—their existence depends on our conscious recognition of real quality. Values thus bring subject and object together in the course of their realization. But I am getting ahead of the story.

For the purposes of this brief introduction to the evolutionary significance of these primary values, suffice it to say that it is by and through our ability to experience and create beauty, truth, and goodness that we are endowed with the privilege of cocreating something spiritually real within the finite universe. As a result of our capacity to comprehend and share these immediate forms of spirit, we become authentic agents of evolution itself.

Summing up what we have covered so far in this chapter, if it is true that the evolution of consciousness and culture is real evolution, then our experience of the evolutionary impulse, which causes us to strive for the improvement of ourselves and the human condition overall, provides direct evidence of what evolution is all about. And from this perspective evolution can be understood as the gradual perfection of the universe, with increasing perfection defined as making ourselves and our world more beautiful, true, and good. The fundamental qualities of beauty, truth, and goodness thus represent more than just our personal preferences or predilections; these primary values are actually the overall directions of evolution itself—it is through these essentially spiritual qualities that we bring the infinite increasingly into the finite. Or perhaps more accurately, it is through these values that the finite becomes transparent to the infinite that is always present, upholding the universe from within.

Purpose and Progress

The next important principle of evolutionary spirituality follows from the three tenets discussed above: (1) humans embody evolution's entire sequence of development, and this emergent structure is continuing to unfold in and through us; (2) the impulse to make things better that we each feel is connected to the larger purpose of evolution overall; and (3) this purpose of evolution is increasingly fulfilled as we gradually perfect the universe by making ourselves and our world more beautiful, true, and good. Contemplating these ideas, interpreting them from a spiritual perspective, leads to the evident conclusion of the next tenet: that we live in a universe of purpose and progress.

As free-will creatures we are endowed with a personal sense of purpose, which suggests that the existence of humanity as a whole has *a larger purpose* in the grand scheme of evolution; we are not a cosmic accident. Likewise, as creatures with self-conscious awareness we are endowed with the ability to reason, which also suggests that humans have *a larger reason* for our existence; we have a cosmic job to do. Our role in the "cosmic economy," if you will, is to discern and pursue the essential directions of perfection by our own lights. In other words, in our capacity as agents of evolution we are recruited to the task of freely discovering what is closer to perfection by our own volition and in our own experience. The unfolding purpose of the universe—the teleology of evolution—thus arises from within us as we are attracted by the potential for new forms of excellence and more inclusive estimates of those worthy of our consideration. We can see this in the way the leading edge of human culture has grown from egocentric to ethnocentric to increasingly worldcentric conceptions of what constitutes "us."

The insight that we are each called to participate in evolution's unfolding points to the conclusion that the finite universe of time and space was actually brought into being so that the *existential* perfection of the preexisting infinite could be supplemented and complemented by an additional kind of perfection—an *experiential* form of perfection gradually achieved by free-will creatures in and through time.

Admittedly, this proposition that the role of humans in the cosmic economy is to perfect the evolving universe of self, culture, and nature is heady stuff, and in *Evolution's Purpose* I devote a chapter to unpacking it. So let me restate this idea another way: according to my understanding of the spiritual teachings of evolution, the purpose of the finite universe is to provide a domain in which conscious beings can freely participate in the experience of perfecting an incomplete cosmos. While this idea may take time to digest or otherwise appreciate, this overview of evolutionary spirituality would not be complete without reference to these big-picture conclusions.

The practical value of these theological observations, however, is found in their affirmation of evolutionary *progress*. One of the main goods that evolutionary spirituality delivers is its sophisticated rehabilitation of the often-maligned notion that evolution is progressive—that evolution creates real value. Despite setbacks and pathologies, evolution is ultimately making things better. And for the last fifty thousand years at least, evolution has been making things better *through us*.

Evolutionary spirituality's clarification of the purpose of the evolving universe affirms that real progress is possible by showing the central significance of beauty, truth, and goodness in the evolutionary process overall. Although these values are always relative to human needs and desires, although they always have a subjective component, as mentioned above, they are not *completely* subjective. Authentic values connect with objective or external qualities, drawing us toward improved conditions and better states of affairs. Although what counts as "better" is partially up to us, the notion of progress cannot be reduced to mere anthropocentric subjectivity because value creation is evident in the structure of evolutionary emergence itself. In other words, evolution's ongoing generation of real value can be seen in the way it has continued to bring forth encompassing layers of development that add value by both including and transcending what has come before. And because this unfolding sequence of emergence is now in our hands, our subjective preferences are connected with evolution's larger movement toward increasing perfection.

Ultimately, the value of humanity cannot be separated from the process that has led to human life. We carry our origins with us in our very being. And we demonstrate the value of those origins as we continue to carry forward the evolutionary process by appreciating and creating value of every kind. Simply stated, as we experience and create value we become more evolved and the world becomes more evolved. Using the sequence of emergence as a gauge of progress necessarily involves the interests of humans, but this is justified by the fact that the very structure of emergence itself demonstrates that humans are an expression of the interests of evolution.

We can thus use this evolutionary understanding of the purpose of the universe to continuously refine our estimates of what counts as authentic progress in this grand scheme of universe development. In short, deepening our discernment of evolution's existential purpose illuminates the directions of further progress.

Panentheism—From Finite to Infinite

The fifth and final major tenet is that the finite universe is related to a larger infinite reality that encompasses and contains the finite universe from without while also permeating the finite from within. Stated otherwise, evolutionary spirituality recognizes that the infinite is both *transcendent* of and *immanent* within time and space. And the theological term that best captures this idea is *panentheism*.

The idea that our finite universe is somehow associated with a transcendent infinite universe is affirmed in one way or another by a wide variety of spiritual paths and traditions. The idea that spirit is infinite is thus a well-respected spiritual principle recognized by Eastern and Western religions in both ancient and modern contexts. Simply put, the infinite is spirit and spirit is infinite. This panentheistic conception of an infinite, spiritual dimension of the universe is also supported by many leading academic theologians who believe it offers a spiritual perspective that is compatible with science but can also accommodate a plurality of religious views.[5] As noted, this transcendent and immanent infinite reality is understood not just as a quantitative or mathematical infinity but also as a qualitative or metaphysical infinity—an infinite realm of pure being in which oneness, or unity, is a primary characteristic. In this context it is also worth mentioning that panentheism avoids the problems of dualism by recognizing that the immanent spirit we find within the finite universe is ultimately a manifestation of the same transcendent spirit that resides in the domain beyond the finite.

Part of what makes this notion of a spiritual infinity so useful is how it leaves room for alternative conceptions of ultimate reality. That is, the infinite can be conceived of as being essentially formless and nondual, or it can be understood as a characteristic of a loving Creator. Both of these views understand ultimate reality to be more than simply infinity, and both develop the concept further in their own directions. But the basic idea that the source and ground of spiritual reality is infinite provides a foundation for the growing cultural agreement of evolutionary spirituality that is both pluralistically open and at the same time fairly solid.

Empirical Evidence for the Infinite

From a scientific perspective we can find support for the existence of an encompassing infinite realm in the circumstances of the big bang. Here I must emphasize that the big bang is no longer just a theory. It is now a well-established scientific fact, supported by four strands of observable evidence, that time and space itself began in an instant 13.8 billion years ago. Science tells us that the big bang emerged out of an "infinitely hot and dense" tiny point known as the *initial singularity*. We have no mathematics or physics that can describe this original state of absolute unity, but the word *infinite* is frequently used.

This distinct and dramatic beginning of our universe in the big bang clearly points to a first cause or "uncaused cause." And because what initiated the big bang necessarily precedes or is otherwise unbound by time and space, it is not a stretch to conclude that this cause is in fact infinite. While this interpretation is certainly not a proof, it does provide a powerful working hypothesis because, again, the premise that the universe has both infinite and finite aspects presents a widely agreeable spiritual ontology—one that is public and potentially acceptable to most spiritual paths. In other words, the idea that the source of the universe partakes of infinity is a proposition that many can accept. Indeed, it seems to me that the existence of an encompassing infinite reality can be generally inferred from what science has now revealed about our evolving universe.[6]

Although some scientists have tried to ignore the staggering significance of the big bang's original emergence, there is really no getting around the spiritual implications of this "first foundational fact"—the birth of finite reality and the beginning of evolution. Even if one subscribes to the multiverse theory (for which there is little evidence), this does not diminish the truth that our evolving universe had a definite beginning and that every evolutionary step since then rests on, and thus includes, this primordial emergence.

This recognition of a first cause, however, does not lead inevitably to the idea of a creator God. The emerging cultural agreement about what constitutes authentic evolutionary spirituality is somewhat flexible regarding the source of creativity in the universe. Within evolutionary spirituality the ultimate cause of our evolving cosmos can be understood alternatively as resulting either from a personal supreme being with a will of its own or from an impersonal creative principle. However, the idea that the universe arose out of nothing for no cause or reason, or the notion that our beautiful cosmic home is just a random accident with no larger meaning, is firmly rejected by evolutionary spirituality.

Experiential Evidence for the Infinite

Evidence for the reality of the infinite, however, is not limited to our scientific and philosophical understanding of the remote big bang. Experiential confirmation of the presence of the infinite is all around us, taking the form of spiritual experience itself (an idea we unpack in chapter 4). Yet even though the infinite can be directly experienced, it remains largely beyond the reach of human mental conception. The experiential evidence for the existence of infinite spirit is thus partially paradoxical—our experience of it is necessarily transconceptual or transrational, even though once experienced its reality cannot be easily denied. Despite this paradox, we can nevertheless begin to grasp and use this central principle of evolutionary spirituality through philosophical analogies that serve to simplify and ground the mind-bending reality of infinite spirit, bringing it into our finite understanding. Indeed, this is the substance of spiritual truth itself: the presence of the infinite within the finite realm of human mind. But, again, I am getting ahead of the story.

These notions of the relationship between an infinite universe of existential *being* and a finite universe of evolutionary *becoming* may at first seem too conceptually dense or philosophically abstract to be useful. But the spiritual truth of the relationship between these two realms is nevertheless impacting us directly in our everyday lives. The infinite is not far off; it is with us here and now—it is present to us in every instance of spiritual experience. And as discussed in the next section, the pursuit and cultivation of spiritual experience in all its forms serves as evolutionary spirituality's essential method and primary practice for spiritual growth. In fact, it is through this enlarged understanding of what spiritual experience is and how it works that evolutionary spirituality makes its advance over the other forms of spirituality discussed in the last chapter.

This overarching panentheistic conception of the interactive structure of the infinite and finite dimensions of reality becomes obvious and practical when we come to see how human consciousness serves to connect the infinite with the finite. It is through our ability to experience spirit that the phenomenal world of appearances becomes transparent to the infinite spirit that is always there. As we will see, the beautiful, the true, and the good, together with all related forms of intrinsic value, serve as windows on the infinite. These glimmers of perfection in time reunite being and becoming through our experience.

From this perspective, time itself can be understood as a gift to us. The finite universe provides an opening, or clearing, within the larger encompassing infinite universe wherein we are privileged to serve as agents of evolution and cocreators of something spiritually real, even in our exceedingly partial and highly imperfect state of human existence.

This concludes our initial overview of the major principles or tenets of evolutionary spirituality as I understand it. While these propositions may tend to contradict some of the venerable spiritual teachings of Eastern traditions, in chapter 6 I will justify the evolutionary necessity of these ideas and show how they are indeed compatible with notions of spiritual reality that point in different or even opposite directions.

THE PRACTICE OF EVOLUTIONARY SPIRITUALITY

Every viable form of spirituality includes practices that contribute to the personal growth of its followers. And in its efforts to carry forward and synthesize some of the best aspects of earlier forms of spirituality, evolutionary spirituality welcomes and includes a wide variety of established spiritual practices. For example, evolutionary spirituality celebrates the beauty and mystery of the rituals and devotions of religious spirituality. It values and respects the powerful practice of critical thinking and the scientific methodology revered by secular spirituality. And, of course, evolutionary spirituality embraces progressive spirituality's emphasis on meditation, contemplation, and the myriad forms of embodied practice that have flourished within the progressive spiritual milieu.

Evolutionary spirituality, however, also helps to establish new forms of spiritual practice, which we examine in this section. At this point in its early emergence, evolutionary spiritual practice is perhaps best summarized as *living the truths* that are now being revealed by the spiritual teachings of evolution. And this "lifestyle" approach to spiritual practice can be categorized under three main headings: (1) the practice of integral consciousness, or "dialectical epistemology"; (2) the practice of beauty, truth, and goodness, or "value metabolism"; and (3) the practice of bearing spiritual fruits, or "perfecting the universe." Although there is considerable overlap and synergy among these approaches, we consider each in turn.

The Practice of Integral Consciousness

Evolutionary spirituality can be generally appreciated and used by both modernists and postmodernists, but the center of gravity of the evolutionary spiritual perspective is found at the post-postmodern, or evolutionary, stage of cultural development (discussed further in chapter 8). Therefore, being able to make meaning from the vantage point of this evolutionary or integral worldview is very useful for getting the most out of evolutionary spirituality. However, practically every attempt to appreciate or practice evolutionary spirituality contributes to the development of an integral perspective within the practitioner, so integral consciousness is not a necessary prerequisite.

For most people, the development of integral consciousness begins by learning the basic tenets of integral philosophy. Although some seem to exhibit integral-level cognition naturally without any knowledge of integral philosophy, an ability to recognize the historical structures of psychosocial evolution in both the minds of our associates and in the current events of our society is very important. And this ability is guided and enhanced by a basic knowledge of integral theory.

Integral consciousness, however, is more than knowledge. It is a way of recognizing the development of human consciousness and culture through time, which leads to deeper understanding, greater compassion, and increased creativity and effectiveness in a wide variety of situations. This enlarged perspective is made possible through the emergent capacity known as *dialectical epistemology*. Dialectical epistemology, also called vision-logic or dialectical seeing, entails the ability to hold two or more opposing perspectives at once, while also recognizing how these opposing positions tend to mutually cocreate each other through their developmental tension. This is not just a matter of both/and seeing; it involves more than a relativistic appreciation of different points of view or a simplistic weighing of alternatives. This method of apprehending reality—an enhanced "depth perception" that recognizes evolution's vertical dimension of growth—requires a sympathetic integration of the natural tensions or developmental dichotomies, which are known within this practice as *polarities.*

Polarities are opposing yet interdependent principles or positions that continually reappear in the course of life. In an existential polarity each side tends to enact or cocreate the other by both contradicting and complementing its opposing pole. Familiar examples include the existential polarity of part and whole or individual and community, wherein opposing interests require continuous rebalancing or reconciling as conditions develop over time.

It is important to understand that the practice of dialectical epistemology is most useful for engaging existential polarities wherein the opposing pairs are both worthy of preservation, such as in the polarity of female and male. There is an important difference between mutually reinforcing positive-positive polarities, where both sides are "good," and positive-negative polarities, such as prosperity and poverty, that present more of a problem to be solved than a developmental system to be managed. According to organizational development consultant Barry Johnson, "Polarities to manage are sets of opposites which can't function well independently. Because the two sides of a polarity are interdependent, you cannot choose one as a 'solution' and neglect the other. The objective . . . is to get the best of both opposites while avoiding the limits of each."[7]

A common mistake is to approach an existential polarity as a straightforward problem with a relatively simple solution. For instance, postmodernists often view the polarity of competition and cooperation as a problem that requires competition to be lessened and cooperation to be increased. While many problematic situations can indeed be improved through greater cooperation, the attempt to eliminate all competitive tension usually results in the stifling of individual initiative and the drive for comparative excellence.

Authentic positive-positive polarities are existential and indestructible because they are woven into the fabric of the universe's becoming. They continually appear as a result of the outworking of evolution itself, which unfolds through the master technique of dialectical development (discussed further in chapter 4). So although such natural conflicts may be temporarily resolved, the underlying polarity that generates the opposition inevitably reappears in a new form.

Although dialectical epistemology can become a daily practice, it cannot be readily reduced to a formula or a simple technique. Dialectical seeing requires more than cognition; it is a process that employs both intellect and intuition to appreciate fully the underlying values that form the foundation of every authentic positive-positive polarity. This method involves literally identifying with both poles simultaneously so as to sense the direction of transcendence implied by their tension. Working with existential polarities in a way that brings out their developmental potential requires that polar opposites be understood within a larger whole that nevertheless preserves their differences. To do this, we have to value personally, or "own," the truth or goodness that inevitably lies at the heart of each pole, making them both "good."

This principle of polar interdependence is illustrated in the positive-positive polar relation between masculinity and femininity. Over the last fifty years or so our idea of what it means to be a "real man" has grown to include being sensitive and even occasionally emotional. Likewise, our ideals of femininity have evolved to include strong and independent women. In short, the realization of both mature masculinity and mature femininity involve a partial integration of the qualities normally associated with the other. When done well, however, such integration does not involve a move toward androgyny. While there is nothing wrong with androgyny, it is a compromise that eliminates creative tension. So in this example of dialectical integration, the cultural ideals of masculinity and femininity remain rooted in their existing gender differences even as each seeks to integrate the strengths of the other side. In this way, both poles use their contrasting differences to "true each other up."

This dialectical method is well explained in the context of spiritual practice by Charles Johnston in his 1991 book *Necessary Wisdom*.

Johnston observes, "Polarity is an inherent dynamic in any process of creation. . . . Seen creatively, polarities are expressions of the tension necessary to bring the new into being."[8] And because creativity—"bringing the new into being"—is an important element of evolutionary spiritual practice, this method of dialectical epistemology (or "bridging polarities," as Johnston calls it) is an indispensable aspect of evolutionary spiritual practice.

After describing the evolutionary context in which dialectical polarities arise, Johnston goes on to point out three errors, or "fallacies," that are almost always implicated in the spiritual practice of creatively bridging any given polarity. These potential errors appear either as a consistent bias toward one of the poles, or as the tendency to simply split all differences. Johnston identifies these three potential pitfalls as "separation fallacies," "unity fallacies," and "compromise fallacies."

According to Johnston, in a separation fallacy

> we side with one half of the polar two. Separation fallacies give ultimate truth to the more form-defined side of life. They express simultaneously a bias toward the archetypically masculine's fondness for distinction and a preferential valuing of the more manifest pole. . . . While separation fallacies are the most common in everyday thought, unity fallacies are most apt to trap us when we consciously try to think in integral ways. Unity fallacies confuse oneness with wholeness. . . . In the name of inclusiveness, unity fallacies quite specifically take sides, here with life's softer, more mysterious hand. When we fall for unity fallacies, in some small way, subtly or not so subtly, we confuse the oneness of the archetypally feminine with the more challenging reality of the creatively 'living' whole.[9]

Using the context of academia for his examples, Johnston cites science's bias for objectivity over subjectivity as an example of a separation fallacy and the humanities' bias for feelings over facts as an example of a unity fallacy.

Johnston then goes on to explain the third type of fallacy that arises in the context of bridging polarities:

> The compromise fallacy is not as sticky, but no less a trap. Such fallacies confuse integration with some additive middle ground. Rather than revealing the rich spectrum of colors that lies beyond black and white, they lead us to conclude that reality simply shows varying shades of grey.
>
> We can use a simple example from organizational theory to contrast the compromise fallacy with its more specific polar siblings. Asserting that organizations should always be hierarchically structured is a separation fallacy. Asserting the opposite, that hierarchies are bad, that decisions should always be made by consensus, brings a unity fallacy. A compromise fallacy would come up with some specific structure that combined hierarchy and consensus and then assert that this is how decisions should always be made. It misses that organizations are unique and evolve, that different contexts and times ask for dramatically different organizational approaches. The key to avoiding compromise fallacies lies in remembering that the task is not to split the difference between truth's two hands, but to live as the rich body or experience that joins them and animates them.[10]

In my experience, Johnston's insightful identification of the traps that can arise in the context of attempting to use dialectical epistemology provides an important tool for practitioners of evolutionary spirituality. This will become more evident when we return to our consideration of polarities in chapter 4, where we further explore the existential conditions of being and becoming that give rise to these natural features of our evolving universe. Then in chapter 7 we will use this understanding of the "three fallacies" to guide our search for a synthesis between the existential polarity of nondualism and theism that arises in the context of spiritual experience itself. But to complete this discussion of the practice of evolutionary spirituality, there are two additional practices to consider.

The Practice of Value Metabolism

In its essence, the practice of evolutionary spirituality is the practice of experiencing spirit. However, this entails more than simply "receiving an experience." To experience spirit in its fullness, we also have to express or share our experiences and thus reproduce them in the minds and hearts of our fellows. Ideally, we need to "take in" the inspiration afforded by spiritual experiences and also "give out" the energy of these experiences creatively in our work.

This process of "metabolizing the energy" of spiritual experience is clarified through an enlarged understanding of what the experience of spirit actually is and how it works. This expanded knowledge of spiritual experience is gained through the deeper appreciation of beauty, truth, and goodness that evolutionary spirituality provides. As we come to understand better the nature and behavior of these intrinsic values, we see how they are literally forms of spiritual energy that manifest through a circuit, like electrical energy. Stated succinctly, getting the most out of these intrinsic values requires both the experience and the creation of these qualities. From this perspective, beauty, truth, and goodness can be understood as essential forms of "spiritual nutrition." Just as maintaining our physical health requires that we take in nutritious food and then use that energy through exercise, we likewise do well to take in the spiritual energy of intrinsic value and then use this energy by bearing spiritual fruit of our own.

As a practical matter, this practice of metabolizing intrinsic values can be understood in terms of the giving and receiving activities through which these values are naturally lived out. For example, truth is practiced through the natural circuit of learning and teaching (with "learning and teaching" understood expansively to include not only communication but also demonstration). We can see this circuit-like behavior of truth in the way that we never really learn something until it "passes through us"—until we share it with another or otherwise give it out. And this energy-like behavior of truth is personally confirmed through the motivation it supplies. That is, when we learn something of real value that we are enthusiastic about it, we often become filled with the energy and desire to relate this truth to someone else.

As with the complementary and mutually supporting practices of learning and teaching truth, the practice of beauty is also optimized by engaging its practice in the circuit of "appreciating and creating." The idea here is that our ability to perceive beauty—to really see it in the world in more variety and with greater intensity—is greatly enhanced by our efforts to create beautiful expressions of our own. For instance, if we set out to paint a picture of a beautiful sunset, we must carefully observe the sunset's subtle details of color and form, as well as the overall majestic feeling produced by its colorful panorama. And this intention to express the beauty of a given sunset helps us see the beauty of that sunset with more depth and clarity than if we did not have a "use" for it. Thus, when we have an outlet for the creation of beauty, whether it involves creating images or music or simply beautifying our homes, we find that the act of expressing beauty opens the aperture of our minds to receive the light of more beauty of every kind.

Even though just about everyone practices some form of beauty and truth every day, the philosophical appreciation of the spiritual significance of these qualities leads to the mindfulness that helps elevate many of our regular activities to the level of spiritual practice. This evolutionary understanding of beauty and truth thus helps us have the spiritual experience that is all around us and always available.

However, the spiritual practice of beauty and truth not only makes the ordinary more extraordinary but also helps us see the highest expression of these values with new spiritual eyes. As we are instructed by the truth that truth itself is a window on the Divine, we may become filled with fresh enthusiasm for the many vehicles of truth by which we can be transported, including scientific, philosophical, literary, and religious truths. All of these forms of truth can literally raise our consciousness by attracting us to new locations—higher elevations—in the topography of consciousness and culture.

Like the practice of truth and beauty, the practice of goodness can also be understood in terms of the circuit-like metabolism of receiving and giving. The spiritual experience of goodness is received as we discern and appreciate instances of authentic quality and moral action in the world. And goodness is transmitted—created or taught like beauty or truth—in the form of service. Understood broadly, service is how we do good—it is how we communicate or give goodness to another person. As the Indian guru Neem Karoli Baba taught, "If you want to grow spirituality, serve someone, love someone."

The spiritual practice of value metabolism thus requires the intention to benefit others and a willingness to take action in the world. This is how the practice is embodied. It is "realized in the body" through the intentional physical action of serving, teaching, and creating the spiritual realities of goodness, truth, and beauty. Figure 2.2 below illustrates the natural circuits, the giving and receiving practice activities, that correspond to the experience and creation of these most intrinsic values.

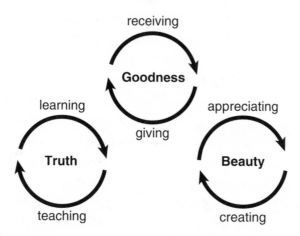

Figure 2.2. Natural circuits of value practice

Ultimately, this approach to spiritual practice through the idea of metabolizing goodness, truth, and beauty really comes alive when we allow ourselves to feel and respond to the inherent magnetism, or gravity, of these intrinsic qualities. Simply put, value metabolism is essentially the practice of cultivating the evolutionary impulse within our hearts, minds, and intentions. Through this method, our spiritual growth may be quickened as we become increasingly pulled by the upward currents of spiritual eros that subtly yet consistently persuade us to strive for ever-higher forms of perfection.

The Practice of Perfecting the Universe

This last point brings us back to the overall purpose of the finite universe and our place in it. As I am arguing, the spiritual teachings of evolution reveal that we are here to serve as agents of evolution and that our role in the cosmic economy is to help perfect the universe of self, culture, and nature through the experience and creation of beauty, truth, goodness, and love. And this "practice of perfecting" can be undertaken wherever conditions can be improved—wherever positive potentials remain unactualized and wherever good can be done, we can use our minds and bodies to make things better. And through this practice, our good works on behalf of others and ourselves—our fruits of the spirit—in turn become the rungs of the ladder of our own ascent.

By expanding and clarifying our understanding of spiritual experience in this way, evolutionary spirituality has the potential to uplift all forms of practice by showing how we can experience and create spiritual realities more efficaciously and more frequently. Through the realization that beauty, truth, and goodness are literally the presence of the infinite within the finite, the practice of evolutionary spirituality can help us see almost every moment as an opportunity to be mindful of the presence of spirit. This beauty, truth, and goodness spirituality thus shows us how to *live* the devotional practice of bearing spiritual fruit and evolving into more perfect beings in the process. As Sri Aurobindo taught, "All life is yoga."

EVOLUTIONARY SPIRITUALITY'S CURRENT STATE OF EMERGENCE

Admittedly, after the foregoing description of the exciting promise of evolutionary spirituality, any account of its current state of emergence is bound to sound comparatively limited or otherwise disappointing. Yet, as with every significant movement in human history, we have to start somewhere. And as of this writing in 2015, evolutionary spirituality is in its infancy. However, in order to connect and relate the rise of evolutionary spirituality to the other contemporary forms of spirituality described in the previous chapter, it is necessary to provide some specific cultural context, even if such context will soon be outdated.

From some perspectives, evolutionary spirituality can be traced all the way back to Jesus of Nazareth's teaching about spiritual growth and perfection. Evolutionary spirituality as I understand it, however, rests on the spiritual teachings of evolution itself. These teachings in turn rely on science's stupendous discovery of the processes of cosmological, biological, and cultural evolution, which have appeared only recently. In fact, the scientific evidence for the big bang was not confirmed until the early 1960s, and our growing realization that evolution is a ubiquitous cosmic process that affects everything is not much older than that. Moreover, evolutionary spirituality is also relying on the cultural accomplishments of progressive spirituality, which only began to appear in the 1970s. And because evolutionary spirituality is only just now emerging out of progressive spiritual culture, many contemporary teachings employing the term *evolutionary* nevertheless remain squarely within the progressive spiritual milieu. As is the case with practically all forms of evolutionary emergence, in the early phases it can be exceedingly difficult to draw hard lines between the "something more" and the "something less."

Distinguishing authentic forms of evolutionary spirituality from teachings that remain within the cultural realm of progressive spirituality is thus fraught with challenges. So even though some important aspects of the spiritual teachings of evolution can now be found within every major category of spirituality we have discussed, authentic evolutionary spirituality as I understand it is still very rare.

However, a reliable marker of authentic evolutionary spirituality is whether or not the teaching in question is informed by integral philosophy. That is, does it take the evolution of consciousness into account? Does it care about what is really true, and is it willing to be self-critical? Does it attempt to harmonize science and spirituality on their own terms? Does it recognize a vertical dimension of growth and allow for healthy forms of developmental hierarchy? Is it willing to recognize comparative excellence among different forms of spirituality? Has it overcome the shortcomings of progressive spirituality described in the last chapter? Although an integral or evolutionary perspective is usually required to answer these questions accurately in the first place, it is important to reaffirm here that evolutionary spirituality itself is emerging as part of the larger evolutionary worldview as a whole.

While there are many writers and teachers working in the wider field of integral theory and its applications, the number of those teaching integrally informed evolutionary spirituality per se is much smaller. In addition to my work, the list of contemporary teachers of evolutionary spirituality in America currently includes Ken Wilber, Andrew Cohen, Craig Hamilton, Terry Patten, Diane Hamilton, Jeff Salzman, Marc Gafni, Carter Phipps, Cindy Wigglesworth, Allan Combs, Roger Walsh, Bruce Sanguine, Ross Hostetter, and others. Although proponents of evolutionary spirituality can differ on many points (and although some carry unfortunate baggage), we are all united by our commitment to the evolution of consciousness and culture and by our common goal of participating in the emergence of a truer form of spiritual understanding that transcends the limitations of progressive spirituality. Of course, there are many other spiritual teachers on the current scene whose teachings come close to evolutionary spirituality or otherwise evince a strong affinity for it. Yet while many of these teachers may soon come to express the new truths of evolutionary spirituality more thoroughly and completely in their work, few do so now. And most of those who are able to make meaning from the perspective of the evolutionary worldview can clearly distinguish between authentic evolutionary spirituality and these less developed forms of progressive spirituality.

We will revisit the question of what distinguishes the fresh perspective of evolutionary spirituality from the most mature expressions of progressive spirituality in chapters 5 and 6. But now in the next chapter we turn to an examination of the foundation of evolutionary spirituality, and indeed the foundation of all future forms of spirituality, the human experience of spirit.

Chapter Three

SPIRITUAL EXPERIENCE FROM AN EVOLUTIONARY PERSPECTIVE

Now we are ready to consider the essential question: what is spiritual experience itself? While the various forms of spirituality we have considered each have their own answers to this question, the fresh insights of evolutionary spirituality shed considerable new light on the subject. The spiritual teachings we have reviewed in the previous two chapters provide an important context for our investigation. But gaining a deeper understanding of spiritual experience also requires us to reflect on the nature of spirit itself. That is, the question of what is spiritual experience cannot be adequately answered without considering the question of what is ultimately real.

While no human can claim to know ultimate reality in its fullness, many saints and sages have glimpsed the ultimate and brought back reports of its character and quality. Yet these reports differ widely. So the project of broadening our knowledge of spiritual experience necessarily involves comparing and contrasting the wide variety of spiritual experiences reported by people down through the ages, together with their varying notions of what is ultimately real. This, of course, is a daunting task, so we need to proceed by first considering spiritual teaching and practice (as we did in the first two chapters), then by considering experience itself (here and in the next chapter), and then by reflecting on ultimate reality (which we come to in chapters 5, 6, and 7). None of these elements can be adequately grasped in isolation; each is reinforced and illuminated by the others. And because these elements form a hermeneutic circle in which each helps explain the others, there is no simple way to start this analysis.

Acknowledging these challenges, in this chapter I will explore the major categories of spiritual experience currently recognized within the religious and academic literature on the subject. This chapter, however, is only a prelude to chapter 4's discussion of the expanded understanding of spiritual experience provided by evolutionary spirituality. Just as chapter 1 surveyed our culture's existing types of spirituality as a precursor to chapter 2's examination of evolutionary spirituality, this chapter likewise provides the context for the wider view of spiritual experience advanced in chapter 4.

If, as I claim, the essential practice of evolutionary spirituality is the cultivation of spiritual experience in all its forms, then the success of evolutionary spirituality's mission of providing more effective spiritual leadership for our culture depends largely on its ability to deliver progress on this critically important subject.

Coming to a deeper understanding of spiritual experience is crucial because as spirituality evolves it becomes increasingly firsthand. As people grow spiritually and become more sophisticated in their relationship to the sacred dimensions of life, their spirituality usually becomes increasingly personal. And as direct spiritual experience becomes the foundation of their spiritual lives, the source of spiritual authority is increasingly found within, in the leadings of the Higher Self. This personal turn does not necessarily result in the abandonment of historically received belief systems or the timeless teachings of spiritual masters about the nature of ultimate reality. But it does place central emphasis on the direct experience of spirit.

Observing this trend toward the increasing personalization of spirituality leads to the conclusion that the spirituality of the future will be based primarily on spiritual experience rather than on the authority of spiritual teachers or texts. Therefore, going forward the spiritual leadership capacity of any given form of spirituality will depend primarily on the quality of its interpretation of what spiritual experience actually is and how it can be most effectively accessed. In other words, to discover and adopt culture-building agreements about spiritual reality that transcend the limitations of the existing types of spirituality currently on offer in our culture, we would do well to start by improving our understanding of spiritual experience itself.

So in pursuit of a more sophisticated and practical interpretation of the nature and behavior of spiritual experience, in this chapter we first consider the reality of human experience and the limitations of what it can disclose. This leads to a brief discussion of the main categories through which spiritual experience is currently understood: mysticism, meditation and prayer, and psychedelic experience. After exploring these well-known kinds of spiritual experience, we briefly examine what the differing perspectives of neuroscience and natural theology can add to our understanding. Once we have completed this overview of our culture's contemporary understanding of the subject, we will be ready to return in the next chapter to our exploration of the spiritual experience that can be found within the good, the true, and the beautiful, which is evolutionary spirituality's central focus.

Experience and Its Limitations

I define *experience* according to the standard dictionary definition, which is "the process or fact of personally observing or encountering something or someone, as given by perception, understanding, intuition, memory, or other cognitive or intuitive input."[1] And while this definition may sound reasonable and straightforward enough, we immediately encounter problems.

The first problem for this notion of experience is found in the philosophical difficulties that arise when we divide reality into a "personally observing subject" and an "externally encountered object." This concept of subject-object dualism has been severely criticized by materialist philosophers who question the metaphysical implications of a subjective reality that is somehow separate from the objective physical realm. These reductionistic conclusions, however, do not pose a problem for integral philosophy, which overcomes this so-called mind/body problem by recognizing how interiority is a natural feature of the universe found at every level of its manifestation. These arguments are discussed elsewhere in my work and there is no need to review them here.[2] Suffice it to say that consciousness is real, that it cannot be reduced to the physical activity in our brains, and that our experience can provide at least a partially veridical account of our world.

Another potential problem for our notion of personal subjective experience is found in the implications of some Eastern spiritual teachings that the idea of a separate self is essentially an illusion. The difficulties arising from teachings that there is no separate self are addressed in chapter 6's discussion of evolutionary spirituality's concept of self, so we will revisit this complicating question about the reality of personal experience later in the book.

Beyond these potential challenges to the concept of subjective experience is the problem arising from the insight that human experience is not a "mirror of nature." Our perceptions are always partially constructed by the frame of reality we use to make meaning. As first argued by Immanuel Kant in the eighteenth century and developed further by postmodern thinkers in the twentieth century, philosophers have shown that perceptions of "reality" are always partially *constructed* by the observer. In other words, we can never know reality simply "as it is." Our apprehensions of the external world are inevitably colored by culture-bound interpretations and filtered through subjective and intersubjective lenses. In short, we are both finders and makers of the real. And while this is true of the physical world of objects and events, it applies even more to our attempts to make contact with spiritual realities.

However, even though we may not be able to apprehend spirit in naked objectivity, it does not follow that spiritual experiences are hopelessly subjective either. As I argue throughout this book, our experiences of spirit *do* make contact with genuine spiritual realities. And while human consciousness may still be far from seeing it clearly, I believe there is ultimately a "unity of truth," a single reality that we can come to know with increasing accuracy as we evolve.

By recognizing how consciousness evolves literally in the direction of truth—how our grasp on truth becomes stronger and thus more objective as we evolve—the evolutionary view helps us avoid the debilitating relativism of staunch "constructionism" on the one hand and naïve realism ("the myth of the given") on the other. The evolutionary perspective makes clear that the human ability to perceive or otherwise experience spiritual realities is tied to the perspective of an always evolving and maturing observer. And as perspectives develop and expand through the evolution of consciousness and culture, new spiritual realities become perceptible. As an example, when the first white men entered Yosemite Valley in 1851, only one of the party of over fifty reported being struck by the beauty of the place. Now, as a result of cultural evolution, the sublime beauty of Yosemite is evident to just about everyone.

Again, while spirit is not a straightforward "object" of experience, it is not merely subjective either. Simply put, as our consciousness evolves we can come to know the nature of reality with increasing depth and clarity. While it may seem obvious, this understanding of how the ability to experience spirit expands as our consciousness evolves is rarely accounted for in the extensive literature on spiritual experience, in both academic and religious contexts. But now, through the evolutionary perspective's insights into the "mobility of the real" we can become increasingly sensitive to the evolving nature of spiritual experience, and to the ultimate referent of this experience—spirit itself.

Contact with Transcendence

Notwithstanding the point that spiritual experiences are always partially constructed by the observer, I must emphasize my conviction that the majority of such experiences are in fact genuine. However, as William James ultimately concluded, the only way to measure the authenticity of such experiences is by the fruits they produce in the lives of those who have them.

Nevertheless, I can affirm that in my own life, as well as in the lives of many others I know and trust, our spiritual experiences are making authentic contact with something that transcends mundane physical reality. This "contact" is usually experienced as a glimmer of something beyond our normal awareness—a glimpse of something more complete or perfect. And these experiential hints of perfection contrast with our current human condition of incompleteness, thereby suggesting the potential for further growth. That is, such experiences confirm that we can and will transcend our current state of development—that transcendence is possible and that we are capable of experiencing spirit more fully and completely as we evolve. This affirmation is one reason why these glimpses of the transcendent are so attractive; they are a kind of a future echo, a foretaste of our destiny as ascendant pilgrims in time.

Indeed, the experience of spirit often goes beyond a sense of the transcendent by providing a taste of the *ultimate*—because spiritual experience is, as I contend, the experience of the infinite itself. And *the infinite is ultimate by definition*—infinity partakes of ultimacy. It is possible for humans actually to experience ultimate reality because, as most spiritual traditions teach, that which is infinite or ultimate actually dwells within us and serves as the foundational essence of who we really are. In such human encounters with ultimacy, the distinction between subject and object itself often becomes blurred through feelings of being enveloped in absolute oneness. Our deepest experiences of spirit can thus provide partial yet reliable access to that which is Absolute. Which means that our inquiries into the nature of ultimate reality cannot be dismissed as mere cosmic speculation. The spiritual experience of ultimate reality is not of something far off; it is of that which is nearer to us than our own breath.

Yet as noted, while most spiritual paths claim to provide authentic access to ultimate reality, their descriptions of the nature of ultimate reality vary widely. And this paucity of agreement among spiritual paths reveals how human experience alone cannot provide a complete or reliable picture of what is finally and ultimately real. The once-fashionable idea of a "perennial philosophy" that lies at the esoteric heart of all religions has now been rejected by many progressive spiritual intellectuals. For example, Jorge Ferrer writes: "The esotericist claim that mystics of all ages and places converge about metaphysical matters is a dogma that cannot be sustained by the evidence. . . . Even though perennialists, to their credit, reject both the exclusivism of exoteric believers and the inclusivism of sentimental ecumenism, their commitment to a nondual monistic metaphysic that is supposed to be Absolute, universal, and paradigmatic for all traditions is ultimately a return to dogmatic exclusivism and intolerance."[3]

A thorough explanation and critique of the perennial philosophy is beyond the scope of our inquiry here. We will, however, return to the subject of spiritual pluralism and the "unity of truth" in chapter 5, where we will further examine how evolutionary spirituality overcomes relativism without falling into the myth of the given. The cautionary point for now is that even as we attempt to deepen our understanding of spiritual experience, we must be mindful of the limitations of what such experience can disclose. The consciousness of humanity faces a long evolutionary road ahead, and our relationship to the spiritual experience we are here to have is only just beginning. While we can indeed experience the infinite partially and fleetingly, comprehensive knowledge of ultimate reality as a definitive whole (or even as an indefinite essence) is beyond the reach of our finite minds. Therefore, the small glimpses of ultimate reality that we can occasionally catch cannot be smoothly identified as confirming a particular spiritual teaching or belief system.

The need to be cautious about drawing definitive conclusions regarding the nature of ultimate reality is particularly important in the case of mystical spiritual experience, to which we now turn.

Mystical Spiritual Experience

The vast majority of writers on spiritual experience have focused on mysticism, which is most often defined as direct contact with the Divine, or the ultimate ground of being. Authentic mystical experiences are usually intense and nonordinary, transporting the subject into an altered state of consciousness wherein feelings of unity, joy, peace, and bliss are frequently reported. The literature on mysticism contains hundreds of detailed firsthand descriptions of mystical spiritual experiences from the reports of both ordinary people and the great mystics of history. But despite the abundant use of effulgent adjectives, the essence of the experience is often said to be ineffable. That is, no matter how evocative and articulate a given account of mystical experience may sound, the authors of such descriptions almost always lament that they cannot adequately depict the profundity of the experience in mere words. This is perhaps because a common characteristic of most forms of mysticism involves an encounter with the "Mystery"—a paradoxical and indeterminate reality that lies beyond the reaches of the human mind. Yet despite its ineffability, many mystics report that encountering the Mystery is a liberating, life-changing event.

Given the alluring and provocative character of the accounts of mystics, it is no wonder that scholars of religion have chosen to focus on this relatively rare subset of spiritual experience in general. Classic or prototypical mystical experiences are thought by many to represent the peak of spiritual experience. And I can attest to having had a variety of such experiences. Some have come upon me unexpectedly while listening to music or riding my bicycle. On these occasions, I have been overcome by intense feelings of joy and gratitude. Love and reassurance wash over me while my spine tingles and tears well up in my eyes. I have also had mystical experiences while backpacking alone in the wilderness. These events were characterized by a sense of timeless absorption into the essence of being, accompanied by a feeling of being watched over and cared for by some higher power.

A common element of my various mystical experiences was a deep conviction of having made contact with an authentically transcendent dimension; I had a strong sense of having witnessed a kind of "parting of the veil" through which I had been allowed a brief glimpse of an underlying spiritual reality. Yet even though I am acquainted with such nonordinary experiences, I would not describe myself as a mystic and am hesitant to hold myself out as an expert on spiritual experience of any kind. Nonetheless, I trust I have experienced enough to undertake this analysis.

Mystical spiritual experience is probably as old as religion itself. Reports of mystical rapture can be found in every traditional religion, as well as in pretraditional accounts of shamanic journeys. Traditional religious mystics in both the East and West penned elaborate descriptions of their mystical states, most of which included distinct categories and hierarchical levels in the approach to ultimate reality.

Although premodern religions sometimes celebrated their mystics, they were just as frequently scorned or ignored. It was not until the emergence of modernism that mysticism began to gain pride of place within Western religious scholarship, spurred by the rise of science and the resulting attempt to delegitimize religious truth claims. In the face of science's challenge to religion, modernist writers who remained committed to a spiritual worldview sought to find evidence for spiritual realities through scientifically respectable methods of empirical enquiry. And the accounts of religious experience reported by mystics seemed to offer such evidence.

This modernist defense of the reality of spirit begin in 1799 with Friedrich Schleiermacher's efforts to change the minds of his Enlightenment contemporaries, whom he called "the cultured despisers of religion." Building on Schleiermacher, spiritually inclined modernists have frequently pointed to the phenomenon of mystical experience to justify their belief in the authenticity of divine realities. As mentioned in the introduction, the most famous and influential attempt at a broadly empirical approach to spirit is found in William James's 1902 book *The Varieties of Religious Experience*. The quality of James's thinking and the success of this book helped make spiritual experience more respectable as a topic of academic philosophical enquiry. And throughout the twentieth century scholars with both traditional religious and secular loyalties attempted to chart the phenomenology of mystical experience.

Their attempts led to a variety of elaborate typologies of mysticism that sought to enumerate analytically the specific elements or levels of mystical experience. As examples, in the 1920s German philosopher Rudolf Otto defined the experience of "the numinous" as being at once fascinating and frightening. Then in the 1960s, English scholar W. T. Stace divided mysticism into two basic categories: "introvertive experiences" that take place entirely within the mind or interior awareness and "extrovertive experiences" that come through the senses, as in mystical encounters with nature. Writing around the same time as Stace, Catholic theologian Robert Zaehner identified three distinct forms of mystical experience, which he called nature mysticism, monistic mysticism, and theistic mysticism. Although often in competition, practically all typologies of mysticism presuppose a kind of universal, cross-cultural experience common to practitioners from every tradition. And this background assumption of naïve realism renders the entire typological approach to the subject somewhat suspect.

The literature on mysticism now contains a large number of alternative typologies, most of which have been advanced in support of a particular spiritual agenda. Some accounts privilege theistic experiences of a separate God. Others argue for a reductionistic explanation that comports with a secular worldview. But the majority of contemporary scholars of mysticism appear to be attracted to the subject because of the support it seems to offer for a nondual or monistic metaphysic of undifferentiated oneness as the ultimate reality.

While there is clearly a wide variety of mystical states of awareness, the limited scholarship on comparative mysticism does not provide a firm foundation on which to chart a detailed empirical map of mystical states or stages.[4] However, despite the lack of agreement in the literature on mysticism, one particular kind of experience (or category of experiences) does stand out in the accounts of mystics East and West and in both ancient and modern contexts. This is what as known as the *unitive experience*, defined by mysticism scholar Jerome Gellman as follows: "A unitive experience involves a phenomenological de-emphasis, blurring, or eradication of multiplicity. Examples are experiences of the oneness of nature, 'union' with God, the Hindu experience that Atman is Brahman (that self/soul is identical with the eternal, absolute being), the Buddhist unconstructed experience, and 'monistic' experiences, devoid of multiplicity."[5] In other words, under the influence of a unitive experience, mystics feel as though they are one with everything; subject-object distinctions collapse into a singular awareness wherein there is no separation between the observer and what is observed, either externally or internally. Although this distinctive category of mystical states of unity is widely reported and fairly well established, the specific types or levels of the unitive experience itself continue to be debated by spiritual teachers seeking to establish the authority of their favored interpretation.[6]

Regardless of its exact cartography (if there is one), the mystical unitive experience of "Absolute Being" is clearly one of the most significant kinds of spiritual experience that humans are capable of having. This profound experience is usually described as being "more real" than ordinary kinds of experience, and the persistent memory of its hyperlucid quality often endures throughout one's life. As we explore in the chapters ahead, the unitive experience serves as the experiential foundation for the family of spiritual paths that recognize nonduality as the ultimate reality.

Nondual, or unitive, states of consciousness sometime arise unexpectedly in the course of everyday life, such as while walking on the beach or simply looking out a window at a distant landscape. Such experiences can also be triggered by neurophysiological anomalies, mental illness, or even near-death events. More often, however, mystical unitive states, and spiritual experiences in general, are brought about through intentional spiritual practices, which we now consider.

MEDITATION AND PRAYER

Over the centuries, people have devised numerous practices and techniques that lead to spiritual experience of one kind or another. These practices include yoga, chanting, fasting, ecstatic dance, tantric sex, contemplative reading or writing, group rituals, nature immersion, and many others. But the most significant and widespread forms of spiritual practice fall under the general headings of meditation and prayer.

Meditation for Enlightenment

The word *meditation* is used to describe a variety of distinct spiritual practices, but within contemporary spiritual culture the most widely practiced form of meditation involves the mental technique known as "open monitoring" or "witness meditation," wherein one cultivates a nonreactive awareness of the content of experience moment to moment.

In America, millions of people meditate every day, and the growing popularity of meditation is a clear sign of cultural evolution. For many, however, the practice of meditation is undertaken primarily to reduce stress or to promote mindfulness. Those who practice meditation for merely physical or psychological wellness may find little about the experience that they would identify as spiritual. But for those who practice meditation with some kind of spiritual intent, spiritual experience usually follows.

The disciplined practice of meditation is said to be the most reliable way to achieve mystical states of consciousness. Yet according to English scholar of mysticism Paul Marshall, "It should be stressed that meditative states are not necessarily mystical states. Meditation leads to a variety of states, many of which bear little or no resemblance to mystical experience."[7] Nevertheless, it seems that the majority of contemporary mystics employ some version of witness meditation as their primary approach to mystical states of spiritual experience. Further, there appears to be significant overlap between the specific states of consciousness described by advanced meditators and the distinct experiences described by mystics throughout history.

There are, of course, many reasons to meditate. But when the practice of meditation is pursued primarily for the purposes of spiritual growth, it usually gravitates toward the well-developed form of spiritual practice best characterized as "meditation for enlightenment." Meditation for enlightenment employs witness meditation as a process for liberating the practitioner's consciousness from identification with the stream of thoughts that usually occupy the mind. This form of practice produces spiritual growth by creating a kind of spaciousness around the mind that is achieved by disidentifying from thoughts, feelings, and normal ego consciousness. By becoming less identified with the ego, practitioners often find that they can see things more clearly because they no longer need to construct or distort their perceptions of reality to defend their individual ego structure.

Meditation for enlightenment is a powerful and venerable spiritual practice that can benefit all who undertake it, regardless of their belief system or spiritual commitments. Yet both the culture and practice of meditation for enlightenment is most often oriented toward a nondual conception of ultimate reality. Put differently, this practice tends to gravitate toward a distinct kind of "attractor basin" within the inner landscape of spiritual experience. As discussed at length in chapters ahead, the world body of spiritual teachings discloses two essential conceptions of ultimate reality, which can be generally identified as "nondual" and "theistic." These alternative visions of ultimacy are more than mere doctrinal differences; they arise from distinctive features of the direct experience of spirit itself. This idea is carefully explained and defended in chapter 5.

The point for now is that meditation for enlightenment is a practice that leads most often to nondual or unitive forms of spiritual experience. Although witness meditation can be a rewarding practice for theists and secularists, and although it can result in a wide variety of spiritual experiences, the unitive state of undifferentiated oneness represents the pinnacle of the spiritual experience that can be realized through this practice.

Communing with the Creator

Just as the practice of meditation for enlightenment gravitates toward nondual conceptions of ultimacy, prayer is a spiritual practice primarily associated with theistic notions of a self-aware Creator as the ultimate reality. And as with meditation, the practice of communing with the Creator can result in a wide variety of spiritual experiences.

Within progressive spirituality, however, prayer is often misunderstood as being merely a traditional-level practice. Opponents of theism sometimes even belittle prayer, characterizing it as a selfish petition for supernatural intervention or a request for special treatment from a capricious deity. But, also like meditation, the practice of prayer deepens and develops as consciousness evolves. At postmythic levels of spiritual development, prayer is increasingly approached not as a method for changing the mind of God but rather as a method for changing the character of the practitioner.

As the practice of prayer matures, recitals of specifically prescribed words or formal petitions for desired outcomes are gradually replaced by sincere and spontaneous expressions of gratitude and affection for the personal Source of all that is. Prayer fosters a living relationship between creature and Creator as practitioners "talk things over" with God in a purely personal way. Although this personal conversation does not usually involve "hearing the voice of God," the communication is nevertheless two-way. God answers prayer by increasing the spiritual receptivity of the practitioner, resulting in deeper realizations of goodness, truth, and beauty.

The practice of prayer is also closely related to the spiritual practice of faith. Like prayer, at postmythic stages of development faith transcends mere belief. Mature faith is a kind of superconsciousness that provides access to levels of reality beyond our normal mental capacity. Faith is the "assurance of things hoped for, and the proof of things not seen"[8] that increasingly brings the realities of spirit into the lives of the faithful.

As we explore at length in chapters 5, 6, and 7, progressive spirituality often resists the theistic premises of prayer, even if for evolutionarily appropriate reasons. Within some progressive spiritual circles, the practice of prayer has accordingly been recast as a form of witness meditation known as centering prayer.[9] While the practice of witness meditation in the context of progressive Christianity or Judaism is certainly a good thing, there are specific forms of spiritual experience that are accessed most effectively through the original practice of prayer, which involves personal communication with the Creator. As we will see, theistic forms of spirituality point to their own distinct "attractor basin" within the inner landscape of spiritual experience, which both complements and contradicts nondual conceptions of ultimate reality. And this essentially theistic aspect of ultimate reality can be directly experienced as the personal love of the Creator for each individual creature. The love of God can, of course, be experienced in centering prayer or any kind of meditation. And states of profound unity can likewise be experienced in the original form of communion prayer. But just as the apogee of witness meditation is nondual realization, the apogee of communion prayer is the direct experience of God's love.

Beyond the categories of spiritual experience explored above, there are certainly other significant kinds of spiritual experience, such as collective spiritual experience, that considerations of brevity prevent me from addressing. This chapter is not intended to serve as a comprehensive catalog of spiritual experiences. There is, however, one more important type of spiritual experience that deserves our attention here—the category of nonordinary experiences produced by psychedelic drugs. Although psychedelic spiritual experience is controversial, it has nevertheless demonstrated the potential to produce positive evolution in both consciousness and culture.

PSYCHEDELIC SPIRITUAL EXPERIENCE

For thousands of years, and perhaps even before the emergence of *Homo sapiens*, humans have altered their consciousness through the use of psychoactive botanicals. While most of these substances produce merely a mild mood-altering effect, a few have been found to trigger profound nonordinary states, which are inevitably imbued with religious significance by the cultures that employ them. The use of psychedelics for religious purposes can be traced to the classical civilizations of antiquity, such as in the Eleusinian Mysteries of the Greeks or the sacred soma used in Vedic rituals. Psychedelic botanicals have also been in continuous use as sacraments in indigenous cultures worldwide for centuries at least. The existence of such mind-altering psychedelic substances, however, was largely unknown to the culture of the developed world until early advocates of progressive spirituality began to extol the virtues of psychedelic experience.[10]

Among the first progressive spiritual intellectuals to write about the mystical merits of psychedelic experience was Aldous Huxley, whose 1954 book *The Doors of Perception* introduced mescaline to a generation of curious spiritual seekers. Interest in substance-induced spiritual experience would later become widespread and highly visible in Western culture in the 1960s as the countercultural youth movement burst upon the scene. As a result of the zealous promotion of LSD and other psychedelics by Timothy Leary and others, these substances soon came to be regarded as a threat to the established social order and were eventually classified together with addictive narcotics as dangerous and illegal drugs. But despite the imposition of strict penalties for their use, these outlawed substances would nevertheless play an undeniable role in the emergence of progressive spirituality as a distinct form of spiritual culture. And having lived through this history myself, I can testify to the authentic spiritual significance of psychedelic experience.

Before going on, I must acknowledge that the following positive portrayal of psychedelic drugs as a legitimate category of spiritual experience will likely offend or otherwise put off some readers whom I care very much about. So let me begin by offering the caveat that psychedelic drugs can be dangerous, that they are still illegal, and that they are certainly not for everyone. Psychedelics, now euphemistically referred to as "entheogens" within progressive spirituality, are neither a central nor necessary feature of evolutionary spirituality. However, as evolutionary spirituality attempts to include and carry forward the best aspects of progressive spirituality in its transcendent emergence, it cannot leave the power of psychedelic experience completely behind. Further, because psychedelic experience has had a profound influence on my own spiritual development, it would be dishonest to avoid or overlook this category of spiritual experience in our discussion, despite the potential cost to my reputation as an author.

Some knowledgeable writers on the subject, such as religious scholar Houston Smith, argue that the nonordinary states induced by psychedelics are largely identical to the classic categories of mysticism. In my experience, however, while there is some overlap between mystical and psychedelic states, the special quality and variety of psychedelic experience warrants its classification as a distinct form of spiritual experience.

Also, as with mystical experience, the spiritual content of psychedelic experience often serves as a kind of Rorschach test for one's spiritual belief system. Such experiences are frequently interpreted in terms corresponding to a particular spiritual teaching about ultimate reality. But despite this tendency, I believe it is possible to use the common features of these experiences to broaden our understanding of the reality of spirit.

As noted, mystical experiences have been overly *universalized* by commentators seeking to interpret a wide variety of distinct encounters with the transcendent as experiences of essentially the same thing. By contrast, psychedelic experiences have been overly *particularized* by claims that such experiences are unique for each person and highly susceptible to contextual influences, known as "set and setting." Yet even though set and setting are important, the experiences produced by various psychedelic substances are relatively predictable and cross-culturally similar. And this commonality is reinforced by the fact that different psychedelic substances produce reliably distinct spiritual experiences, especially when such substances are taken with a sacramental intention.

For example, those who take a proper dose of ayahuasca (a brew made from two rainforest botanicals) inevitably embark on an inward journey of deep personal insight and discovery that frequently results in positive life changes. I can attest that after taking ayahuasca for the first time in 1994 I felt a little like Saint Francis of Assisi the next day. The experience left me with an extraordinary sense of love for each person in my life; I felt more free, more gentle, more reassured, and more open to the synchronistic assistance of larger spiritual forces that I could not understand but nevertheless knew were active in my life. Even though this elevated feeling wore off after a few days, the ayahuasca experience did in fact result in a "course correction" in my life that proved to be an important step in my personal spiritual development.

Now in my fifties, having practiced many forms of spirituality and having had a wide range of spiritual experiences going back to my youth, I can affirm that both natural and synthetic psychedelic substances are capable of producing intense encounters with undeniable spiritual realities. Although, as noted, different substances produce distinct experiences, most entheogens have a strong "noetic quality" that provides access to profound insights beyond the reach of normal cognition. In most cases, the onset of a psychedelic experience brings a palpable sense of cosmic consciousness in which the spiritual nature of the universe is almost laughably obvious. And even after coming down from the drug, the profundity of the insights and the conviction of having made contact with higher spiritual realms strongly remain. Indeed, I have found that every one of my psychedelic journeys has had a moral—a practical lesson seemingly tailored to my personal spiritual needs at the time.

Although beyond my personal experience, some users actually report psychological and even physical healing resulting from psychedelics. While I could certainly go on about the spiritual phenomenology of various psychedelic substances, suffice it for now to conclude that entheogens provide authentic and reliable access to undeniably spiritual experience. Yet if this is the case—if life-changing spiritual experience can be produced simply by altering our brain chemistry—then what does this mean for spiritual experience in general? Can spiritual experience be reduced to a neurological explanation?

Spiritual Experience and the Brain

Secular spirituality, of course, has a strong interest in denying or otherwise refuting the apparent metaphysical referent of every kind of spiritual experience. Freud, for example, categorized mystical experience as a remnant of the pre-separative ego state of infants. Other materialist authors have analyzed spiritual experience from the perspective of evolutionary psychology, arguing that the religious impulse is merely a functionalist mechanism that promotes group solidarity and thus species survival. Evolutionary psychology, however, is merely one of many strategies used by materialists to explain away spiritual experience as simply being "all in the head." Over the last two decades this materialist explanation has been seemingly fortified by advances in brain-imaging technologies, such as PET, SPECT, and fMRI machines. These technologies have spurred a now-immense scientific project of discovering "the neural correlates of consciousness," and many expect the findings of this research to eventually reduce the explanation of mental states of awareness to the electrical-chemical activity of the brain.

Using these techniques, some researchers have studied the brains of advanced meditators in an attempt to isolate or explain spiritual experience in purely neurophysiological terms.[11] And I believe these investigations, sometimes called "neurotheology," are certainly worthwhile. In fact, according to integral philosophy there is a strong connection between the interior and exterior (or mental and physical) dimensions of evolution, with the complexity of consciousness generally corresponding to the complexity of the brain it inhabits.[12] So we would naturally expect to find many correlations between states of conscious awareness and brain states. However, such correlations do not provide grounds for gross reductionism. Indeed, the spiritual teachings of evolution clearly reveal how reductionism in all its forms is essentially false. This is shown by the very structure of emergence, wherein something more keeps coming from something less. Just as life cannot be reduced to matter, conscious awareness—ordinary or nonordinary—cannot be reduced to brain states. According to philosopher Evan Thompson, neuroscience's foundational assumption that the mind is in the brain is confused. "It's like saying that flight is inside the wings of a bird. . . . You need a brain, just as the bird needs wings, but the mind exists at a different level."[13] Moreover, despite the loose correspondences that can be found between subjective consciousness and objective brain activity, the entire project of charting the neural correlates of consciousness is called into question by numerous, carefully documented near-death experiences demonstrating that consciousness and even perception can continue when the brain is effectively dead.[14]

Interestingly, the idea that spiritual experience cannot be reduced to the brain may at first seem to be challenged by the case of psychedelic drugs, which appear to act as powerful triggers of such experiences merely by the ingestion of certain brain-altering chemicals. Researchers have found that psychedelic substances mimic the brain's natural neurotransmitters, either blocking or releasing chemicals naturally produced by the brain, such as serotonin, dopamine, and norepinephrine. Different psychedelics result in distinct experiences by producing unique combinations of inhibition and release, altering the brain's chemistry in a manner that can be compared to the playing of a musical instrument. Extending the analogy, we can see how each kind of entheogen plays a unique set of "chords on the keyboard" of the brain's neurotransmitter receptor sites, which results in the distinct versions of psychedelic experience.[15]

Neurophysiologists who have never experienced a powerful psychedelic journey may be attracted to the reductionist implications of these chemical triggers of spiritual experience, but most of those who have actually had such experiences know better. That is, entheogens clearly reveal an expanded dimension of reality, and becoming aware of the very presence of such an enlarged reality serves as a spiritual teaching in itself. And despite some claims to the contrary, such experiences cannot be induced in their fullness through breath work, ecstatic dance, meditation, or other nonpharmacological techniques. That is why psychedelic spiritual experience must be recognized as a distinct category of its own and not merely a shortcut to classic mystical experiences better achieved through natural practices.

Initiation into the spiritual insights provided by entheogens reveals how we are truly "behind a veil" in our ordinary state of awareness. From the inside, the phenomenology of practically all psychedelic substances points to a conception of the brain not as a generator of consciousness itself, but as a filter or "reducing valve" limiting our perception of the larger reality that is all around us, so we can function in the everyday world. In fact, neuroscience may eventually show that the brain can be more accurately conceived as a receiver or "antenna" for consciousness rather than as an original generator of it.[16]

Regarding the relationship between neurotheology and spiritual experience in general, it must be acknowledged that much of what we experience is clearly determined by our physiology. We are also determined to a great extent by the larger cultural structures we use to make meaning. But in between the deterministic influences of both our brains and our culture, we each have a small degree of freedom. And it is through this gift of freedom that we are privileged to serve as authentic agents of evolution.

SPIRITUAL EXPERIENCE AND NATURAL THEOLOGY

In this chapter so far we have considered spiritual experience through conceptually familiar frames of reference. As we have seen, within the culture of progressive spirituality at least, spiritual experience is most often understood in terms of mystical encounters or nonordinary epiphanies. And as we have also discussed, although these extraordinary-state experiences occasionally occur spontaneously and unexpectedly, they are most often achieved through disciplined spiritual practices or through entheogenic substances used with sacramental intent.

Up until now, however, we have not focused on the more common-place spiritual experience that occurs "along the way"—the experience that is around us all the time, like the proverbial water around the fish. The idea here is that if spirit is real, then it should be something we can live and breathe, something we can use in our work, and something that enlivens and nourishes us as the sustenance of our very existence. While disciplined spiritual practices such as meditation can certainly help integrate spiritual experience into daily life, as we discuss in the remainder of this chapter and in the next chapter spirit can also be abundantly experienced in our normal waking states and in our regular frames of mind.

Down through the ages humans have consistently encountered indications of the influence of spirit in their everyday experiences and in the natural world at large. These apparent forms of evidence for spirit have served as the basis for a variety of classic arguments for the existence of God, which have been made again and again by sensitive thinkers in almost every generation. Even before the emergence of Christianity, ancient Greek philosophers developed teachings that attempted to prove the existence of divinity. While such arguments for God have never proved entirely persuasive or decisive—while they do not work as formal proofs—they have never been decisively refuted either. And not only do these lines of reasoning continue to attract proponents, they also continue to compel atheist philosophers to attempt to explain why these forms of evidence for the Divine do not actually confirm a spiritual reality. In other words, even those who are hostile to the idea of spirit can nevertheless feel the force of these classic forms of spiritual evidence.

Now, in my opinion, the powerful experiential realities of beauty, truth, and goodness provide the best evidence for the reality of God, or spirit, and, again as promised, we will focus on these elements of spiritual experience in the next chapter. But before going to the heart of the matter, it is worth briefly exploring the philosophical approach to spiritual reality found in the recently reemerging field of natural theology.[17]

Although numerous arguments for God continue to be debated by academics, there seem to be three main types that get the most traction: *cosmological arguments*, which point to the sheer existence of the universe; *teleological arguments*, which point to nature's intricate order or apparent purposiveness; and *moral arguments*, which contend that the widespread human sense of moral duty or obligation is best explained by the existence of God. While these arguments continue to be made by contemporary theologians, they are effectively marginalized within mainstream academia and appear to be of interest only to specialists.

Recently, however, these classic arguments for God have been reframed in a way that better connects them with the spiritual experience available to the average person. In his insightful book *Natural Signs and Knowledge of God*, Christian theologian C. Stephen Evans recasts these philosophical arguments, viewing them not as convincing proofs in themselves, but rather as indications of underlying forms of natural spiritual experience (which he calls "natural signs of God") that can be felt by believers and unbelievers alike.

Evans focuses on four such natural signs, which he identifies as (1) our sense of cosmic wonder that the universe actually exists; (2) our perception of the beneficial order found in nature; (3) our recognition of the fundamental value of human persons; and (4) our sense of moral duty or obligation. According to Evans, these natural signs consistently elicit universal human responses to the presence of divinity in the universe. He notes that while signs 1 and 2 can be explained scientifically as arising from purely physical causes and while signs 3 and 4 have been subject to evolutionary psychology's attempts to explain them away, the authentic spiritual communication or experience provided by these signs cannot be entirely defeated or extinguished by naturalistic explanations.

Evans goes on to observe that each of these natural signs of spirit evince the common characteristics of being both *widely accessible* and *easily resistible*. The signs are widely accessible in the way they can evoke spiritual experience without requiring any special knowledge or specific beliefs. Even children can feel cosmic wonder and the beneficial order of nature, and some children as young as two have been shown to have a sense of fairness or moral duty. Yet even though these signs of divine presence or divine influence are available to everyone, they do not compel us to believe or overawe us in a way that forces us to conclude that reality has a spiritual source.

Further, Evans shows how these apparent principles of spiritual experience—wide accessibility and easy resistibility—were originally identified by the seventeenth-century French philosopher Blaise Pascal, who wrote: "[God wishes] to appear openly to those who seek him with all their heart and hidden from those who shun him with all their heart;

he has qualified our knowledge of him by giving signs which can be seen by those who seek him and not by those who do not."[18]

Notwithstanding the Christian convictions of Pascal and Evans, I think it is possible to receive the "messages" of these natural signs and benefit from the spiritual experience they provide without interpreting them according to a theistic conception of God as the ultimate reality. As we explore further in the chapters ahead, authentic spiritual experiences can be interpreted as leading to either theistic or nontheistic conclusions about the nature of ultimate reality. Indeed, "cosmic wonder" is a form of spiritual experience now being widely promoted within secular spirituality. And as Evans points out, there are many additional kinds of natural signs of spirit that have nothing to do with arguments for any kind of spiritual ontology. In fact, from certain perspectives practically everything within our evolving universe of nature, self, and culture can be interpreted as a natural sign of spirit.

Yet, as I hope this discussion is beginning to show, there are certain types of experience that do reveal the presence of the infinite more profoundly than others. So in furtherance of the goal of evolving our understanding of what it means to experience spirit, in the next chapter we explore essential forms of spiritual experience that are even more basic than those disclosed by Evans's natural signs. That is, to get in touch with the most palpable, usable, and transformative aspects of spiritual experience, we need to try to come as close to the actual presence of the infinite as possible, while remaining grounded in the finite. This involves getting at the root of spiritual experience found in the most fundamental forms of intrinsic value that humans can know. And this investigation is the focus of the next chapter.

Chapter Four

THE SPIRITUAL EXPERIENCE OF
PERFECTING THE UNIVERSE

Now we come to the heart of our inquiry, which is how we can broaden and deepen our understanding of what spiritual experience is and how it functions in our evolving universe. The emerging evolutionary perspective allows us to see something new and say something more about spiritual experience because it clarifies how the infinite and the finite interact in the process of evolution. And this clarified understanding results in useful insights into the nature and behavior of beauty, truth, and goodness. Moreover, as we come to see how these intrinsic values are literally the presence of the infinite within the finite, this knowledge helps explain what spirit itself actually is, which helps "naturalize" both spiritual experience and its ultimate referent. In other words, when we begin to recognize how the infinite moves the finite realms of self and culture toward perfection through its influence on the consciousness of free-will creatures like us, the metaphysical and supernatural are revealed as being actually quite natural and intelligible.

The promise of this expanded knowledge of spiritual experience is that it could eventually lead to a relatively universal agreement that spirit by whatever name actually exists. Even as it retains respectful pluralism and allows for a diversity of convictions about what is ultimately real, such a new agreement could foster greater social solidarity and cooperation and thereby supply some of the spiritual leadership our civilization needs.

This hope for greater spiritual solidarity within our society transcends wishful New Age thinking when we begin to see how evolutionary spirituality's enlarged understanding of spiritual experience can actually lead to a pragmatic new method for raising consciousness. As we will explore in chapter 8, the evolutionary perspective's insights into the spiritual experience of intrinsic values provide an enhanced ability to reproduce such experience in others. And this new power to cultivate spiritual experience in the minds of our fellows may eventually bring about an effective technique for producing large-scale evolution within human consciousness and culture.

Admittedly, this chapter is philosophically dense. In fact, this investigation into the deeper aspects of the spiritual experience of beauty, truth, and goodness is the most intellectually challenging chapter in this book. But despite the mental effort required, the work of improving our theoretical understanding of spiritual experience is indispensible because, as Einstein wrote, "Whether you can observe a thing or not depends on the theory which you use. It is the theory which decides what can be observed."[1] So in furtherance of our efforts to better "observe" the phenomenon of spirit moving in the world, this chapter explores some of the further reaches of the spiritual teachings of evolution. Although this theoretical discussion may be challenging in places, it is designed to make the experience of spirit more vivid, more frequent, and more fruitful.

As I will argue, the most important spiritual experiences—those providing the most growth for ourselves and the most impact for our world—are experiences of the good, the true, and the beautiful, together with similar forms of intrinsic value. And the experience and practice of these intrinsic values becomes significantly enhanced through the realization that the beautiful, the true, and the good are the "currency of the cosmos"—the means by which the finite universe of time evolves toward its ultimate end of experiential perfection.

As an overview, first I introduce a philosophical frame for the discussion by describing how the infinite interacts with the finite. We then revisit the evolutionary spiritual practice of perfecting the universe initially discussed in chapter 2. This is followed by an in-depth exploration of the reality of beauty, truth, and goodness, where we consider further how these values represent comprehensible elements of divinity in the realm of time. Then, after a close examination of the nature and behavior of these intrinsic values, we contemplate the essential function of human consciousness in the evolutionary perfection of the universe. This discussion of consciousness explores how the freedom of our human wills provides "an opening in the finite" through which the actuality of the infinite—the perfect being of the infinite—can "enter" the finite and thus improve and evolve our world. The chapter then concludes with a brief consideration of how evolutionary spirituality's enlarged understanding of the nature of spiritual experience can lead to a more unified knowledge of physics and metaphysics.

THE INTERACTION OF INFINITE BEING AND FINITE BECOMING

I believe that the key to a deeper understanding of spiritual experience in general, and beauty, truth, and goodness in particular, is found in evolutionary spirituality's panentheistic insights into the interactive relationship between the finite and infinite aspects of the universe. According to panentheism, the overall structure of reality can be broadly understood as consisting of *infinite being* and *finite becoming*. And, as noted before, this idea that our finite universe of time is encompassed and permeated by a larger infinite reality is affirmed by a wide variety of spiritual paths and traditions. Moreover, all of these various forms of spirituality connect this notion of metaphysical infinity with their own definitions of spirit in one way or another.

It thus bears repeating that according to my interpretation of evolutionary spirituality our finite realm of evolutionary becoming has evidently emerged so that the preexisting and perfect realm of infinite being can be augmented and supplemented by the creaturely experience of gradually becoming perfect in and through time. In other words, infinite being has called forth the evolving universe of time wherein free will creatures like us may cocreatively participate in achieving perfection through the process of spiritual growth—the process of perfecting the universe of self, culture, and nature. This creative gift of time allows the self-aware citizens of the universe to participate in the grand adventure of integrating the infinite back into the finite through our own experience and creation of the relatively more perfect. And that which is relatively more perfect is best conceived as that which is more beautiful, true, good, and loving.

Transforming the Transcendent into the Immanent

At the human level of existence we can make contact with infinite spirit in two basic ways: first as our consciousness experiences spirit, and second as we create spiritual experience in others in the many ways we can, and especially through the perfecting quality of beauty, truth, and goodness. Our experience of these realities puts us in touch with the transcendent. And when we then share these realities by making things better and creating spiritual experiences for others, we help transform the transcendent into the immanent. This is how we perfect the universe.

Recognizing how our mental, emotional, and even physical experiences of spirit serve to reveal the infinite also suggests that the "presence of the infinite" is more accurately conceived as the "absence of the finite." The Indian sage Ramana Maharshi described the relationship of the infinite and the finite using the analogy of a film being projected onto a screen. According to Maharshi, the infinite does not "enter the phenomenal world"; rather, in the experience of the infinite the phenomenal world partially withdraws, becoming translucent to the oneness that lies underneath, like the screen that underlies a movie. We find similar ideas in many other traditions that understand their sacred sites as "thin places" where the realm of normal appearances becomes transparent to the spiritual reality that lies underneath. This idea was expressed by the Christian contemplative Thomas Merton, who wrote, "We are living in a world that is absolutely transparent, and God is shining through it all the time."[2]

This idea of the finite becoming transparent to the underlying infinite helps us understand beauty, truth, and goodness as *windows into divinity*. In the same way that a window is less than a wall, which lets the light shine in, these primary forms of intrinsic value render the finite realm diaphanous, allowing us to see through it to the light of infinite spirit that is always already there. Yet, as we explore further below, in their most sublime instances, these primary values are more than structures that let the light shine into our experience. They are also the light itself, which suggests that the common notion of the "light of truth" is more than simply a metaphor.

The Dialectical Polarity of Infinite and Finite

Our philosophical understanding of the interaction of the infinite and the finite is further clarified when we begin to see how this process occurs most often at the level of human experience through the developmental function of *existential polarities*. This idea of existential polarities was first introduced in chapter 2 in the context of the evolutionary spiritual practice of dialectical epistemology. There we saw how polarity is an inherent dynamic in any process of creation. Now we revisit this idea to consider further how these macroaspects of the universe—the infinite and the finite—interact at the microlevel of human experience.

According to my understanding, infinite being and finite becoming can be understood as a kind of *primordial polarity*, which first came into existence when the finite was differentiated from the infinite in the big bang. Most Western religionists recognize this prime polarity in terms of Creator and creation, while many Eastern religionists acknowledge it as Absolute and relative. This primordial polarity functions as a kind of master pattern, or birthmark, that can be detected throughout the universe. Traces of this existential birthmark of the original emergence of the finite within the infinite are found at every level of the universe in the form of existential dialectical polarities that characterize the pattern and process of evolution itself.

Familiar examples of these natural, indestructible, positive-positive polar realities include part and whole, self and community, male and female, order and freedom, competition and cooperation, simplicity and complexity, and many similar dichotomies. And it is through the ongoing integration of polarities at every level that the finite universe grows toward ever-higher states of development. For instance, the integration of the polarity of male and female results in the reproduction of life, and the integration of the polarity of self and community results in the establishment of fairness.

This ubiquitous polar constitution of our evolving universe—the yin and the yang—arises from the partial, temporal, imperfect, and gradually becoming character of our finite home. In other words, the dynamic relationship between the two sides of every existential yin-yang-like polarity subtly reflects the overall structure of our evolving universe. Through the microcosmic recapitulation of the overarching prime polarity—the primordial relationship of the infinite whole and the finite part that arose with the big bang—these permanent positive-positive polarities function as miniature systems of development. Simply put, existential polarities are localized engines of evolution that mirror the dialectical function of the evolving universe as a whole. And this fractal, or self-similar, relationship between the polarities we encounter daily and the original prime polarity is itself a kind of unity—unity across scale—which is another marker of the spiritual character of these existential polarities.

However, I do not mean to imply that these existential polarities are perfect literal models or exact replicas of the prime polarity of the infinite and the finite. The common polarities we find here on earth merely exhibit the faint traces or echoes of the original creative emergence. But what they do usually retain of this origin event is the general character of part and whole. That is, the finite became *a part* of the infinite 13.8 billion year ago through the primordial emergence that marked the beginning of time. And this original creative act continues to be subtly reflected in practically all the positive polarities we encounter in our journey. Indeed, this act of creation is ongoing moment to moment as "the new" is continuously brought into being.

It is also important to acknowledge in this context that while all existential polarities may exhibit opposing yet interdependent relationships, their poles are not necessarily equal or otherwise perfectly balanced. Some polarities, such as male and female, are equal in many important respects, even while they continue to reflect the creative motif of part (male) and whole (female). But other existential polarities are decidedly less balanced, such as the polarity of part and whole itself. Obviously, just as the finite is not equal to the infinite, the part is not equal to the whole.

The process through which polarities bring forth value and serve as engines of evolution is further explained through the observation that almost every positive-positive polarity we encounter is a *dialectical system of development*—a portal for growth that we can use to evolve.

The idea of a dialectical system is usually understood through the simplified construct of thesis-antithesis-synthesis: we start with an existing condition—the thesis. But as time passes, the thesis decays and becomes increasingly inadequate. This situation is initially remedied by the appearance of an antithesis—a condition or thing defined through its opposition to the problems or inadequacies of the original thesis. Once an antithesis emerges, it usually reveals an authentic polarity. The antithesis represents an attempt to move beyond the limitations of the prevailing conditions represented by the original thesis. However, because the antithesis and the thesis are interactively locked together, defining each other by what they are not, the way forward lies in a move that transcends the opposition, while continuing to include the best of both sides of the original polarity. In other words, as shown in figure 4.1, out of the energy of tension produced by the polarity of thesis and antithesis, a creative emergence often occurs—a novel event or new condition synthesizing the best qualities of the thesis and antithesis into a transcendent new whole.

An evident example of this dialectical process in action can be seen in the relationship between the thesis of modernism and the antithesis of postmodernism. As first described in the introduction, and as will be discussed further in the chapters ahead, the postmodern worldview defines itself largely through its opposition to the shortcomings of modernism. And this cultural opposition between modernism and postmodernism is now supplying the tension energy that is giving rise to the synthesis that the evolutionary perspective represents.

Through this technique of dialectical development, evolution is able to solve problems creatively and achieve progress. Eventually, however, any improved synthetic condition becomes a new kind of thesis through which the process continues.[3] This is how evolution grows from within itself, always building on what has come before. And as we are here

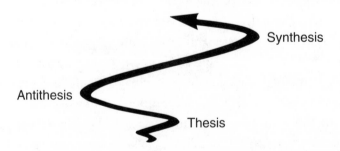

Figure 4.1. The synthetic trajectory of the dialectic pattern of development

exploring, this technique of creative advance into novelty takes its pattern and process from the macrostructure of being and becoming itself.

This philosophical understanding of existential polarities as systems of development begins to explain how the infinite enters the finite through our experience. We will revisit this subject toward the end of this chapter in the crucial section on the role of consciousness in perfecting the universe. Moreover, this understanding of existential polarities will serve as a foundation for our discussion of the spiritual experience of ultimate reality in chapters 5, 6, and 7.

THE PRACTICE OF PERFECTING THE UNIVERSE REVISITED

As I contend, the spiritual teachings of evolution reveal that the purpose of the finite universe is to evolve gradually toward ever more perfect states of existence. Yet what constitutes "a more perfect state" is not completely predetermined. Because we can experience spirit—because we can discern ever-deepening levels of intrinsic value—our job in the cosmic economy is to discover the meaning of perfection for ourselves, in this life and in our ongoing universe careers. That is why we are here. In other words, the realization that we are agents of evolution illuminates the spiritual purpose of our lives and helps us grow into this purpose. Simply stated, according to evolutionary spirituality we are in the universe to participate in its perfection through evolution. And as we come to understand the larger purpose of evolution overall, we become more effective agents of evolution, increasing our powers to solve the urgent problems we face at this time in history.

While this notion of perfection may at first seem unattainable or excessively utopian, the practice of perfecting the universe can be pursued in a wide variety of contexts and actually provides a practical approach to personal spiritual growth. The spiritual teachings of evolution clarify how spirit can be experienced in our everyday lives and in our work in the world. Authentic spiritual experience is not reserved only for mystics or adepts. All of us experience the influence of spirit in the things we adore and the things that most concern us. Our fondest hopes and desires, as well as our sense of moral obligation, can help us tune into the directions of further perfection. And our hunger for greater perfection, the inkling we feel of a greater good lying beyond our current circumstances, is kindled by what we find to be most beautiful, true, and good. As moral philosopher Iris Murdoch understood, "We are spiritual creatures, attracted by excellence and made for the good."[4]

By framing both the purpose of creation and the purpose of each creature in terms of beauty, truth, and goodness, the spiritual teachings of evolution can help us recognize every experience of intrinsic value as an experience of spirit. These experiences are how spirit most often speaks to us, communicating to us from the inside, through the evolutionary impulse, which in its deepest and most intimate essence calls to us as that "still small voice" that says, "This is the way, walk therein." Although both the experience of spirit and the ontological reality of spirit obviously consist of more than simply these most intrinsic values, these "matters of ultimate concern" constitute an essential aspect of spiritual reality that evolutionary spirituality can help us better comprehend.

While some aspects of intrinsic value are presented to us with immediate and obvious clarity, practice is required before many forms of intrinsic quality can be recognized or otherwise appreciated. The process of discerning real value involves more than simply looking; we have to practice *seeing* it. Yet we come to see it most clearly—we find it most abundantly—when we know what it is good for and how to use it. Here we can recall the example from chapter 2 of how the intention to paint a beautiful sunset helps the artist perceive the sunset's beauty with greater depth and insight.

Further, as we become accustomed to this approach to spiritual reality and our practice develops, we can increasingly tap into the motivational energy of intrinsic value. The beautiful, true, and good have a kind of gravity, which we can feel through our impulse to evolve. And like a muscle, the evolutionary impulse becomes stronger as we respond to it and use it. The practice of working with the evolutionary impulse kindles our passion, and by pursuing what we are naturally passionate about we can discover and develop our innate talents and gifts. Offering these gifts in love and service, however, involves not only creating fresh and original forms of intrinsic value but also working to fix problems and to fulfill unmet needs. In fact, that which draws us and that which troubles us are often directly related.

Moreover, it is important to emphasize that perfection can be approached through either greater complexity or greater simplicity. While the idea of perfecting something is most often conceived as "adding more," the process of perfecting can also involve paring down or taking away. For example, the idea of a "perfect boat" can be conceived of as either a luxury yacht that lacks nothing or as a kayak whose perfection is found in its sparely efficient simplicity.

In reflecting on how we can experience spirit by participating in the gradual and incremental perfection of the universe, it is important to keep in mind evolutionary spirituality's understanding of evolution itself as unfolding within nature, self, and culture. As we are coming to see, the gradual perfection of human culture is bound together with the gradual perfection of our selves, and vice versa. The perfection of nature, however, is not as straightforward. From some perspectives, the natural world is already perfect; humans cannot improve on it. And unless humans have caused damage, intervening in the course of natural evolution is uncalled for. Yet, while we are usually not called to participate in the natural evolution of matter or life, we can increasingly perfect our *relationship to nature*—we can learn to better understand it, respect it, use it, and care for it.

Enlarging our understanding of spiritual experience in these ways, so as to better include the beautiful, the true, and good, is not just a theoretical or theological project. Again, the goal of this evolutionary exploration of spiritual experience is to provide better spiritual leadership for our culture and to develop a method for sharing spiritual experience that actually raises consciousness and solves difficult social problems. As we saw in the last chapter, our culture's current conception of spiritual experience is murky and still largely bound to the century-old ideas articulated by William James in his *Varieties of Religious Experience*, which focuses primarily on mysticism. While mysticism remains an important category of spiritual experience, the time has now come to use the fresh insights of evolutionary spirituality to expand and improve our notions of what it means to experience spirit.

Our initial exploration of the interaction of being and becoming, together with the considerations of practice described above, has now set the stage for our primary inquiry in this chapter. So far, our focus has been on the process or context of spirit's unfolding. But now we are ready to return to the consideration of intrinsic value itself.

What Are Beauty, Truth, and Goodness?

While it is always easy to identify particular instances of goodness, truth, and beauty, the answer to the question of what these values are in themselves has proved elusive. In fact, this question has been pondered by philosophers for millennia. Yet despite the attention of some of humanity's best minds, no satisfactory definition of these intrinsic qualities has ever been agreed upon. I have written extensively about these primary values in my previous books and have been reflecting on the nature and behavior of these qualities for over forty years, and from my work so far I have been able to conclude the following: The beautiful, the true, and the good are the basic *directions of evolution*. They are not things or substances or preexistent Platonic forms. But neither are they merely subjective preferences or individual choices. Again, they are neither purely subjective nor simply objective—they bring subject and object together in the course of seeing and being seen.

One way to describe these most intrinsic qualities is as *aliveness* or perhaps even as *the flowering of the real*. These values are realized in their fullness in those momentary climaxes of total excellence that provide flashing glimpses of perfection. In fact, in the case of beauty, the appearance of shimmering perfection can sometimes actually be seen. In its most concentrated expressions, such as in an exceptionally beautiful person or in a sublime scene in nature, beauty has a recognizably luminous (or even numinous) quality. These instances of perfection are what the Bhagavad Gita calls "the splendor of the splendid and the goodness of the good."[5] Simply put, spirit manifests in our experience as that which has the special fleeting quality of how things should be at their best.

Sometimes, these experiences can take our breath away, such as when we witness a virtuoso artistic performance, visit a sacred site, or have an "aha" moment of profound realization. But at other times these qualities appear to us in less dramatic ways, which we may even take for granted, such as in the loving-kindnesses we receive from our family. We may also find intrinsic value in the unshakable consistency of our loyalties to what is noble or in our appreciation of what is exceedingly original or even intriguingly clever. And these intrinsic qualities can also be found in the warm fellowship of lasting friendship, in the thrill of epic adventure, or even in the glow we feel from an afternoon of hearty good fun.

My contemplation of the concepts of beauty, truth, and goodness has also helped me see that the experience of these primary values is perhaps the most important and useful kind of spiritual experience humans can have. These intrinsic values can not only be experienced, they can also be *created and shared*. As initially explained in chapter 2 in the discussion of the practice of value metabolism, we experience these "comprehensible elements of divinity" most fully in the process of sharing them with others. Thus, when we expand our conception of spiritual experience in a way that places special emphasis on these intrinsic values, we shift our foundational assumptions about spirituality from something we *get* to something we *give*. Stated otherwise, the natural hunger for perfection we feel—the eros of evolution that urges us to grow spirituality—is satisfied most completely through the gifts of value that we bring into the world. As Jesus taught, it is better to give than to receive, and by their fruits you shall know them.

Although they have distinguishing features, the beautiful, the true, and the good can also be recognized as differentiated expressions of the same thing. They are best understood together because these three concepts reflect and define each other in a way that discloses their relationship as a unified dynamic system. But even as we recognize the underlying unity of these three ideals, we can also see how this threefold "jewel of truth" has many facets. We began to examine this conceptual jewel in chapter 2, and in the subsections that follow we explore some of its other facets, which inevitably overlap and reflect each other. And as we now continue to contemplate the great evolutionary attractor constituted by this primary value triad, turning it over in our mind's eye to consider one facet after another, its exquisite spiritual luster may become increasingly apparent.

My aim in this section is to show how our experiences of the beautiful, the true, and the good are literally encounters with the presence of the infinite in the finite and thus authentic experiences of spirit. First we explore how beauty, truth, and goodness are each forms of unity that serve to connect the infinite with the finite through the gateway of consciousness itself. Next we examine the pragmatic aspects of the primary values; not only do these intrinsic qualities make the reality of spirit comprehensible, but they also help make spirit actionable and useful for our work in the world. This is followed by a discussion of how the primary values can provide spiritual experience in even their most ordinary or mundane occurrences. Then we briefly explore the shadow of beauty, truth, and goodness to see how the relative absence of these qualities in any given situation can be recognized as a positive opportunity and even a sacred gift. Finally, we consider how these intrinsic values communicate messages of spirit that take the form of both *instructions* for making things more perfect and *assurances* that we are loved and cared for.

Primary Values as Manifestations of Dynamic Unity

Beauty, truth, and goodness can be understood as forms of *unity in action*. For example, beauty unifies contrasts and represents the fleeting unification of the real and the ideal. Truth unifies our thoughts with reality. And goodness unifies people and things in the right relation, the fairest or most optimal arrangement. Goodness also unifies objects and events with their fullest potential—a condition of excellence that can be approached but never completely achieved.

This proposition that the beautiful, the true, and the good are essentially forms of dynamic unity is supported by the following chain of reasoning: (1) spirit is infinite; (2) spirit can be experienced; (3) all experiences of spirit provide a fleeting glimpse of the infinite; (4) the infinite is the ultimate form of unity; and (5) spiritual experiences of intrinsic value are essentially experiences of various aspects of the infinite's unity as perceived from within time and space.

However, it is important to make clear that beauty, truth, and goodness are not simply the presence of the infinite in its fullness. These values are like the *rays of the infinite* that shine into the finite universe—aspects of infinity that are down-stepped enough to be experienced by finite creatures like us. And this analogy of the beautiful, the true, and the good as rays of light has affinities with the color analogy mentioned in chapter 2 comparing these primary values to primary colors that can represent the entire visible spectrum of color through their combination. Recognizing these most intrinsic values as colors of spirit or rays of infinity can help us see how they *connect* the infinite with the finite in our experience. Extending this connecting ray analogy further, we may come to appreciate how at one end, in their most sublime expressions, these values make contact with the pure being of the infinite, while at their other end they reach all the way down to the ground by making things better at the finite level.

The idea that intrinsic values serve to connect or unify the infinite with the finite finds support in the common observation that these three primary values themselves can be both unified and distinct. That is, in their highest expressions these qualities can be almost indistinguishable, but as they become more definitely associated with finite realities they become increasingly differentiated. Put another way, the more they approach their infinite end—the more purely spiritual they are—the more they are the same. As the poet Keats famously wrote, "Beauty is truth, truth beauty." But as they approach their finite end—as they become concretely manifested in the world—they can be more readily distinguished as separate qualities.

An example of the unity of the primary values is seen in the way physicists and mathematicians frequently evaluate the truth of their equations or theorems by how elegant or beautiful they are. And it is often the case that the more fundamental the truth, the greater the beauty.

This unified quality of the primary values was expressed by Harvard sociologist Pitirim Sorokin, who wrote: "Though each member of this supreme [value] Trinity has a distinct individuality, all three are inseparable from one another. . . . The genuine Truth is always good and beautiful. . . . Goodness is always true and beautiful; and the pure Beauty is invariably true and good. These greatest values are not only inseparable from one another, but they are transformable into one another, like one form of physical energy, say, heat, is transformable into other kinds of energy, electricity or light or mechanical motion."[6]

Yet we can also find examples where the primary values appear as distinct and even opposed to each other. This idea is expressed by another Harvard professor, Howard Gardener, who writes: "In my view, the three virtues [values] are conceptually distinct from each other—each must be considered on its own merits (and demerits). As an example, we realize that something can be true (the fact that over fifty-seven thousand

Americans lost their lives in the Vietnam War) without being beautiful or good. By the same token, something can be good without being beautiful—consider a gruesome documentary about prison life intended to shock people into embracing prison reform. And a scene of the natural world, after the demise of all human beings, can be cinematically beautiful, even though it is neither true historically or good, at least for the species that has been annihilated—that is to say, us."[7]

This discussion begins to show the multiple levels on which beauty, truth, and goodness reveal their nature as actual, literal forms of unity. Each value demonstrates a specific kind of unity in the unique way it unifies the real with the ideal. And all three values together demonstrate unity with one another, even while they retain their distinct identities. Yet their most profound demonstration of unity can be seen in their cosmic role as the directions of evolution that unify the finite with the infinite, step by step and experience by experience. We will continue to contemplate the unifying structure, function, and nature of these intrinsic qualities later in this chapter. But now we turn to a more practical facet of the primary values.

Primary Values as Useful Handles on Spirit

The previous subsection's discussion of how intrinsic values connect the infinite with the finite helps us recognize these qualities as "handles" on spirit. Because the primary values are comprehensible and actionable, because we can grasp them in our experience and use them in our work, they serve as the aspects of the infinite that we can literally pull into the finite.

For example, one of the finite handles of beauty is *pleasure*. Practically everyone values pleasure in one form or another—regardless of people's stage of development, there are some things they find pleasurable and thus some things they can recognize as beautiful. And those of us who want to bring more beauty into the world can ensure that our creations will be valuable to others by endeavoring to give pleasure and delight to those whom we seek to serve.

Similarly, one of truth's most useful handles is the *reason* it usually embodies. Reason explains things; it gives us access to how and why things are the way they are. As with beauty, the increased understanding provided by the reason of truth can be useful for people at every level of development. Even children are served when they are taught forms of reason they can understand—when they learn the how and the why of any given condition or event, their grasp of reality is expanded. And for those of us who seek to provide more effective spiritual leadership for our society overall, making our spiritual teachings more reasonable, and thus more in harmony with science and logic, can help make such teachings more widely agreeable.

Goodness too has finite handles that make it useful and valuable within real world conditions. Among the many ways that goodness is valuable, perhaps the most directly experiential is the way this form of unity often contains *kindness*. Although "what's good for us" may not always be kind, kindness is usually associated with authentic goodness, and kindness is something that most of us really value deep down. Even the higher mammals show kindness to their mates and offspring; kindness helps bind families together. And as we strive to bring about the universal family of humanity here on earth, our kindness provides a tangible expression of the goodness that motivates us. Kindness is thus very useful in establishing the trust among people that is required to build organizations and create the agreements that lead to increased forms of social solidarity.

Pleasure, reason, and kindness are not the only practical and useful features of beauty, truth, and goodness, but these specific examples help show how the presence of the infinite almost always improves what it touches.

Primary Values Can Be Spiritual at Every Level

If we think about the highest forms of beauty, truth, and goodness we can know, there may be little disagreement that the experience of these things clearly rises to the level of authentic spiritual experience. As examples, in tender moments of affection between parent and child we may find the spiritual experience of loving-goodness; when quietly walking in a lovely natural setting we may have a spiritual experience of beauty; and when contemplating how we embody thirteen billion years of evolutionary emergence in our very being, we may recognize the spiritual experience of truth. For those who have felt the depths of experiences such as these, their spiritual quality is unmistakable.

Within our language and culture, however, the notion of what is good, true, or beautiful can also stand for entirely mundane realities. For instance, *good* can mean a simple economic good, such as two dollars being better than one; *truth* can be understood as what is merely a fact, such as the direction of true north; and *beautiful* often signifies something that is merely pleasant or pretty. Given that in their regular usage these words stretch from the common to the sublime, we may question whether we need new words to stand for the more authentically spiritual aspects of these realities.

In answer to this question I can say that while the emergence of evolutionary spirituality will inevitably result in the appearance of new words and the overall growth of our language, I think the definitional flexibility of the words *beauty*, *truth*, and *goodness* is something we can retain. This is because even in their most mundane expressions, these words continue to connect to the spiritual process of perfecting the universe. Simply put, even the least spiritual manifestations of these intrinsic values stand for quality or improvement of some kind.

For example, for someone living in poverty who subsists on two dollars a day, the gift of a dollar and a smile could produce a profound spiritual experience of being cared for by others. Likewise, for someone who is lost, the simple truth of which way is north could be of great service. If someone noticed you were lost and cared enough to give you the simplest fact of the right direction, this could indeed result in the subtle but significant spiritual experience of being cared for by others.

Similarly, even the most common expressions of beauty can make a big impact. As one further example, recall the iconic image from the 1960s of the hippie placing a flower into the barrel of a National Guardsman's gun during a Vietnam War protest. The flower—probably just a weed picked from a nearby lawn—was only mundanely beautiful, yet the gesture it made of the power of peace over violence will be remembered a thousand years from now. The point is that just about any kind of beauty, truth, or goodness can cause an improvement. Ultimately, it is the intention and timing involved in providing intrinsic values that makes the giving of these qualities a spiritual contribution to the perfection of the universe.

That being said, it is important to acknowledge that there are, of course, *levels* of spiritual experience. So it is not my intention to conflate astonishing and life-changing encounters with some apparently supernatural reality (such as the Apostle Paul's history-changing vision of Jesus on the Damascus road) with more common experiences of aesthetic or moral excellence. But just as light itself can be experienced in extremes that range from the blinding desert sun to the faint twinkling of a far-distant galaxy, the experience of spirit can likewise appear in both bold and subtle forms. And given the unified character of spirit, at least regarding beauty, truth, and goodness, it may be best to understand the levels of such experience by reference to the states and stages of human consciousness through which such experience occurs and evolves. In short, levels can be found more readily in the experiencer than in the experience itself.[8]

The Shadow of the Primary Values

This examination of the facets, or spiritual features, of the primary values would not be complete without some consideration of the negative aspects, the dark side, of the spirituality of beauty, truth, and goodness.

My exaltation of these intrinsic values as forms of perfection perfecting may cause some readers to feel that this spiritual philosophy is overly optimistic or unrealistically idealistic. Admittedly, by describing the good, the true, and the beautiful as forms of light I have begged the question, what about the shadow? Indeed, wherever there is light there is also a shadow. However, while there are many ways to think about the idea of the shadow, I hesitate even to bring it up because it is a thorny subject that cannot be adequately treated in a short subsection such as this. Nevertheless, here I will briefly touch on the subjective side of negativity, as seen in the psychological shadow, and on the objective aspects, as framed by the "problem of evil."

Within progressive culture the idea of the shadow is most often associated with Jungian psychology, which defines the shadow as the unconscious part of the mind lying "outside the light of consciousness." In this context, the shadow is understood primarily as the dark side of the psyche—the aspects of ourselves that have been repressed or denied and that often reappear as negative projections on others or as forms of neurosis. And this recognition of how unacceptable drives often become repressed can help us better understand our inherent urge to grow and become better. As noted, we experience the "evolutionary gravity" of goodness, truth, and beauty through the evolutionary impulse, the drive or hunger for spiritual growth and greater perfection. But when our natural desire to evolve becomes frustrated or stymied, this hunger can result in self-destructive tendencies. For example, if in the course of life our personal potentials are not being actualized and our unique gifts remain ungiven, the unfulfilled desire to bear spiritual fruit can become lodged in the shadow of our psyche where it may actually prevent our further self-actualization.[9]

However, when our psychological shadow is adequately understood and worked with appropriately, the practice of shadow work can ensure that the urge to evolve remains aligned with the gravity of intrinsic value and thus attuned to the directions of perfection the primary values represent. The practice of shadow work has received a great deal of attention within progressive spirituality, and there is no need to review it here.[10] Suffice it to say that being aware of repressed fears and drives—working to own our shadow so that it does not own us—is part of the practice of these primary values.

Now we turn from the negative aspects of our subjective consciousness to the more objectively negative features of our troubled world. The real pain and suffering caused by the presence of evil, falsehood, and ugliness may cause some to question the teaching that the purpose of the universe is to evolve toward beauty, truth, and goodness. Although I have argued that intrinsic values are neither purely subjective nor straightforwardly objective, they are nevertheless real entities that powerfully influence the evolution of both consciousness and culture. So if values are real, what does this imply about the reality of evil and other disvalues?

Unlike the positive-positive existential polarities we have discussed, which function interdependently and cocreate each other, I do not think that the positive-negative polarity of goodness and evil is cocreative in the same way. Rather, I understand the polarity of values and disvalues in the same way that I understand physical light and darkness. As Saint Augustine taught, evil is simply the absence of goodness and not an equivalent or counterbalancing reality. While light cannot be perceived without darkness, light has a physical presence of its own, whereas darkness does not. As an illustration, we can produce light with a flashlight, but there is no such thing as a "flashdark" that can project a beam of shadow. And in the same way that darkness is merely the absence of light, evil can be understood as the absence of goodness.

This shadow analogy also helps explain how disvalues only come into being as the result of our powers to recognize the good and choose to do it. Just as the potential for suffering emerges only when animal consciousness gains the capacity to feel pain, the potential for evil and cruelty really emerges only when humans gain a sense of morality. But as our consciousness evolves, the growing potential to be troubled by immorality, ignorance, and ugliness serves as a strong psychological motivator to improve the human condition. And the more developed our consciousness becomes, the more we become aware of the extent to which our development is partial and incomplete.

Clearly, the shadow, or absence, of beauty, truth, and goodness is painfully obvious in the realms of human consciousness and culture—the finite universe remains far from perfect. But this is the whole point of the finite universe. The fact that it lacks perfection is what gives it the capacity to evolve, and this in turn gives us the opportunity to experience and participate in evolution's growth toward more perfect states of existence by our own volition. These ideas may help us begin to sense how, in the long run of evolution, all things work together for good—even the bad things.[11]

Primary Values as Messages of Love

As a final consideration, in this subsection we explore how spirit actually communicates to us through our experience of these primary values. As discussed at the end of chapter 3, certain kinds of spiritual experience can be understood as natural signs that disclose the presence of divinity in the universe. And in my experience, goodness, truth, and beauty are themselves natural signs that communicate meaningful spiritual messages. These messages take the form of both *instructions* for making things more perfect and *assurances* that we are loved and cared for.

Understood as *instructions*, the primary values communicate the directions of perfection. For instance, our intuitions of beauty tell us how to make our creations more elegant or complete. Our sense of truth guides us toward the direction of increasing accuracy and reality. And our moral compass instructs us about the right relation or optimal arrangement of things. Conversely, we are also instructed by our sense that beauty, truth, or goodness may be lacking in any given situation. The relative absence of these qualities alerts us to opportunities for improvement.

The primary values instruct us through their dynamic demonstration of what we are ultimately trying to bring into being in our work. In other words, the "juice" that makes the results of our actions effective and persuasive—excellent and convincing—is found in and through these essential qualities.

Through their ability to attract our attention and point the way forward, these intrinsic values teach us about the directions of evolution itself. That is why Whitehead thought of them as "lures." And by following the guidance of the beautiful, the true, and the good, we may find instructions for fulfilling our purpose in life.

Our experiences of the primary values can also be understood as *assurances* in the way they communicate personalized messages of love. These messages are discovered in the pleasure and satisfaction provided by beauty, in the confirmation and clarity provided by truth, and in the security and well-being we find in goodness. These messages of assurance are accordingly found in the wider dimensions of value experience the primary values ultimately stand for. In other words, while the distinct concepts of beauty, truth, and goodness can signify narrow and specific instances of quality, they can also be interpreted as standing for larger aesthetic, rational, and moral domains of value. And it is in these more general dimensions of quality that we may discern the intimate messages of assurance that spirit has for each of us.

For example, understood expansively, the concept of beauty opens into a larger dimension of delicious satisfaction and even bliss, which might be called Dionysian. This Dionysian dimension of satisfaction is one of the great joys of life, and as such it conveys a message that we are loved. That is, beauty makes us feel loved in the way it lets us in on the thrilling delight the universe can provide. The experience of beauty is thus a way of ensuring that our erotic desires—both physical and spiritual—can find periodic contentment along the way. And through beauty we are also given a taste of the greater perfection we are yet to find.

Conversely, just as beauty opens into a larger dimension of Dionysian pleasure, truth evokes a larger dimension of Apollonian achievement. Understood broadly as its own direction of perfection, truth represents the quest for heroic discovery and the glorious accomplishments we will inevitably make in our spiritual ascent through time. Truth makes us feel loved by assuring us that the way is open and intelligible and that we can actually make things better by discovering the truth. And as our truth recognition grows, our very selves become more real in the process. Our ever-enlarging grasp of truth thus affirms that we are free to grow and pursue value by our own lights.

And, above all, the expansive idea of goodness—including all related forms of moral quality and general excellence—evokes the wider embrace of the universal family of sentient creatures to which we all belong. In its essence, goodness is relational, and the highest relation is *love*—"love is the desire to do good to others." The existence of goodness in the universe thus makes us feel loved as it manifests in the milk of human kindness and the potential for goodwill that is always available for our choosing. Through the ministry of goodness we find that we are secure, cared for, and included in the circle of communion that makes us all one. And where such care is lacking, we may find our best opportunities to serve.

From this we may see how the perfecting currents of intrinsic value transform everything they touch. These vectors of improvement encompass the descending currents of delightful beauty, the ascending currents of exquisite truth, and the overall synthetic flow of goodness itself. Goodness is perfection's plumb line, as revealed by the pull of value gravity upon our evolutionary impulses. And even though we find ourselves in a world that can often be jarringly ugly, appallingly false, and tragically unkind, our evolutionary impulses unfailingly point to the presence of intrinsic value, both actual and potential.

Recognizing that beauty, truth, and goodness are actually communicating messages of love may help us see how the infinite is more than an impersonal creative force. The infinite cannot be conceived of accurately as something akin to a law of physics. As we explore further in chapter 6, because the infinite is the source of everything—including the source of personal, self-aware beings like us—it almost certainly possesses some kind of awareness of its own. It is thus from this self-aware aspect of the infinite that these personal messages of love are communicated. And in their most intimate essence, these messages of assurance that can be found in our experiences of beauty, truth, and goodness are urging us to "feel loved," "grow," and "love others."

THE ESSENTIAL ROLE OF CONSCIOUSNESS IN PERFECTING THE UNIVERSE

A central tenet of most of the world's great religions is that each person possesses a divine spark, or spirit. Christians know it as the Holy Spirit or the "Kingdom of God within." In Judaism it is often called the "indwelling Spirit of the Lord." Hindus know it as the Atman. And within many contemporary forms of progressive spiritual teaching it is referred to as the Absolute Self, the True Self, or the Higher Self. Carl Jung called it the "splinter of divinity" that lives within each one of us. Looking closely at these various spiritual teachings, we can certainly find important differences, but the notion that humans are indwelt by some form of spirit is a widely accepted idea.

As biological beings we are clearly part of nature, but we also contain something that elevates us above nature, connecting us to supernature—to the infinite itself. This concept of an indwelling spirit within humans is crucial for evolutionary spirituality's recognition of the interaction of the infinite and the finite aspects of reality. Our ability to recognize the presence of the infinite within the finite depends on the presence of the infinite within us. Succinctly stated, "it takes the infinite to see the infinite."

As discussed in the previous section, intrinsic values are like vectors or lines that connect the infinite with the finite; they are the rays of spiritual light, the glimmers of infinity that can be seen from within the finite realm of time. And through our ability both to apprehend and to share these spiritual realities, we are empowered to perfect the universe. The perfecting function of intrinsic values is accordingly achieved by and through *us*. As we have seen, values depend on the recognition of consciousness for them to come fully into being. For instance, the discernment of beauty usually requires intuitive assessment and wise appraisal, and the discernment of truth and goodness also usually requires considered intuition, careful judgment, and conscientious decision. In short, to be fully real, values require *evaluation*.

Again, the essential role of consciousness in perfecting the universe is clarified when we see how intrinsic values have both an objective pole and a subjective pole. Like electricity, their circuit-like behavior is enacted when a subjective person recognizes the objective presence of authentic quality in his or her world. And also like electricity, when intrinsic value is realized, the experience provides both light and power— the light to see the way forward and the power to make things better. It is thus through our very recognition and appreciation that the spiritual energy of the infinite supplies the power that propels evolution within the finite realms of self and culture. An example of the power of spiritual energy to improve the world can be seen in the American civil rights movement of the 1960s. Martin Luther King's eloquent illumination of the fairness and equality that all Americans deserve energized a generation to strive for racial justice.

Experiencing Spirit through the Process of Perfecting

Recognizing how subjective recognition is a component of the reality of values leads to a subtle but important point about how the infinite interacts with the finite. As noted, infinite spirit cannot be properly conceived of as a finite object or thing because its being remains outside of time. Yet the infinite's perfect being can nevertheless be experienced by our partial and incomplete consciousness. While we cannot experience perfect being "as it is in itself," we can experience a temporal approximation of it in the *process of perfecting*—the process through which the finite universe evolves toward more perfect and complete states of existence. In other words, the perfect being of the infinite is experienced in time when and as the finite is *moved in the direction of the relatively more perfect*.

This helps explain why our temporal experience of the infinite through beauty, goodness, and truth is always dynamic and fleeting, and how these values often grow stale and lose their vitality when they are not actively improving things. We cannot hold onto the infinite; we can only experience it as it moves through us, perfecting us incrementally in the process of its very recognition. The presence of the infinite in the evolving universe of time is almost always experienced as a gift of improvement— a service of goodness, a lesson of truth, and an expression of beauty. The infinite in the finite is always a verb; it is always *perfection perfecting, unity unifying*.

Considering this from another angle, the perfect infinite's encounter with the finite is always developmental because the finite is imperfect by definition, so every encounter with the infinite is a kind of criticism by comparison that reveals the finite's incompleteness and partiality. But the presence of the infinite in the finite, the presence of intrinsic value, is what overcomes the inherent entropy of the material universe, driving evolution's creative advance into novelty.

This perfecting process of value recognition and attraction begins with life, which strives for the basic yet intrinsic values of surviving and reproducing. Then with the emergence of humans, the intrinsic values of beauty, truth, and goodness begin to gain traction on our consciousness, causing us to strive for ever-higher levels of perfection. And this universal response to value gravity shows how evolution itself is a process of spiritual growth at almost every level of its manifestation.

Free-Will Consciousness: An Opening for the
Infinite to Enter the Finite

This insight about how the infinite only appears in the finite as a dynamic process of perfecting leads to another important point about the essential role of consciousness in this process. The aspect of the infinite that resides within each of us is like an *opening* into the eternal realm of pure being. In other words, the fragment of infinity that dwells within us acts as a kind of semipermeable membrane that we use to discern or decide what is more or less valuable. As spirit enters the finite through the subjective pole of value that is our consciousness—as the infinite perfects the finite incrementally through us as we experience spirit and help create such experience in others—this opening within us is *enlarged*. When the light of the infinite shines into the world through our experience and creation of spiritual realities, this action of perfecting the finite helps perfect us, making us more spiritually real. It thus bears repeating that we become more evolved and the world becomes more evolved as we experience and create intrinsic value.

As a result of our creative freedom, we can act as authentic cocreators of real value—we are agents of evolution empowered to improve the human condition. So even though the infinite can only really exist in the finite in the form of spiritual experience as explained above, when we help produce a spiritual experience in another person, when we bring intrinsic value into the lives of our fellows, we are creating something "objective" that is spiritually real and worthwhile. However, the intrinsic value itself—the spiritually real element of what we bring into the world— does not originate with us. The kernel, or most essential aspect, of the beauty, truth, and goodness that we manage to create remains connected to its infinite source. We may see the aftereffects of the perfecting process of spirit moving in the world—we may recognize that things have been objectively improved, and we may feel the subjective satisfaction of having played a part in the process—but the intrinsic value itself is always a dynamic improvement and is thus always fleeting.

Using a somewhat different analogy to describe this phenomenon, we could say that the finite universe is like a near vacuum, or void, because the infinite has been partially removed. But this vacuum is permeated by tiny holes, openings of consciousness, through which the surrounding infinite is rushing back in. And as the perfect being of the infinite is increasingly pulled back into this finite vacuum, these openings are widened in the process. Taking this analogy further we can say that these tiny openings in the finite are made possible by the indwelling spirit's gift of *freedom*—the freedom itself, the freedom of our wills, is what actually creates these openings in the finite.

The Higher Self that serves as the spiritual core of our consciousness is thus like a crack in the fabric of the finite through which the light of the infinite shines. And as we grow spiritually, expanding the crack and letting in more light, we become increasingly useful to our fellows. This usefulness is actually one way to gauge the state or status of our own personal spiritual growth. The more we bring the light of intrinsic value into the world, the more we serve to widen this opening in others so that their light may shine forth more abundantly as well.

Admittedly, these ideas are philosophically dense and conceptually difficult. But please allow me to make one more point, building on the above insight that the freedom of our wills creates an opening into the infinite. As mentioned above, the infinite that resides within us is a semipermeable membrane, and we are usually in charge of deciding what comes through the membrane and what is screened out. In order for our consciousness to serve as the subjective pole of value, we have to meet spirit halfway; it rarely makes contact with us unilaterally. Spirit reaches down to us as we reach up to it.

Indeed, this is an essential function of our freedom within the cosmic economy—our autonomous sovereign choices are required in the project of perfecting the universe. It is our original discovery of perfection by our own lights that adds something spiritually real to the preexisting form of existential perfection that preceded the big bang. Stated differently, the inherent perfection of the preexisting infinite is augmented and enhanced through the process of our direct experience of becoming more perfect by our own choices and efforts. Through this process, the gradual achievement of *experiential perfection* occurs as a result of our participation in finite evolution. And it is this achievement of experiential perfection that enhances the existential perfection of infinite spirit. This is our purpose. We are evolution's agents, indwelt by spirit and engaged in the cosmic adventure of increasingly perfecting ourselves, the cultural world we live in, and our relationship to nature itself.

Yet, we are not compelled to evolve; we usually only grow spiritually when we make the effort. And this is why even though spirit is widely accessible—even though spirit is all around us in the beauty, truth, and goodness pervading our world—it remains easily resistible for those who are not ready. As Whitehead understood, the perfecting influence of the infinite on the finite occurs through the "gentle persuasion of love."

OUR EMERGING UNDERSTANDING OF THE "PHYSICS" OF SPIRIT

In this chapter, we have used evolutionary spirituality's newly available light to wrestle with some advanced spiritual concepts. But no matter how far our spiritual knowledge may advance, our human understanding of the purpose of the universe will present only a rudimentary picture pieced together from the shadows cast by spirit into the realm of reason and experience.

Nonetheless, realizing philosophically that "the presence of the infinite" is an actual, ontological description of the referent of spiritual experience reveals how the metaphysical and supernatural are actually quite "natural" under this broadened understanding. This spiritual reality is confirmed when we begin to see how it influences the evolution of self, culture, and nature. As I have argued, the infinite moves the finite toward perfection through its influence on the consciousness of free-will creatures, drawing us like iron filings toward a magnet. And as spirit appears to us in the form of the beautiful, the true, and the good, we can feel its palpable gravity—its peculiar magnetic aspect. As philosopher John Cottingham has observed, these intrinsic values somehow have "to-be-pursuedness" built into them.[12]

This emerging knowledge of what spirit is and how it works enhances our ability to have and share spiritual experiences. And as we come to better understand what it is, the reality of spirit can be increasingly confirmed through phenomenological experience, just like other widely accepted facts. Moreover, as this kind of experience becomes more familiar and understandable, attempts to explain it away or reduce it to the physical activity in our brains will be increasingly recognized as merely the rhetoric of an outworn belief system.

However, even as our understanding of spirit becomes more "naturalized" and we accordingly achieve a more unified knowledge of physics and metaphysics, we must remain circumspect. The perhaps worthy but naïve goal of developing a science of spirit that establishes a particular form of belief as factually confirmed and objective (thus eliminating spiritual pluralism) may never be achieved. And even if such a spiritual science were theoretically possible, it is still well beyond the current horizon of our cultural evolution.

Nevertheless, the goal of building cultural agreement around the spiritual authenticity of the beautiful, the true, and the good is certainly achievable in our time. Although such an emerging agreement about the transcendent reality of intrinsic value would not constitute a science of spirit in itself, it could take us beyond the currently impoverished state of spiritual ignorance that prevails in much of the developed world. The metaphysics of such an agreement would necessarily be modest and minimal, and subject to different interpretations, but such a new form of concurrence around the basic reality of spirit would help us overcome the blindness asserting that the universe is nothing more than matter in motion. And the emergence of a relatively universal agreement that spirit by whatever name actually exists would indeed result in a greater sense of social solidarity and cooperation, and thereby supply some of the spiritual leadership our civilization needs.

The kind of minimally metaphysical understanding of spiritual reality that I am advocating, however, will involve more than just a static agreement about what is ultimately real; it will also illuminate a method. As will be explored in chapter 8, this method promises to provide new techniques for raising consciousness through the skillful provision of spiritual experience itself. Even those who are already using this kind of method intuitively can be guided and encouraged by the enlarged understanding of spiritual experience we have been exploring here. In fact, all attempts to bring intrinsic value into the world are inevitably strengthened by the knowledge that such efforts are not only satisfying individual needs and solving localized problems but are also fulfilling the larger purposes of the universe.

We will return to the exciting idea of using the "spiritual physics" of beauty, truth, and goodness to help solve the problems of the world at the end of the book. But before we get to that discussion, the next three chapters address the important subject of how evolutionary spirituality can emerge beyond the limitations of progressive spirituality.

Chapter Five

CONTEMPORARY SPIRITUAL CURRENTS: PROGRESSIVE AND NONDUAL

In this chapter we shift the focus from the content of evolutionary spirituality to the cultural context of its contemporary emergence. This chapter picks up where chapter 1 left off by exploring progressive spirituality in greater detail. This cultural analysis begins with a closer look at progressive spirituality's origins and accomplishments. We then consider the most recent trends in this alternative form of spiritual culture that have become evident since the turn of the millennium, leading to the conclusion that progressive spirituality is reaching a kind of maturity or culmination through its growing agreement regarding the nondual nature of ultimate reality. And this agreement itself is arising from the partial merger of the practices and truth teachings of Advaita Vedanta Hinduism and Westernized progressive Buddhism.

After describing these relatively recent developments, I then contend that progressive spirituality's illumination and consolidation of a wide variety of nondual spiritual teachings reveals an existential polarity within humanity's understanding of ultimate reality. As I will argue, this polarity is not simply a matter of doctrinal distinctions or different conceptual approaches to spirit; it is confirmed by the direct experience of spirit itself. And because evolutionary spirituality can work with and build upon this existential polarity in new and effective ways, our emerging understanding of this essential opposition presents an exciting opportunity for further spiritual development.

Once we have examined the recent maturation of progressive spirituality and the evolutionary opportunity this creates, we will be ready to explore in the next chapter how evolutionary spirituality can use this opportunity to transcend the limitations of progressive spirituality and thereby achieve the next dialectical step in our society's cultural evolution.

PROGRESSIVE SPIRITUALITY IN CONTEXT

Progressive spirituality has emerged in the developed world primarily as a subset of the larger postmodern worldview, as defined in the introduction. And as mentioned, the postmodern worldview now provides the cultural center of gravity for approximately 20 percent of the US population. While some postmodernists have no interest in spirituality of any kind, the majority, in America at least, do seem to evince an affinity for one form of progressive spirituality or another. Yet I must also quickly add that today many who identify with progressive spirituality nevertheless maintain traditional, modernist, and even post-postmodern cultural centers of gravity.

Although the cultural accomplishments of progressive spirituality are usually overlooked or dismissed by the modernist mainstream, progressive spirituality's ongoing influence on the culture of the developed world has actually been considerable. Beyond the sizable market for books and workshops in this field, the impact of progressive spirituality's rise, which began in the 1970s, can be clearly seen in the ways it has influenced the larger marketplace of ideas, especially in America.

For example, the emergence of progressive spirituality has effectively dissolved the once large and vibrant center of mainstream American religion. As a result of the new pluralistic mores and emphasis on personal development brought about by progressive spirituality over the last forty years, most of America's once-liberal Protestant churches have been culturally polarized, becoming either more conservative and traditional or more progressive and postmodern. This trend can also be seen to a lesser degree within American Catholicism, where a split along these lines has recently occurred between some nuns and the male clergy.[1]

Progressive spirituality has also been influential in the arts and in America's entertainment industry, as seen in the many celebrity endorsements of progressive spiritual teachers. The impact of progressive spirituality on the larger society can also be recognized in American business, as evidenced by Silicon Valley's affinity for Western Buddhism, seen, for example, in the Wisdom 2.0 conference. Progressive spirituality's influence on business can also be seen in the prevalent use of progressive spiritual practices in the corporate world. In fact, many of progressive spirituality's techniques for personal development and team building have become the mainstay of the organizational-development consulting field.

Academics and scholars of religion often have a difficult time recognizing or appreciating the historical significance of progressive spirituality because they are accustomed to analyzing religious culture in terms of church attendance or adherence to creedal beliefs. Yet in contrast with religious spirituality, progressive spirituality is generally not characterized by membership organizations or doctrinal affiliations. Progressive spirituality's syncretic and pluralistic character has resulted in extensive cross-pollination such that the teachings of once-distinct paths are now mixed together. So even though some types of progressive spirituality claim to represent ancient traditions, in practice virtually all of its forms have been transfigured by the postmodern context of their cultural expression. Thus, in order to appreciate what this new form of spirituality is and how it manifests in our society, we have to approach its understanding through a broad cultural analysis that takes into account the larger dialectical currents of history that have given birth to the postmodern worldview.

Chapter 1's description of the three major forms of spirituality currently on offer in American culture—religious, secular, and progressive—briefly noted the origins of progressive spirituality. However, because this relatively new family of spiritual views is indeterminate and hard to pin down, and because a basic recognition of both its accomplishments and its shortcomings is crucial for understanding evolutionary spirituality, a closer examination of the history of progressive spirituality will be helpful.

A Brief History of Progressive Spirituality

As previously mentioned, precursors of progressive spirituality can be clearly seen in the American transcendentalist movement of the nineteenth century. Prominent transcendentalists such as Emerson and Thoreau were among the first Westerners to recognize the appeal and mystique of oriental religions. Another historical source of progressive spirituality can be found in the Theosophy movement of the late nineteenth and early twentieth centuries, which was highly influenced by Tibetan Buddhism and Eastern esotericism in general. It was also around the beginning of the twentieth century that Advaita Vedanta Hinduism became popular within American intellectual circles.

These various currents of countercultural or alternative religion remained relatively obscure until the emergence of the youth culture of the 1960s. Interest in alternative forms of spirituality exploded in the late sixties and early seventies, largely as a result of spiritual experiences induced by psychedelic drugs. Then as the hippie movement faded in the mid-1970s, much of its emergent momentum was channeled into the birth of progressive spiritual culture.

Citing some examples, it was originally during the 1970s that Indian gurus such as Maharishi Mahesh Yogi gathered large followings, and Vedic spirituality in general became popular among many Westerners. At the same time the practices of Tibetan and Zen Buddhism were also adopted by many progressively minded Americans. This growing popularity of Buddhism and Hinduism was spurred by countercultural icons such as Alan Watts and Ram Dass, who extolled the virtues of Eastern mysticism.

The establishment of the wisdom of the East as the leading view within progressive spirituality was also aided by the rise of transpersonal psychology. The eclectic culture of progressive spirituality, however, also included from the beginning many strains that did not arise in the Far East. For example, shamanism and Native American spirituality became popular through best-selling books by authors such as Carlos Castaneda.

Counterculturalists in the seventies were experimenting with new spiritual forms, some of which were venerable and others quite silly. Yet even though it was composed of many different strains, progressive spirituality did cohere as a distinct and identifiable form of culture because just about everyone involved had been significantly influenced by the events of the sixties and accordingly shared strong postmodern loyalties. In other words, practitioners of the various forms of progressive spirituality that became popular in the seventies were generally united by the fact that they were all countercultural outsiders looking for alternatives to the religious conventions of the mainstream establishment.

By the late seventies intellectuals such as Fritjof Capra and Marilyn Ferguson began calling attention to the similarities that could be increasingly found between leading edge science and Eastern religious teachings. Their work marked the beginning of progressive spirituality's largely unsuccessful attempt to align itself with science. Despite its ongoing efforts to link mysticism with quantum physics and despite more recent attempts to establish the benefits of meditation and yoga for health, the inability of many progressive spiritual authors to distinguish credible science from pseudoscience has only served to alienate many in the larger society who might otherwise be attracted to alternative spirituality.

Although it remained relatively countercultural and underground, progressive spirituality continued to emerge and evolve in America and elsewhere throughout the 1980s. It was during this time that the popular spirit-channeled book *A Course in Miracles* became influential, and the self-help and human potential movements continued to bring many into the orbit of progressive spirituality. It was also during the eighties that

Buddhism became established as the leading form of organized religion among postmodernists, largely through the efforts of Tibetan Buddhist teacher Chögyam Trungpa, as well as through the work of Zen masters Shunryu Suzuki-roshi and D. T. Suzuki. But a variety of Western-born teachers, such as Jack Kornfield and Pema Chödrön, also played important roles. And many of the luminaries who originally contributed to the rise of Western Buddhism in the eighties remain highly influential to this day.

Then in the early 1990s progressive spirituality began to experience a florescence. Popular authors such as Deepak Chopra and Marianne Williamson rose to prominence, and progressive spirituality became the publishing industry's largest category by far. By the late nineties thousands of New Age bookstores had opened across America. Although the label "New Age" has now become a term of derision that is usually reserved for the least sophisticated forms of progressive spirituality, during this decade a large demographic segment of American society readily identified themselves as New Age.

I was an enthusiastic participant in this flowering of progressive spirituality in the 1990s. And I know that for myself and many others it felt like the dawning of a spiritual renaissance. Although I eventually grew out of my progressive spiritual identity to follow an evolutionary spiritual path, this was a heady time that I will never forget. Like me, the majority of people involved in the progressive spiritual culture of the period were baby boomers, but a significant percentage of younger people were also involved.

By the time of its heyday in the late nineties, progressive spiritual culture had come to include an even wider variety of forms than had originally been part of its emergence in the seventies. And many of these various spiritual paths were essentially incompatible with one another. However, while some sought to distance themselves from the more magical or commercial elements of progressive spirituality, postmodernism's staunch pluralism and intensive relativism generally ensured that almost every alternative form of spirituality was welcome.

As a result of this nonjudgmental cultural climate, Western practitioners of Eastern religions, those seeking personal development, deep ecologists, eco-feminists, progressive Christians and Jews, pagans, channelers, practitioners of psychedelic shamanism, and those interested in transpersonal psychology or alternative medicine or sacred geometry or the paranormal, as well as millions of others who became interested in the myriad postmodern flavors of self-actualization offered at the time, were all included uncritically within America's countercultural spiritual milieu.

As we discuss further in the next section, progressive spirituality continues to constitute a significant demographic segment of American society in this century. Although it is no longer growing as fast as it was in the 1990s and may even be leveling off in numbers, it remains a large movement. The handful of academics who have studied the phenomenon of progressive spirituality have made various estimates of its size, but no hard data is available on how many people are actually involved. But in America at least, it is clear that the size of this progressive spiritual subculture numbers in the tens of millions.

The Culmination of Progressive Spirituality in Nonduality

While no one can credibly claim to fully understand or otherwise objectively describe the current state of progressive spirituality as of 2015, we can begin to make out some of the more significant developments that have occurred since the beginning of the present century. Although they are still in evidence, some of the more outlandish aspects of the New Age, such as crystal healing or belief in "indigo children," seem to have faded in popularity. Since the turn of the millennium, however, the practice and culture of yoga has become much larger. While many of those who have been attracted to yoga see it merely as a form of exercise and not as particularly spiritual, at its core America's growing yoga culture is clearly a form of postmodern progressive spirituality.

But beyond yoga, the most significant development within progressive spirituality since 2001 has been the ascendency of *nonduality* or *nondualism*, which can be loosely understood as a family of related views about the nature of ultimate reality. While various teachings of nonduality have been part of progressive spirituality from the start, this "grand tradition" has recently become the focus of a more widespread agreement within progressive spirituality about what is ultimately real and spiritually true.

The evidence for this development can be found in subtle cultural cues such as which thought leaders are getting the most attention and respect in the progressive spiritual marketplace of ideas. The rise in popularity of nonduality can accordingly be recognized in the conferences that are being promoted, in the books that are selling, and in the overall discourse of this countercultural demographic segment of American society. The emergence of this nondual agreement, however, is difficult to recognize unless one is actually participating in the culture of progressive spirituality. Nevertheless, although there are a diversity of opinions about the essential meaning and implications of nonduality, this basic conception of ultimate reality has now become the leading and most respected form of spiritual teaching within progressive spiritual culture in America. And as I will argue in this section, this growing agreement regarding nonduality represents the mature expression or culmination of progressive spirituality as a cultural movement.

What is Nonduality?

Nondual spirituality can be difficult to describe or encapsulate because (1) it represents a variety of perspectives rather than a singular belief system; (2) its teachings are spread out along a continuum from the staunchly doctrinaire to the vaguely suggestive; (3) it traces its roots to partially conflicting teachings originating in Hinduism and Buddhism; (4) some of its Western expressions blur the important distinctions between nondual and theistic conceptions of ultimate reality; and (5) many of its teachings are transconceptual and thus cannot be easily reduced to a definitive theology subject to straightforward explication. Notwithstanding these nuances, practitioners of nondual spirituality often summarize it as "fundamental oneness and nonseparation."

Nondual teachers rooted in the Advaita Vedanta Hindu tradition encapsulate the teachings of nonduality as "thou art that" or "I am this," meaning there is only one unified being and all perceptions of separation are an illusion. However, while agreeing with their Advaitan colleagues on many points, nondual teachers rooted in the Buddhist tradition often reject this formulation because it implies the retention of the concept of the self, or Atman, which Buddhism disavows. Yet even this seemingly straightforward distinction between Hindu and Buddhist versions of nondual teaching becomes tentative in the context of the partial merger of Buddhism and Hinduism (described below) now occurring within contemporary progressive spirituality.

Discussing the emergence of nondualism as the leading form of progressive spirituality is also fraught with difficulties because this teaching originated primarily in the writings of Indian philosophers who lived over a thousand years ago. Among these philosophers, the Hindu Shankara and the Buddhist Nagarjuna are the most prominent. These sages have been followed down through the centuries by a long line of nondual religious philosophers who have developed an extensive scholarly literature within traditional Buddhism and Hinduism. As a result of this complex history, the importation of this aggregate of traditional religious teachings into the progressive spiritual culture of the West, even at the hands of the most intellectually sophisticated progressive spiritual authors, has resulted in the assertion of philosophically contradictory propositions. This is especially evident in the case of nondual teachings about the self and the illusory nature of the phenomenal world (discussed in the next chapter).

This occasional lack of philosophical coherence, however, has not been a major barrier to nonduality's success within progressive spirituality because nonduality attempts to deemphasize its beliefs; it does not depend on philosophical arguments or doctrinal creeds. Rather, it is presented as a method for achieving enlightenment through the experience of ultimate unity behind all appearances. In other words, nondual spirituality is based on the encounters with absolute unity described by mystics East and West, and in both ancient and modern contexts. This is the same phenomenon described in chapter 3 as the quintessential unitive mystical experience. These archetypal encounters with the unitary dimension of being that seems to underlie all reality have thus provided the authentic and powerful spiritual experiences that serve as the foundation for practically all forms of nondual teaching. According to nondual philosopher David Loy, "The argument for nonduality is actually reduced to the experience of nonduality—either our own or that of someone else whose testimony we may be inclined to accept."[2]

Although this mystical unitive experience is rare, it is clearly universal. And while many other kinds of mystical experience can be distinguished from this archetypal unitive encounter with nondual being, there seems to be widespread agreement among mystics themselves that this unity experience represents the apogee of their realization.

The nondual conception of ultimate reality that has emerged from this universal and perennial form of mystical spiritual experience has many features making it particularly appealing to progressive spirituality. Consider these examples: (1) it is the animating principle of major forms of Buddhism and Hinduism; (2) it can also be found in many Western mystical teachings; (3) it points to the values of interdependence and interrelatedness, which are key values for postmodernists; (4) it provides an attractive alternative for those who cannot accept mythic conceptions of a judgmental God as the ultimate reality; (5) it is a powerful revelatory experience that can actually be achieved through dedicated spiritual practice; and (6) a stable realization of nonduality is said to result in personal enlightenment. Before going further, however, I must mention a caveat. There are certain forms of Buddhism that resist or deny the idea of any kind of ultimate or absolute reality whatsoever. But as I argue in chapter 7, despite Buddhism's "suspicion of absolutes," most Buddhists end up recognizing ultimacy in one form or another.

The Partial Merger of Buddhism and Hinduism

Given the appealing elements listed above it is easy to see why nonduality has come to represent the mature expression of progressive spirituality. Moreover, because the unitive experience of nonduality is foundational for both Buddhism and Advaita Vedanta Hinduism, this powerful experience lends itself to a kind of synthetic amalgamation of these traditions. Although only experienced by a few practitioners, the very existence of the unitive experience provides a strong sense of cultural solidarity for most of those who identify with nondual forms of progressive spirituality. And within this consolidation of Buddhism and Hinduism under the umbrella of nonduality, purportedly nondual versions of the other great traditions have also found a welcome home. For example, nondual, or "contemplative," interpretations of progressive Christianity, Judaism, and Sufi Islam are now included within progressive spirituality's nondual complex. While the mores of postmodern pluralism remain in place and many of the distinctive aspects of these religions are preserved, contemporary nonduality does provide an interreligious common ground for all the forms of spirituality that identify with it.

The emergence of nonduality as the culmination of progressive spirituality can be attributed to many factors, but the most successful popularizer of this synthetic agreement is undoubtedly Eckhart Tolle. As discussed in chapter 1, Tolle's books have sold millions, and his teachings are highly influential and relatively well respected. His spiritual teaching is essentially a blend, or harmonization, of Hinduism and Buddhism, with some theistic terminology included in deference to pluralism. Yet, although Tolle's teaching is mostly a popularization of the work of other writers, his realization of some degree of enlightenment is undoubtedly authentic, as evidenced by the spiritual fruits his work has borne.

Beyond Eckhart Tolle, we can also attribute the rise of nonduality to the less popular but more rigorous work of progressive spiritual intellectuals such as Huston Smith, Ken Wilber, Stanislov Groff, A. H. Almaas, David Loy, and Georg Feuerstein. The commitment of these authors to a nondual spiritual path has provided leadership within postmodern culture, showing the way forward into more credible and respectable forms of spirituality that transcend the limitations of earlier and less mature versions of progressive spirituality.

Nondual spiritual teachings, however, have not become the mature expression of progressive spirituality solely by dint of their purported truth quality. Other cultural currents and pressures have also contributed to the consolidation of this conception of ultimate reality as the leading form of progressive spiritual understanding. Postmodernism in general and progressive spirituality in particular are communally oriented forms of culture. And postmodern religionists find cultural solidarity within progressive spirituality in ways that have nothing to do with their respective conceptions of what is ultimately real. For example, most of them prefer to eat natural and organic foods, and a large number are vegetarians. Most have faith in the efficacy of alternative medicine. Many wear clothing that reflects their countercultural loyalties, and most are staunch environmentalists and left-of-center politically. As a result of this common sense of cultural identity, practitioners of practically all forms of progressive spirituality generally have a sense of the contemporary movements and fashions within their culture and seek to solidify their sense of belonging by "going with the flow." This observation is not meant to imply that nonduality is merely a fashion. But the larger, extrareligious cultural momentum it has achieved within progressive spirituality over the last two decades has definitely contributed to its current popularity.

Despite the continued existence of extensive pluralism, a cultural analysis of the current state of progressive spirituality does reveal that something significant has definitely occurred since the turn of the millennium. Although it has been moving in this direction from the beginning, this partial but powerful synthesis of Western Buddhism and Advaita Vedanta Hinduism can now be clearly seen at the cultural level. And although it includes other nondual religious forms, it is the amalgamation of Buddhism and Hinduism that is primarily responsible for the emergence of this unifying nondual agreement.

Teachers and scholars working within the traditional institutions of these historical religions may deny that Buddhism and Hinduism are merging and may even contend that such a merger is impossible. But unlike traditional or academic contexts, progressive spiritual culture is highly syncretic, and it is in this context that the merger is occurring. Within this emerging cultural milieu some practitioners remain closely tied to the specific teachings of their main tradition, while others identify with the looser hybrid teachings of nonduality in general. But for those who have transcended traditionalism and relate to their spirituality from a postmodern perspective, a certain amount of blending between forms is inevitable.

Therefore, even though these respective spiritual paths retain much of their distinct identities within progressive spirituality, and even though the significance of this partial fusion of Western Buddhism and Hinduism can be fully appreciated only when viewed through a cultural rather than a doctrinal lens, I do think this merger represents a kind of culmination of progressive spirituality as a historically significant movement in the evolution of human religion.

In fact, some of the world's greatest religious traditions have come about through similar kinds of mergers. Zen Buddhism, for example, emerged as a result of the combination of older forms of Buddhism with Taoism, and many of the doctrines of Christianity resulted from the merger of Judaism and Greek philosophy. While the merger of

Hinduism and Buddhism has been both promoted and resisted for centuries (Buddhism originally emerged from Hinduism), this most recent synthesis within progressive spirituality represents more than simply the return to an older form.

The Truth Value of Concepts

Some may object to this conclusion that the growing cultural agreement about the nondual nature of ultimate reality represents the culmination of progressive spirituality. Progressive Buddhists or Hindus may point out that their spirituality is about the direct experience resulting from practice, and thus the culmination of their spirituality is defined as authentic personal realization and not as a cultural agreement about mere concepts of nonduality. According to Alan Watts, for example, "Buddhism is not interested in concepts, it is interested in direct experience only."[3]

To this potential objection I can reply that, notwithstanding all assertions to the contrary, there is no getting away from concepts of ultimate reality—even the rejection of such concepts is still a concept of ultimacy itself. And even the least conceptual forms of spirituality inevitably include teachings about what is ultimately true and real. Moreover, the quality or usefulness of such teachings largely determines the service value and thus the cultural power of any given form of spirituality.

As we explore further below, a spiritual path's concept of ultimate reality impacts the lives of its practitioners in subtle but profound ways. Teachings about ultimate reality thus color the character of the culture in which such teachings are practiced. Indeed, the main purpose of this book is to explore the emergence of a new form of spirituality that has the potential to create greater social solidarity within the developed world. And this greater solidarity depends on the formation of new agreements that will result from the emergence of a more evolved understanding of spiritual truth.

In the context of teachings of spiritual truth, concepts function like the branches of a tree. When a teaching's conceptual branches are living, spiritual truth flows through them, delivering authentic spiritual experience. But when concepts become dead branches through which no living truth flows, teachings lose their vitality. And the existence of many such dead conceptual branches in our culture's tree of knowledge have understandably caused many religionists to discount the value of concepts overall. However, as I hope this discussion is beginning to show, evolutionary spirituality's emerging concepts of spiritual truth do provide authentic spiritual experience.

A thorough account of the enduring truths and personal benefits of a nondual spiritual practice is beyond the scope of our inquiry here, but in concluding this section I can affirm my belief that nondualism is an important and authentic spiritual path because of the spiritual fruits it bears in the lives of its practitioners, such as gentleness, poise, self-discipline, and compassion. Again, as Jesus taught, "By their fruits you shall know them." And as William James also concluded, in our evaluation of spiritual experience it is best "to turn our attention to the fruits of the religious condition, no matter in what way they have been produced."[4]

Like practically all historically significant forms of spirituality, nonduality is best conceived of as a *line of development* within human culture.[5] And this ancient line of religious development has now grown beyond the traditional level of its origin to become the leading line of spirituality within the postmodern level of cultural evolution.

An Existential Spiritual Polarity Becomes More Clearly Visible

The rise of nonduality as the mature expression of progressive spirituality provides new insight into the landscape of spiritual experience itself. As discussed above, the teaching that ultimate reality is essentially nondual has now brought together most of the major strands of progressive spirituality into a widespread cultural agreement. And the emergence of this agreement itself makes clear that nonduality is a vital and authentic aspect of spiritual reality.

However, no matter how popular this teaching may become and no matter how authentic the spiritual experience of nonduality may be, this does not negate or subordinate the experiential authenticity or cultural significance of other current forms of spirituality that are not nondual. In other words, within the spiritual marketplace of ideas, both contemporary and historical, other equally venerable kinds of spirituality can be found whose teachings point in a somewhat different direction. While some proponents of nondual spirituality contend that such alternative teachings are simply lower, or less true, the experience of nonduality itself does not justify such a conclusion. In fact, one of the virtues of a nondual unitive experience is that it is completely transconceptual, so it does not lend itself well to conceptual claims of belief system superiority.

As a result of its welcoming pluralism, the culture of progressive spirituality continues to embrace a wide variety of convictions regarding the character of ultimate reality. Yet even when we account for the full spectrum of diversity and acknowledge the myriad ways that people can experience spirit, when we survey the field of contemporary spirituality a clear pattern can be discerned. And as I will argue through the rest of this chapter, this evident pattern within spiritual experience points to two fundamental ways in which ultimate reality is most often experienced by spiritual practitioners: either it is experienced as unqualified unity, or it is experienced as a transcendent Creator. Simply put, spiritual experience itself reveals two essential kinds of ultimate reality, which can be loosely identified as *nondual* and *theistic*.[6]

These two fundamental conceptions of ultimate reality, however, are not just lying next to each other as alternative possibilities. Their dynamic relationship produces an interactive structure that takes the form of an *existential polarity*. That is, within the ideational and experiential terrain of humanity's search for ultimate meaning and value a dialectical tension exists between two essential conceptions of ultimate reality. And as discussed in chapters 2 and 4, existential polarities such as this can be recognized as *systems of development* providing openings for further evolution.

Challenges of Discernment

This polarity is clearly visible at the level of culture. But as soon as we try to define it or distill its essence at the level of actual teaching, significant difficulties arise. For example, between the two fundamental poles, which again consist of a nondual oneness on one side and an intelligent Creator on the other side, we can find teachings that are closer to the nondual pole but nevertheless use theistic terminology. Examples include nondual belief systems such as *A Course in Miracles* or the teachings of Neale Donald Walsh. Conversely, we can find teachings that claim to be nondual but are actually closer to the theistic side, such as the modified nondualism of the Hindu sage Ramanuja, which is more panentheistic than pantheistic.

However, despite well-meaning attempts to smooth over these differences or otherwise explain away their contradictions, for those who care about spiritual truth there is no getting away from the fact that many of the core tenets of nonduality and theism stand in opposition to each other, even in their most advanced expressions.

The recent maturation of progressive spirituality helps us see this existential polarity more clearly than ever before because progressive spirituality is really the first type of spirituality able to draw upon all the great religious traditions of history. As a result of the extensive religious scholarship and translation during the twentieth century, coupled with progressive spirituality's intensive interest in Eastern, esoteric, and indigenous spiritual teachings and practices, for the first time in history we have now effectively assembled much of the wisdom of the ages. And as we compare these treasures of spiritual wisdom and experience, we can begin to see how this body of knowledge naturally divides into two major kinds of spirituality.

This polarity can be seen in the history of Hinduism in the fierce debates between the followers of the pantheist Shankara and the panentheist Ramanuja.[7] And although it is not as starkly defined, this polarity can also be seen in the history of Christianity. The teachings of the Christian mystic Meister Eckhart, for example, clearly show the existence of the nondual pole within a Western religious context. Again, although we can identify multiple variations along the continuum between these poles, the cumulative body of spiritual experience discloses two distinct "attractor basins" for the human encounter with spiritual reality. And these distinct poles of spiritual experience have resulted in the development of alternative polar conceptions of what is ultimately real.

Regarding this apparent opposition between nondualism and theism, it is important to add that the existential polarity we are coming to find within the human experience of ultimate reality is deeply embedded in the fabric of being. Within these poles of experience something much larger and more permanent than our current understanding of either nondualism or theism is being encountered. So I do not mean to imply that the contemporary doctrines of nondualism and theism are permanent or indestructible. These forms of spirituality will inevitably change and evolve. But the deeper polarity that their opposition points to will likely endure as long as our minds remain within the finite realm of time.

Nonduality and Postmodernity

Even though the existential polarity I am labeling nondual and theistic has been repeatedly encountered in the history of religion, one of the ways progressive spirituality makes it more evident than ever before is how as this spirituality has grown into its maturity it has come to favor or emphasize the nondual pole. Progressive spirituality does not just favor Buddhism and Hinduism; it particularly favors the most nondual versions of these religions. Among the various forms of Buddhism found in the ancient canons, Tibetan and Zen Buddhism are the most popular by far. Likewise, among the varieties of Hinduism, Advaita Vedanta has found the most success in the West. Moreover, advocates of progressive spirituality have sought out and assembled practically all the other kinds of spirituality in the historical record that are compatible with a nondual vision of ultimate reality. As additional examples, the mystical oneness of Plotinus, the unitary ecstasy of Saint Teresa, Sufi mystic traditions, and the nondual visions of Kabbalistic theology have all been given pride of place within progressive spirituality.

Despite the polarizing limitations of this focus, progressive spirituality's preference for nondual teachings is actually evolutionarily appropriate for its task in history. As postmodernism emerged as a significant cultural force in the sixties and seventies, spirituality had been nearly extinguished within modernist intellectual circles. Cultural sophisticates and thought leaders eschewed ideas of the transcendent, and many academics concluded that religion itself was largely a thing of the past. The way forward for postmodernism thus involved a redefinition of the sacred that could make progress beyond the seemingly worn-out religious traditions of the Judeo-Christian establishment. Postmodernists accordingly embraced Eastern religions and other forms of spirituality that had a distinctly different feel and flavor than the traditional Western religions they were attempting to transcend. So now as progressive postmodern spirituality has matured and naturally refined its focus and its preferences, the nondual pole of spiritual experience has been brought into greater relief, showing this side of human spirituality more clearly than ever before in history.

Here it bears repeating that this is a cultural analysis of the frothy leading edge of human spiritual development, so the picture must necessarily be painted with broad brushstrokes. And, again, many exceptions and counter examples can be cited. But for those familiar with the contemporary currents of progressive spiritual culture in America, the dialectic pattern of an existential polarity can be clearly seen. This conclusion is supported by the fact that even though nondualism is now preferred by the majority of those involved with progressive spirituality, a strong minority of theists can still be found within postmodern spiritual culture.

Before going further with this discussion, I must briefly address potential objections to the perhaps somewhat ironic idea that nonduality remains linked to theism and its allies in an existential polarity. Nondualists may object that the whole point of nondual spirituality is to transcend the pairs and leave all forms of polarity behind through the realization that our perceptions of separation are illusory. Yet we are all here within the finite evolving universe, and as long as we exist in time, the primordial polarity of infinite and finite will continue to condition our reality. We may catch glimpses of ultimate unity beyond time, but our work in this world will always be bound by evolution's sequential unfolding. Therefore, we cannot get away (not permanently at least) from the existentially dialectical constitution of our evolving reality. The dialectical character of evolution, which we find refracted throughout the universe at every level, means that our spiritual growth must almost always proceed by polar steps—one foot after another—on our journey toward perfection.

The Polarity Exists within Spiritual Experience Itself

The experience of spirit itself seems to divide naturally into two distinct categories that provide the foundation and determine the teaching themes for the nondual and theistic forms of spirituality we are exploring. As we have seen, nondual versions of spirituality are founded primarily on the universal mystical experience of *formless unity*. As Advaitan teacher Nisargadatta Maharaj wrote, "When you go beyond awareness, there is a state of non-duality, in which there is no cognition, only pure being. In the state of non-duality, all separation ceases."[8] Conversely, theistic versions of spirituality rest upon another kind of deep and foundational spiritual experience—*the love of God*. For those who have a direct relationship with God, the experience of being personally known and cared for by the Creator of the universe is a thrilling confirmation of their faith. As Saint Augustine wrote, "God loves each of us as if there were only one of us."[9]

But while formless unity is the experiential foundation of the nondual pole and the love of God is the experiential foundation of the theistic pole, the experience of God's love is not a perfect polar mirror of the nondual unitive experience. The experiential basis for theistic spirituality is more varied and not always mystical in character. Theistic spiritual experiences can include awareness of loyalty and duty, as well as the other "natural signs" discussed at the end of chapter 3. Such experiences can also include a sense of love, not just from God but from other spiritual sources, such as from Christ. For example, philosopher and mystic Simone Weil described her experience of Jesus as "the presence of love, like that which one can read in the smile on a beloved face."[10]

Some have argued that the apparent differences found in descriptions of essential spiritual experience can be reduced to interpretive constructions designed to justify previously established belief systems. Others contend that such differences are due to the indeterminate nature of spiritual reality, which is said to be best understood as a wide ocean of diversity rather than as a structured polarity. However, after reflecting on this subject for quite some time, it seems to me that the polar opposition I am describing does not result simply from previously held biases toward doctrinal commitments. My conclusion is that the polar tension between theism and nonduality reflected in the overall world body of spiritual teachings about ultimate reality results from a polarity in the human experience of ultimate reality itself, rather than the other way around. In short, the experiences produce the polarity in the teachings more than the teachings produce the polarity in the experiences.

From an evolutionary perspective, however, the recognition of this polarity need not lead to further division. A clearer understanding of the dialectical structure of spiritual experience can actually increase the degree by which these poles mutually enact one another. Quoting Friedrich Schleiermacher, Christian scholar Eric Reitan concludes, "Perhaps the proper attitude is not to choose sides but to adopt a 'beautiful modesty' which recognizes that religious experience carries with it 'a feeling of man's utter incapacity ever to exhaust it for himself alone'"[11] Indeed, practitioners of nondual spirituality can and do experience the love of God, just as theists can and do experience the absolute unity of all things. Yet there remains an important difference between nondual spirituality and forms of spirituality that relate to a personal God. And as we will explore in chapter 7, the natural polar tension between these essential forms of spirituality provides an opening for the further evolution of consciousness and culture.

Recognizing and understanding the inherently dialectical structure of the spiritual experience of ultimate reality can be useful in many ways. But one of the most interesting features of this polarity of nonduality and theism, and one that clearly demonstrates the polarity's existence, can be seen in the way these alternative conceptions of ultimate reality present somewhat different opportunities for spiritual growth and cultural evolution. That these two poles of spiritual experience tend to lead to somewhat different notions of what it means to live a spiritual life is well understood by the renowned German theologian Hans Küng. In his seminal book *Christianity and World Religions*, Küng identifies two basic kinds of "higher" religion, which he calls the "mystical" and the "prophetic." He then goes on to describe their distinct notions of what it means to live a "pious life":

> *Mystical piety* is . . . primarily turned inward; it strives to be free from desire, to extinguish affective and volitional life. It is a process of self-transformation, in which the mystic appears as one who goes without but, in the end, as one who knows. The high point of a life of mystical piety is reached in extraordinary experiences beyond

normal consciousness . . . in which sensory excitement blends with purely spiritual experience, and the everyday subject/object split is abolished. . . .

Prophetic piety, by contrast, is characterized by a strong will to live: an instinct for affirmation, a condition on which one is gripped by values and responsibilities, a passionate striving for the realization of certain goals and ideals. Prophetic piety is thus primarily turned outward, stands up to confront the world, and aims to prevail in it. Emotions are not suppressed, but awakened: The will to live asserts itself and seeks to triumph even amid external defeat. In this respect the prophetically oriented person is a fighter who struggles through from doubt to the certainty of faith.[12]

While Küng may seem to give preference to the theistic, or prophetic, pole in this passage, *Christianity and World Religions* as a whole demonstrates his thorough understanding and deep sympathy for both Buddhism and Hinduism. And regardless of his preferences, his scholarly recognition of the two basic kinds of higher religion underscores my argument that an existential polarity exists between nondual and theistic spirituality.

The idea that these alternative poles of spiritual truth lead to different orientations toward living one's life is also confirmed by "dual belongers" who identify with both Buddhism and Christianity. In her insightful book *Buddhist and Christian? An Exploration of Dual Belonging*, religious scholar Rose Drew writes: "Christianity emphasises love (*agape*) as the most crucial aspect of transformation and fosters loving engagement with the world. . . . Buddhism, by contrast, emphasises wisdom (which in Mahayana terms means direct non-conceptual, non-dual awareness of the emptiness of all phenomena) as the most crucial aspect of the salvific/liberative transformation and fosters the eradication of attachment to all phenomena."[13] After exploring the contrast between Buddhism's emphasis on wise nonattachment and Christianity's emphasis on loving engagement, Drew ultimately agrees with the Sri Lankan Jesuit theologian Aloysius Pieris that "it is the dialectical interplay of wisdom and love that ensures a progressive movement in the realm of the human spirit."[14]

However, progressive spirituality's natural tendency is to claim that the teachings of these different forms of spirituality are all essentially saying the same thing—that they are simply "different paths to the top of the same mountain." But this homogenizing or leveling tendency is actually a shortcoming of postmodernism's otherwise commendable pluralism, which we must resist if we are to effectively transcend progressive spirituality's limitations.

As we have seen, one of the major strengths of evolutionary spirituality is its ability to recognize and work with polarities more effectively than ever before. The evolutionary perspective's emergent capacity of dialectical epistemology gives it the power to harmonize and synthesize existential polarities—such as the polarity of nonduality and theism—in ways that allow opposing poles to true each other up. As will be explored further in chapter 7, nonduality and theism can complement and even mutually enact one another in significant ways. But there are also important ways in which these poles remain in tension or conflict, even under the most sympathetic interpretations. Therefore, the growing recognition of the polarity of theism and nonduality presents evolutionary spirituality with an unprecedented opportunity to work with this polar tension in a way that synthesizes its strengths without erasing its differences. The synthetic bridging of this existential polarity is thus a task for which evolutionary spirituality is particularly well suited.

By clearly identifying and effectively working with the existential polarity of nondual and theistic forms of spiritual experience, evolutionary spirituality can begin to overcome progressive spirituality's stifling relativism through the development of a more evolved criterion of evaluation for spiritual truth. This important project of working with both essential poles of spiritual experience begins by showing why nondual conceptions of ultimate reality and the spiritual teachings they entail are not sufficient in themselves to provide the more effective forms of spiritual leadership the developed world now requires. In other words, to work with an existential polarity in a way that realizes its developmental potential, the inherent conflicts that naturally exist between its poles must be critically engaged.

Accordingly, in the next chapter I will undertake a constructive critique of progressive nondual spirituality with the aim of furthering the emergence of evolutionary spirituality.

Chapter Six

A Constructive Critique of Nondual Spiritual Teachings

An evolutionary understanding of human history and culture helps us appreciate how practically every perspective has a piece of the truth. Once we see how truth itself is like a ladder of distinctions whose rungs lead step by step to an ever-widening conception of what is real, we can see the importance and enduring necessity of every rung on the ladder. Adding to this inclusive perspective on the true, an evolutionary understanding of the good affirms that despite the inevitable differences and disagreements that arise in trying to discern what is ultimately real, all those who are honestly seeking spiritual truth are really members of the same family. In other words, almost everyone is seeking beauty, truth, and goodness in one way or another, and this recognition of our common quest for value provides a foundation for our solidarity. Indeed, this is a central truth of evolutionary spirituality.

Another central feature of evolutionary spirituality, however, is its vigorous pursuit of excellence and its relentless striving for improvement. This penchant for progress creates a sense of restlessness and discontent with current conditions. And this discontent becomes particularly acute with regard to the developed world's current state of spiritual evolution, which leads to this chapter's critique of nondual spirituality.

Recall that in chapter 1 we identified both the need and the opportunity for more agreeable and inclusive forms of spiritual leadership in the developed world. And in chapter 2 we began to explore how the rise of evolutionary spirituality could supply such leadership. Also in chapter 2, we examined how harnessing the developmental potential of an existential polarity involves using its inherent conflicts to discover the transcendent synthesis implied by the existence of its dialectical tensions. Then in the last chapter we explored how the maturation of progressive spirituality has revealed more clearly than ever before the existence of such an existential polarity within the world's spiritual teachings (both ancient and modern) and also within human spiritual experience overall.

So now in this chapter we will use evolutionary spirituality's method of dialectical epistemology to help facilitate the emergence of evolutionary spirituality itself. In the context of contemporary spiritual culture, this dialectical method involves working with the essential contradictions between nondual and theistic teachings about the nature of ultimate reality. When we evaluate the respective truth teachings of these two poles in light of the spiritual teachings of evolution, we can begin to recognize certain underappreciated propositions of spiritual truth (underappreciated within progressive spirituality at least) most often associated with theistic spirituality. As I will argue, these truths are confirmed by the spiritual teachings of evolution themselves and are thus rehabilitated and reclaimed by evolutionary spirituality.

As a preview, the teachings of spiritual truth that can be recognized as necessities from the viewpoint of evolutionary spirituality include: (1) the necessity of a spiritually real evolving soul; (2) the necessity of human free will; (3) the necessity of a spiritually real evolving finite universe; and (4) the necessity of recognizing that ultimate reality possesses the personal powers of intention and love. I believe these propositions of spiritual truth are necessary elements of evolutionary spirituality because they follow directly from the spiritual teachings of evolution. Simply put, the universe does not really make sense unless we acknowledge a place for these truths within our spirituality.

While the recognition of these evolutionary necessities inevitably results in a constructive critique of some of the teachings of nonduality, my arguments do not attempt to invalidate nondualism. As I hope will become clear in the next chapter, the purpose of this critique is to help establish a more "roomy oneness" within nondual teachings that can better accommodate the *spiritual parts within the spiritual whole*. However, the same practice technique that allows us to engage effectively the polarity of nonduality and theism in an evolutionary context also requires us to reaffirm and preserve the core teachings of nonduality, even in the face of paradox and contradiction.

This dialectical practice of bridging polarities does not provide tidy conclusions or static rest. Rather, this practice involves a dynamic, iterative, back-and-forth process wherein the inherent contradictions of an indestructible polarity such as this are held in a dynamic tension—a tension that serves to true up both poles over time. However, this chapter's critique of nondual spiritual teachings, together with the next chapter's exploration of a potential synthesis of the two poles, is only the beginning of a process that will require many such iterations. And thus I trust that as evolutionary spirituality emerges, this process will continue through the work of others.

DIALECTICAL STEPS OF PROGRESS

Those who are relatively new to progressive spirituality may ask, what's wrong? Its defenders may contend that it represents the most open, inclusive, diverse, and compassionate form of spiritual culture that has ever appeared. The general opinion within progressive circles seems to be that it is the mainstream materialistic culture that needs to change. It is they who need to become "more conscious" and adopt the practices and values of progressive spiritual culture. And I think that if the majority of modernists were somehow able simply to "wake up" and embrace one or more versions of progressive spirituality, this would indeed represent cultural evolution. However, for reasons we are here considering, progressive spirituality is not good enough—its teachings are generally not true enough—for it to present an attractive alternative worldview for significant numbers of secular American modernists or for others who identify as spiritual but not religious.

As a counter to this point, defenders of progressive spirituality may claim that attracting modernists is not really their aim. While most would certainly like to see a more enlightened society, their goals are focused primarily on personal enlightenment and the cultivation of a community of like-minded religionists. And from this perspective perhaps there is nothing wrong. But as we come to appreciate the spiritual teachings of evolution, we see where progressive spirituality is most in need of improvement, which in turn motivates us to work toward our society's further spiritual evolution.

Therefore, I believe the kind of critical evaluation we will undertake in this chapter is warranted because, as noted, the leading edge of contemporary spirituality is not adequately fulfilling the spiritual needs of our society. That is evidenced by progressive spirituality's fringe status and ongoing lack of influence, which renders it incapable of providing the kind of inclusive spiritual leadership the developed world requires. Yet if we are to follow evolution's own technique of dialectical development, to *transcend* progressive spirituality we must also *include* its important accomplishments. Transcending *and* including involves a two-step process. First we acknowledge where progressive spirituality has succeeded in producing cultural evolution, and how these very successes are now making the emergence of evolutionary spirituality possible. Then the next step involves pushing off against the shortcomings of progressive spirituality to create something better.

Step 1: The Maturation of Progressive Spirituality Presages Further Emergence

Admittedly, as discussed in the last chapter, the relatively recent mature culmination of progressive spirituality in nondualism is an important evolutionary step in itself. Nondual spirituality's focus on practice and its de-emphasis of belief have helped rescue spirituality from death at the hands of modernism by offering a form of spirituality that can be clearly distinguished from the traditional forms of Judeo-Christian theism the West has inherited from its history. The progressive nondual complex is thus seen by many as being free from some of the more objectionable aspects of historically received Western religion, such as its patriarchal character and its reliance on myths and miracles.

Even though the historical significance of the rise of progressive nondual spirituality has not yet been adequately recognized by the mainstream, I believe that in the future this cultural development will be loosely compared to other major religious emergences, such as the Protestant Reformation in Europe. And just as the Reformation set the stage for the subsequent Enlightenment, the partial merger of Buddhism and Hinduism within progressive spirituality's nondual complex may similarly serve as a precursor for a kind of *second Enlightenment*—the emergence of the evolutionary worldview. But while the accomplishments of progressive spirituality are necessary prerequisites for a second Enlightenment, they are not sufficient in themselves to produce such an emergence.

However, now that we can recognize progressive spirituality's culmination—now that this important step has been taken—we can begin to see the next step looming on the horizon of evolutionary possibilities. While such further progress will not be found by simply returning to a preference for the theistic pole, neither will it be achieved by remaining primarily within the opposing pole of nonduality. For evolutionary spirituality to fulfill its promise of becoming the next authentic step in the evolution of spiritual culture, it must move toward an unprecedented synthesis that preserves the best of both kinds of spirituality, better integrating the two poles while simultaneously transcending their respective limitations. In other words, as evolutionary spirituality emerges as a fresh kind of spirituality, both poles will be needed and both poles will be put to good use.

Step 2: Evolutionary Spirituality Offers a Way Forward

Evolutionary spirituality, however, is only just now emerging out of progressive spiritual culture. For it to make further progress beyond our current cultural conditions, it has to distinguish itself clearly from progressive spirituality—it has to explain how and why these two forms of spirituality are different and actually dialectically separated. In fact, this dialectical move beyond progressive spirituality mirrors the larger historical movement of which the rise of evolutionary spirituality is only a part. And this larger dialectical movement involves the overall transcendence of the postmodern worldview through the emergence of a post-postmodern or evolutionary worldview that can better appreciate and integrate the accomplishments of modernism.

As first discussed in chapter 4, evolution's primary process and technique is dialectical development. In our discussion of this dialectical process we saw how it is most often understood in terms of thesis-antithesis-synthesis. But Hegel originally described this three-step process as affirmation, negation, and negation of the negation, and recalling his essentially negative characterization of the process helps us understand that for evolutionary spirituality to emerge it not only has to synthesize; it also has to negate. Yet the idea of the negation of the negation does not entail the complete invalidation of the original negation. Nevertheless, evolutionary spirituality's negation of progressive spirituality's original and ongoing negation of traditional theism must create enough separation to effectively break the grip of step one so that step two can emerge. Showing why and how evolutionary spirituality should make this move is the purpose of this chapter.

TRANSCENDING PROGRESSIVE SPIRITUALITY:
INHERENT CHALLENGES

Those of us who are attempting to supply a truer and more useful vision of humanity's existential purpose by helping to develop evolutionary spirituality inevitably have to push off against the shortcomings of progressive spirituality's current state of cultural development. As noted, however, this is tricky because even in its mature and culminating expression in nonduality, progressive spirituality remains complicated. Any attempt to point out its shortcomings must thus grapple with the following challenges: (1) contemporary progressive spirituality is an amorphous and indeterminate hybrid of different spiritual traditions; (2) nondual spiritual teachings are often transconceptual and can thus be paradoxical or philosophically problematic; and (3) even as it attempts to transcend progressive spirituality's limitations, evolutionary spirituality must preserve and include nondualism's essential truths. In this section we address these challenges in turn.

Progressive Nondual Spirituality Is an Indefinite Cultural Hybrid

This chapter's suggestions for improvement are not aimed specifically at either traditional Buddhism or traditional Advaita Vedanta. Although these venerable religions have already been somewhat modified through their contact with Western culture, they are obliged to be loyal to the heritage of their respective lineages, which will undoubtedly continue to edify humanity for centuries to come. Therefore, critiquing the core doctrines of these traditions is uncalled for and unlikely to result in any improvements. Rather, this critical appraisal focuses on progressive spirituality's synthetic nondual cultural agreement, which is broader and more inclusive than either Buddhism or Hinduism alone and which has recently come to represent the leading edge of our society's spiritual development.

As discussed in the last chapter, unlike the teachings of traditional religions, this indeterminate but nevertheless identifiable and attractive (to postmodernists at least) nondual cultural agreement is more flexible and more subject to evolutionary improvement than historically received religions in themselves. This flexibility can be seen over the course of the last forty years in which this cultural agreement structure has adopted the doctrines that suit its needs and discarded the ones that do not.

And this process now has the opportunity to continue through another round of expanded realization and doctrinal refinement made possible by the emerging evolutionary perspective.

As also noted, nondual spirituality can now be understood as a line of development that has grown from the traditional level into the postmodern level. And this line will undoubtedly continue to grow into the evolutionary level and beyond. But to evolve beyond the countercultural limitations of progressive spirituality, the leading edge of spirituality has to move beyond the nondual pole's antithesis toward a synthesis that makes room for the enduring truths of Western civilization's philosophical and religious heritage. Nonduality's essential realization of the absolute oneness of the universe will certainly continue to be the touchstone of its focus. But there are other aspects of its truth teachings that will need to be modified (or at least challenged) as this line of development grows into the evolutionary level.

Spiritual Truth Becomes Slippery in the Face of Philosophical Indeterminacy

Many forms of contemporary nonduality pride themselves at being transconceptual or even nonconceptual, which often results in logical inconsistencies being ignored or glossed over. For example, teachings of love and compassion are ubiquitous within nondual spiritual discourse, but because love is a relational feeling or quality that requires at least two separate entities, grounding this quality within a body of teachings that denies the reality of all such relations—because it denies all separation in the first place—presents philosophical difficulties. This problem has been acknowledged by nondual philosopher David Loy, who admits, "Love as ordinarily experienced and understood is undeniably dualistic in that the lover is distinct from the beloved. Love, as much as hate, seems to be the relation between two things and in order to sustain that as a relation they must remain distinct."[1] Yet even after lamenting the philosophical difficulties of finding a place for love within a non-dual ontology, two pages later Loy asserts the contradictory conclusion that nondual conceptions of ultimate reality can nevertheless be loving: "The Mahayana Dharmakaya [Buddha-essence] radiates love and compassion to all, impersonally like the sun, but many are not receptive to it."[2]

A similar philosophical difficulty arises with the idea of creativity within a nondual context. The Buddhist teaching of "dependent origination," that all things and events mutually cocreate each other, is said to eliminate the need for conventional notions of cause and effect. This teaching is advanced in the context of the traditional Buddhist cosmology of eternal beginninglessness. But even if we allow that the infinite and eternal aspect of the universe is in fact beginningless, we now know that the finite evolving aspect of our universe had a distinct and dramatic beginning, which is unmistakably causal and creative. And since the big bang our evolving universe has demonstrated an unfathomable outpouring of creativity in which something more keeps coming from something less.[3]

However, nondualism's seemingly difficult problem of grounding the presence of creativity within its monistic conceptions of reality is usually explained away by nondual philosophers. For example, Kitaro Nishida, the eminent founder of the Kyoto School of nondual philosophy, claimed that his conception of ultimate reality, which he termed "Absolute Nothingness," is in fact a "creative principle." Nishida justified this seemingly self-contradictory assertion through the teaching that nothingness, or emptiness, "is that by which everything is constituted." But exactly how this teaching can be reconciled with the scientific facts of the causally creative big bang and the teleological evolutionary unfolding that has followed remains unclear at best.[4]

These examples illustrate the difficulties of trying to evaluate or evolve teachings of spiritual truth containing performative contradictions that render such teachings partially self-deconstructing. For instance, even the concept of experience itself, which nondualists claim as the primary argument for their beliefs (according to Loy), is unavoidably dualistic. Experience has little meaning if there is no subject who can have such an experience in the first place. Similarly vexing, the basic concept of improvement is also unavoidably dualistic in the way it requires a movement from a less valuable condition to a more valuable condition. All concepts of improvement thus necessarily recognize two separate states or conditions—the less and the more.

Nondualists often counter such philosophical objections by invoking some version of the "two truths doctrine," which holds that there is an absolute level of truth in which reality is nondual and a relative level of truth in which concepts of separation can be properly recognized. But while this apologetic teaching acknowledges the problem, it does not really solve it—at least not to the satisfaction of those not already committed to a nondual belief system in the first place.[5]

This discussion is meant to show how trying to critique a system of thought that is highly transconceptual is difficult at best and perhaps even futile. But we cannot escape the conclusion that our civilization stands in need of better forms of spiritual leadership. So we cannot neglect the crucial task of trying to improve even the best versions of the forms of spirituality currently on offer in our culture. And this is where the crucial recognition of the existential polarity of nonduality and theism comes back into play.

Evolutionary Spirituality Must Preserve Both Poles of Spiritual Truth

Much of the last chapter was devoted to the argument that the landscape of human spiritual experience reveals an existential polarity of two essential but different conceptions of ultimate reality—nonduality and theism. And now, as a result of the evolutionary achievements of progressive spirituality, we can see the nondual pole more clearly—we can see how it has been realized in both the East and the West and how it is grounded in the mystical experience of absolute unity. As I hope I have made clear, the rise of nondual spirituality in America over the last fifty years in general, and over the last fifteen years in particular, is a positive development in spiritual culture.

Yet as I argue below, there are important spiritual truths rooted in the theistic pole that conflict with the teachings of nonduality. And as we come to appreciate the spiritual truth revealed by our growing scientific and philosophical understanding of our evolving universe—as we begin to recognize evolution's spiritual teachings—we begin to rediscover the ongoing veracity and enduring necessity of many of theism's spiritual truths. Thus, in light of what we can now see, we can begin to reaffirm the truth of a spiritually real evolving soul, the truth of human freedom, the truth of the spiritual value of nature and history, and even the truth of a loving Creator. These spiritual teachings are each discussed in the sections that follow.

But again, even as we attempt to develop an evolutionary synthesis that reaffirms some of the essential truths of theism, we must simultaneously preserve and deepen our hold on the spiritual truths of nonduality. Notwithstanding their contradictions and tensions, both kinds of spirituality are affirmed by evolutionary spirituality. Evolutionary spirituality, however, does more than simply affirm both truths. It also attempts to show how we can use both the complementary aspects and the conflicting aspects of these two essential kinds of spiritual experience to further the spiritual evolution of our culture. In other words, the evolutionary practice of working with polarities involves engaging dialectical tensions in a way that synthesizes and strengthens opposing poles without erasing their differences.

According to this understanding, whenever we are faced with an existential polarity wherein two sides are in tension but nevertheless both worthy of preservation, we need to avoid the natural proclivity of each pole to try to dominate, exclude, or invalidate its opposing pole. Yet we also need to avoid the attempt simply to split the difference in some kind of mediocre or superficial compromise. Preserving the tension is crucial because the tension itself is the source of energy needed for transcendence. As we have seen, this method is how dialectic relationships serve as engines of evolution.

Progressive theologian Hans Küng has written about such a potential integration of Eastern and Western religion, calling for a "tension-rich synthesis" that includes the truths of both while preserving and honoring their distinguishing elements: "The goal is not a compounding of various features from various religions, . . . nor a fusing of religions, but, rather, a dialectical 'transcending' of conflicts through inner mediation, which at once includes affirming, denying, and overcoming antagonistic positions."[6] Küng's understanding of the need for a tension-rich synthesis thus affirms the ongoing necessity of both poles.

This same sentiment was expressed a decade earlier by John A. T. Robinson, the Dean of Trinity College, Cambridge, who wrote, "The two centres . . . are but two poles in an interrelated mass. From whichever one we start, whether from the I-Thou or the *tat tvam asi* [thou art that], we must maintain the tension with the other. They are not saying the same thing (and to claim that 'ultimately' they are, or that all religions lead to the same point does not help). Moreover in isolation or in fusion they lose their charge. The aim is not syncretism or absorption, but more like what has been called a 'unitive pluralism.'" As an example of this approach, Robinson ends his insightful book *Truth is Two-Eyed* with a quote from Indian theologian Pandippedi Chenchiah: "The photographic negative plate of Jesus, developed in a solution of Hinduism, brings out hitherto unknown features of the portrait and these may prove exactly the 'Gospel' for our time."[7]

Evolutionary Spirituality's Dialectical Opportunity

Evolutionary spirituality, however, cannot escape the dialectical currents of history. Even as it values synthesis—even as it defines itself as essentially synthetic in character and method—it must nevertheless work with the opportunities handed to it by the achievements of the previous stage of cultural evolution. And as we have discussed, progressive spirituality's most significant accomplishment can now be seen in its important and continuing work of illuminating and refining the nondual pole of spiritual experience.

This achievement allows us to take the next crucial step in the evolution of spiritual culture, which involves reclaiming some of the enduring truths of the theistic pole by showing how they reappear in the light of the spiritual teachings of evolution. These crucial truths, however, are ungrounded at best and denied at worst by most forms of nondual spirituality. Therefore, the move toward an evolutionary spirituality that can effectively transcend progressive spirituality's limitations must begin by wrestling with the natural tensions and conflicts between the nondual and theistic poles of spiritual experience. Although religionists have been grappling with these polar tensions for millennia, the emerging evolutionary perspective allows us to see these contradictions in a new light and at a new level. And from this more evolved vantage point new progress becomes possible.

In the next chapter we will reflect on the possibility of a temporarily stable synthesis of nondual and theistic spirituality. But before we can begin to consider such a synthesis, we need to explore further the problems creating the need for such a synthetic advance. And this inevitably takes the form of a constructive critique. In other words, evolutionary spirituality recognizes certain necessary spiritual truths that can be problematic for nondual spirituality. So it is to these problems that we now turn.

THE EVOLUTIONARY NECESSITY OF A
SPIRITUALLY REAL EVOLVING SOUL

Exactly what the spiritual teachings of evolution consist of is certainly subject to a variety of opinions. But one thing that seems fairly certain is that the evolution of our universe of nature, culture, and self is a real and valuable project resulting from the movement of spirit in time. Simply stated, a foundational truth of evolutionary spirituality is that evolution has a genuine spiritual purpose. And if this is the case, then our personal spiritual growth must be recognized as an important part of the value evolution is creating.

The word *soul* is most often used to designate the spiritual reality of what is growing within us as we evolve, but alternative terms such as *spiritual nature* or *character* are also sometimes used. Yet even though the notion of a developing soul can be understood or defined in a variety of ways within evolutionary spirituality, the spiritual teachings of evolution make clear that as our consciousness evolves we become more spiritually real. So regardless of whether we use the word *soul* or some other term, recognition of the growth of spirit within us is a necessity for evolutionary spirituality. But this is hard to reconcile with the nondual teaching that there is no real self or that the real self we do possess is already perfect and thus does not evolve. As an example, according to Ramana Maharshi, "It is false to speak of realization. What is there to realize? The real is as it is always. We are not creating anything new or achieving something which we did not have before."[8]

As noted, one point of relative agreement among the world's great religions is that humans are indwelt by spirit. Whether it is called the Higher Self, the Atman, Buddha-nature, or some other name, practically all religionists will affirm that the infinite lives within us, and this is what makes us spiritual creatures. Further, there appears to be general agreement that humans also possess an individual ego or mental vestige of our animal origins that can be distinguished from our true spiritual nature. And the idea that through spiritual growth we come to identify with our spiritual nature rather than with our ego is a teaching found in some form within most spiritual paths. However, if the process of transcending the ego-identity is conceived of as simply a matter of waking up to the true spiritual nature of who we have been all along, then the value of what emerges through our spiritual growth becomes largely, if not completely, overlooked.

The commendable focus of the nondual pole is on connecting with universal oneness. But within contemporary nondual spiritual teaching, the spiritual aspect of ourselves that is growing, the part that is gaining spiritual knowledge and experience, which I'm calling the soul, is often implicitly conflated with the ego-identity and thus relegated to the status of illusion. As another example, popular nondual teacher Adyashanti writes: "Stop pretending to be someone, or something! You are no one, you are no-thing! You are not this body or this mind. This body and mind exist within who and what you are. You are pure consciousness, already free, awake, and liberated. Stand up and walk out of your dream."[9]

While there may be important truths in the approach to awakening articulated by Adyashanti, these teachings leave little room for the evident truth of the evolving soul that is growing out of the interplay of the Higher Self and the ego-identity. As discussed in chapter 4, the infinite and the finite interact in the process of our personal spiritual development. But if our spirituality has no place in its teachings for an evolving soul—if our conception includes only the relatively unreal ego and the everlasting and unchanging absolute self (or no-self)—then the spiritual value of what is evolving in our consciousness goes missing. Stated another way, if the goal is simply to overcome our identification with the lower self and recognize that the always-already-perfect nature of the Higher Self is who we are, then the spiritual reality of the "becoming" is collapsed or reduced to timeless "being" alone.

The necessity of including the idea of an evolving soul in our culture's spiritual agreement is not just a theological fine point. This idea is very important because it is central to evolutionary spirituality's teaching that we are here to create something good, true, and beautiful—that we are in the world to make it better. But if this process of working to evolve our world does not create something of lasting value within our selves that did not previously exist, then this essential teaching is undermined. Unless some version of an evolving soul is included in its teachings, evolutionary spirituality will fail to provide the foundational reasons and motivations we need to support our work as agents of evolution. Moreover, for evolutionary spirituality to accomplish its mission of providing a more evolved form of spirituality that can lead to greater social solidarity, its teachings must recognize the real spiritual value created by evolution in all three realms of its becoming—nature, culture, *and self.*

While personal spiritual growth is certainly recognized and encouraged in nondual spirituality, the relative absence of the concept of an evolving soul creates philosophical problems for nondualism that can cause confusion and diminish its capacity for spiritual leadership. By pointing out the need to better account for the evolving soul, evolutionary spirituality shows where the nondual pole can benefit from the moderating and even challenging influence of the theistic pole of spiritual teaching and experience. But, again, we need not reject the important truths of nondual teachings or otherwise contend that they are simply wrong. The evolutionary practice of dialectical seeing allows us to hold conflicting truths in a kind of developmental tension, as described above and as explored further in the next chapter.

However, when progressive culture's most influential spiritual teachings tend to subtly undermine the important work of perfecting the universe, an opportunity is presented to use the spiritual teachings of evolution to refine and improve the cultural agreements we inevitably use to construct our identities and guide our choices.

THE EVOLUTIONARY NECESSITY OF FREE WILL

Related to the necessity of recognizing an evolving soul is the necessity of recognizing that humans possess varying degrees of relatively free will. While many of our actions are influenced (and often coerced) by material and social forces beyond our power to resist, we all nevertheless directly experience our powers of choice. Moreover, a strong affirmation of relative human freedom is not only central for evolutionary spirituality; it is also a cornerstone of our civilization. If we have no real choice we cannot be responsible, and without personal responsibility the entire concept of morality becomes meaningless.

Nondual spirituality, however, often has difficulty with notions of personal responsibility and the relative freedom of choice this idea necessarily entails. Obviously, if there is no self or if the one universal self is the only real thing, then the concept of individual free will is effectively ruled out.

In the process of rejecting free will, some nondual teachers try to avoid the opposite implication of total determinism by denying there are objective causes in the first place by which we could be "determined." For example, David Loy writes, "If there is no subject then there are also no 'objective' causal factors."[10] Loy's extreme position does not represent all nondual views. Many nondual teachings hold that it is possible to alter one's karma through the choice of right action. But the notion of free will nevertheless remains philosophically problematic within a nondual ontology. The result is that most forms of nondualism continue to deny free will either implicitly or explicitly. For instance, Jewish nondual writer Jay Michaelson calls the idea of free will "the last gasp of the unenlightened mind."[11]

However, if we have no authentic agency and we are just going along for the ride—if our choices make no real difference in the evolutionary process of perfecting the universe—then the spiritual value of both ourselves and the evolutionary process overall is clearly undermined. That is, without free will it is hard to imagine what purpose or value humans may have within the cosmic economy. If our spirituality finds it philosophically difficult to account for our authentic freedom or creativity, then this begs the question, what do we add and why are we here? Conversely, if our interpretation of the spiritual teachings of evolution affirms that we are cocreators of the universe, then our spiritual philosophy must be able to explain how our creativity is something we are at least partially responsible for. Stated differently, the existence of a finite evolving universe is left without a spiritual reason or purpose if the infinite—the preexisting, eternal state of perfect being—is not actually advanced or otherwise benefited by the human experience of evolving in time. And if our own experience of this process is merely a passive witnessing wherein we have no real opportunity to participate voluntarily in the creation of evolutionary perfection by our own lights, then what is the point? In response to the challenge of this question, evolutionary spirituality emphatically affirms that the universe *does* have a point and so do we. But unless we have authentic agency, then this point is essentially lost.

There are few nondual teachers who are willing to go as far as Michaelson in baldly declaring that the idea of free will is "unenlightened." But it seems that many nondualists do acknowledge the problem of finding individual freedom within an essentially monistic ontology. Nondual teacher A. H. Almaas, for example, explains that free will is a "delusion" that is part of the mistaken notion of a separate self. But he nevertheless attempts to preserve the idea through some countervailing nuances in his teaching, explaining, "We are not saying that you don't have free will, but that you don't have a free will separate from the whole."[12]

While Almaas's position leaves me somewhat mystified, I am heartened by the clarity with which renowned Zen Buddhist teacher Thich Nhat Hanh affirms the freedom of human will:

> Everything evolves according to the principle of interdependence, but there is free will and the possibility to transform. Free will is mindfulness.... We don't want to take a path leading to ill-being; we want to take the path leading to the cessation of ill-being, to well-being. Free will is possible in Buddhism, because we know that we can handle our thinking, we can handle our speech and we can handle our action. We are responsible for our action and it is possible to assure a good continuation. Freedom begins with mindfulness, concentration and insight. With insight, with right view we can practice right thinking. We can change ourselves; we can change the world. Everything is the fruit of action.[13]

This quote by Thich Nhat Hanh, however, does not represent the majority view on the freedom of human will among nondualists, and he has recently come under fire for contradicting established Buddhist teachings.[14] According to Buddhist scholar Riccardo Repetti, "The Buddha's teachings implicitly endorse a certain type of free will and explicitly endorse something very close to determinism."[15] And this ambiguity has prevented the question of free will from being settled within Western Buddhism, as demonstrated by ongoing debates in *Journal of Buddhist Ethics*.[16] Despite Thich Nhat Hanh's affirmation of human freedom, it remains difficult to establish a working concept of free will within the context of the teachings of no-self.

As with all these points of critique, many of the arguments come down to the question of what is real and what is illusion. And this brings up the next element of the critique.

The Evolutionary Necessity of a Spiritually Real Finite Universe

Both Buddhism and Hinduism include teachings that the phenomenal world is essentially an illusion. In Buddhism the illusion is called *samsara* and in Hinduism it is known as *maya*. The idea that the world of appearances is unreal arises partially as a logical consequence of a nondual view, but this philosophical proposition is reinforced by the unitive experience itself, in which the difference between subject and object collapses into the perception of a singular unified reality. There are, of course, important differences between the notions of maya and samsara within the traditional teachings of these religions. For example, Indian religious scholar T. R. V. Murti explains that "Madhyamika [Buddhism] is epistemological in its procedure while the Vedanta is ontological. The former is an *advayavada* (no two views), while the latter is an *advaita* (no two things)."[17]

At a superficial level of criticism, many have pointed out that the Hindu doctrine of maya and the Buddhist doctrine of samsara are both clearly part of the world and thus part of the illusion themselves. But the essential paradox, or performative contradiction, that arises from claiming the world is an illusion from within that very world is perhaps illustrative of the paradox such claims are endeavoring to describe.

Going beyond such superficial critiques, professional philosophers of religion have carefully explored the deeper meaning of these Indian doctrines of illusion in an attempt to reconcile such claims with Western philosophical and scientific notions of an empirical reality. For example, Vedanta scholar J. G. Arapura explains that the concept of maya is a dialectical device used in discourse about Brahman, which is said to be otherwise beyond discourse. According to Arapura, "Maya does not mean denial of the world. The ultimate non-being of the world does not have to be stated as a theory, as it is strictly implied in the very definition of Brahman itself. . . . Maya, therefore, is a provisional recovery of the world so that its ultimate non-being, along with Brahman's being, may be spoken of."[18] As this quote suggests, these ancient religious teachings about the illusion of the world have engendered significant debate and scholarly apologetics, but such analysis tends to be highly labyrinthine. The result is that almost anything that can be said about these doctrines of illusion can be contradicted or dismissed as a misinterpretation.

However, as explained above, this critique is not aimed at the doctrines of either Buddhism or Hinduism proper. Here I am pointing out the problems of the larger and looser agreement about nonduality that has emerged as the leading form of spirituality within progressive culture in America. And within this culture, the subtleties of the more scholarly interpretations of these doctrines are rarely taken into account. That is, within progressive spirituality people generally take these nondual teachings of illusion at face value. So at this popular level of understanding at least, these teachings cannot help but contradict and undermine evolutionary spirituality's teaching that perfecting the universe is an important spiritual practice and indeed a moral duty.

However, it is important to acknowledge that progressive nondualists are in fact working to improve the human condition in countless ways, regardless of any teachings to the contrary. Nevertheless, the nondual teaching that the world is a "beautiful illusion" remains largely philosophically incoherent, and this rejection of reason has a cost.

That being said, let me again affirm that certainly aspects of both nondual spirituality and theistic spirituality are commendably transconceptual; teachers from both traditions generally agree that much of ultimate reality is beyond the grasp of the finite human mind. But while the accommodation of the transconceptual is necessary, this should not be seen as a license to embrace a completely nonconceptual view. Every form of spirituality has important work to do in the world and must eventually connect with the world through teachings that employ concepts and reasons. Indeed, even the rejection of all conceptual spiritual teachings is itself a conceptual spiritual teaching.

As we have discussed throughout this book, the developed world needs more effective forms of spiritual leadership. And the provision of such leadership depends on teachings demonstrating that the modern truths of science and the ancient truths of religion are complementary and subject to harmonization. While nondual spiritual teachings do connect with science on a variety of points, their perceived denial of the self and the phenomenal world renders such teachings difficult to accept for the majority of American modernists.

Whether they recognize it or not, modernists are in need of better—truer—kinds of spirituality than those currently on offer in the marketplace of ideas. But at this point in history it is clear that progressive spirituality, even in its mature nondual expression, is not capable of meeting this spiritual need by itself. The project of harmonizing and synthesizing science and spirituality ultimately requires the mediation of philosophy, which itself depends on conceptual reason and the conviction that our experience of the phenomenal world is relatively veridical and reliable.[19] While evolutionary spirituality readily admits that the finite is *less real* than the infinite, it cannot accept teachings that the finite universe is an illusion.

For the limited purposes of this critique of the nondual doctrine of worldly illusion, suffice it to conclude that staunch nondualism is too nonconceptual to adequately harmonize science and spirituality by itself. Despite the mystical appeal of the idea of ultimate oneness, for most scientifically minded modernists at least, strict nonduality doesn't really make sense. Spiritual leadership for the developed world thus requires that progressive nondual spirituality be supplemented—transcended and included—by the larger and more science-friendly perspective of evolutionary spirituality.

The Evolutionary Necessity of Ultimate Reality's Self-Awareness

The idea that the source or ground of reality is somehow conscious or aware is denied or resisted by many forms of progressive spirituality, not to mention by all forms of secular spirituality. This is understandable given that both of these cultures have been tasked by history with the job of transcending the objectionable aspects of traditional Western religion. And at the heart of all the Abrahamic religions is the teaching that the universe is created and upheld by a self-aware being—a God with personal attributes. Although there are many positive and charming features of these traditional characterizations of a personal ultimate reality, such teachings are also freighted with anthropomorphic conceptions of a jealous, judgmental, and even vengeful deity, which are abhorrent to modernist and postmodern sensibilities.

So it is no wonder that most versions of progressive spirituality either rule out or at least tone down and deemphasize notions of a personal God.

Evolutionary spirituality, however, does not share progressive spirituality's need to distance itself from traditional religious spirituality because this has been largely accomplished by modernism and postmodernism. Because evolutionary spirituality is "post-postmodern" it is two dialectical steps removed from the traditional level, so the outworn mythical conceptions of the traditional stage are not as threatening.

Evolutionary spirituality accordingly finds that the important task of moving beyond mythical notions of God as judgmental—as evoked in Michelangelo's painting of a stern and bearded judge in the sky—has been largely accomplished by previous stages of development. In other words, even though the majority of the world still makes meaning at a premodern, traditional stage of cultural development—even though both modernists and postmodernists are still in the process of pushing away from the pathologies of traditionalism—those at the evolutionary level are presented with a different set of opportunities for progress. As a result of having achieved the requisite conceptual distance from the more objectionable aspects of the notion of a conscious Creator, evolutionary spirituality can now take a fresh look at the crucial idea of ultimate reality's self-awareness.

As we have seen, most forms of nonduality conceive of ultimate reality as unqualified and formless. The Buddha generally declined to include ideas of God within his teaching, and most versions of Buddhism either disavow notions of a self-aware Creator or remain agnostic on the matter. In Advaita Vedanta the ultimate concept of Brahman is characterized as being without attributes and strictly impersonal. And while some Advaitans consider ultimate reality to be "transtheistic," positing the existence of a subultimate personal godhead, most forms of progressive nondual spirituality generally eschew all notions of a self-aware ultimate reality.

However, as it transcends progressive spirituality's biases against traditional Western religion, evolutionary spirituality finds that there are at least two features of ultimacy pointing to its self-awareness. As explored below, these apparently personal aspects of ultimate reality are (1) will or intention manifesting as *creative causation*, and (2) the personal connection between Creator and creature manifesting as *love*.

Self-Awareness and Creative Causation

Unlike many forms of nondualism, which conceive of the universe as beginningless, evolutionary spirituality follows mainstream science in recognizing that our finite universe of time had a distinct and dramatic beginning in the big bang. The infinite reality that existed prior to the big bang is indeed beginningless, but the universe of evolution—the universe we live in—definitely had a finite beginning. Further, evolutionary spirituality also recognizes the divine lure of intrinsic value, which draws evolution forward through its influence on consciousness. Our human consciousness and culture continue to evolve because we can always imagine how things can be better. And as discussed in chapters 2 and 4, intrinsic values such as the beautiful, the true, and the good exert a kind of evolutionary gravity on consciousness.

Both of these tenets of evolutionary spirituality—the universe's finite beginning and the human sense of a better way that lies beyond current conditions—point to the apparent fact that ultimate reality has not only created the universe, but it is continuously creating it moment to moment. And acknowledging the initial and ongoing creative power of ultimate reality leads us to the conclusion that ultimate reality is intentionally causal. Stated in philosophical terms, the causal influence of ultimate reality is both the *first cause* of the big bang and the ongoing *final cause*, which gently persuades us to grow toward increasing perfection. It is thus through evolutionary spirituality's recognition of these causes of evolution that ultimate reality is shown to possess will or intention. And for ultimate reality to be willful or intentional in this way, it is necessary for it to have some kind of self-awareness, which makes it personal in at least some sense.

Self-Awareness and Love

The spiritual teachings of evolution also point to ultimate reality's personal, or self-aware, qualities by recognizing the authenticity of the ubiquitous *spiritual experience of the love of God*—the experiential foundation of practically all forms of theistic spirituality.

However, as explained above, love is a relational quality; it cannot really exist where there is "no separation." For the concept of love to have its full meaning there must be at least two entities—that which loves and that which is loved. While that which is loved may be impersonal (as in "I love nature"), the original source of love is inevitably a personal entity with something equivalent to a heart (nature cannot love me). Admittedly, nondualists can be filled with love without any apparent need of the concept of a personal God as the ultimate source of that love. But the necessary denial that ultimate reality possesses qualities of any kind, and especially the quality of the heartfelt affection of a loving creative parent, is philosophically problematic for nondual spirituality.

In the context of Buddhism, the philosophical problems arising from notions of an impersonal or unqualified ultimate reality are well articulated by academic theologian Stuart Hackett, who writes:

> To the transformed bodhisattva, the qualities of love, wisdom, and firm resolve are actualized in his new moral quality of being. . . . [Yet] in his more speculative moments, he sees that somehow, in its absoluteness, the ultimate Reality is beyond all such determinate qualities. . . . But can such an enlightened individual reasonably cling to that awkward and cramping speculative posture? Can the unassailable authenticity of these moral qualities really manifest unless these qualities constitute, in part, the intrinsic and essential nature of the absolute Reality? And can these qualities themselves be understood adequately unless they are viewed as possible only for a Being that is itself a completely actualized personal

being? The bodhisattva has realized his own true personhood through these qualities: can he reasonably continue to regard their ultimate ground as anything less?[20]

While philosophical consistency is not something that nondual spirituality always requires of itself, one of the ways evolutionary spirituality transcends strict nondualism is by reclaiming the value of philosophical consistency. And to be consistent with spiritual reason and experience, evolutionary spirituality recognizes that ultimate reality is not strictly impersonal or completely unqualified. On the contrary, ultimate reality possesses the qualities of awareness, intelligence, intentionality, creativity, and love—qualities that are unmistakably personal.

Every human possesses these qualities; indeed these are the qualities that actually make us real persons. And if we also possess the undivided nondual whole as our true nature or essence—if "thou art that" or "we are it"—then the nondual whole in itself must also possess these personal qualities. Stated differently, if we *are* the whole and we have self-awareness, how could the undivided whole of ultimate reality itself lack such awareness? Viewed in this light, the idea that humans are self-aware but ultimate reality is not self-aware strains credibility as a spiritual teaching.

Beyond philosophical argument, however, it is clear that the teachings of the Buddha are saturated with love, and there is no doubt that Buddhism is a beautiful religion. But no historically received religion—not Buddhism or Hinduism or Christianity—is true enough by itself to provide the spiritual leadership our civilization needs in the twenty-first century. To fulfill such needs, we must draw upon the truths of every major form of spirituality and attempt to synthesize these religious truths with the scientific and historical truths of evolution. But to be effective, such a synthesis must also transcend the limitations of progressive spirituality's polite spiritual pluralism. And as we have discussed, going beyond such relativistic pluralism involves better engaging the evolutionary potentials of the polarity between nonduality and theism.

The Disvalue of Anthropocentrism

On this point about recognizing the evolutionary necessity of ultimate reality's self-awareness, it is important to address concerns that this idea is too anthropocentric. Anthropocentric notions of God, which attribute human qualities to ultimate reality, provide a kind of ideational crutch for many forms of religious spirituality. At the traditional level of cultural evolution, abstract thinking is not always well developed, and thus many need a human-like image of God they can relate to. And, as mentioned above, those attempting to transcend traditionalism's more objectionable aspects find that purging anthropocentric notions of ultimate reality is often the first order of business. As consciousness evolves and we become more conscientious about the limitations of our ego-self, it is only natural that we want to keep our human shadow off God. From a modernist or postmodern perspective, the more human qualities God is thought to possess, the more imperfect God becomes.

However, while evolutionary spirituality rejects mythic notions of a God who has human tendencies, it does not throw out the personal baby with the mythic bathwater, if you will pardon the cliché. Indeed, in our human experience it is the personal aspects of life that are among the most real and spiritually rewarding. For example, when we contemplate death it is usually the idea of parting from loved ones that concerns us most. And these feelings show how loving personal relationships are the most spiritually real aspects of our experience. Yet, as I am arguing, for love to be real at the ultimate level, "somebody has to be home." In other words, as the creative source of everything, ultimate reality is also the source of personhood. And if ultimate reality is understood to be perfect, then it can also be understood to be the perfection of personhood.

That is, God is not only the perfection of being or the perfection of truth; God is also the perfection of personality. And as the perfect source of personality, God is free from all of our anthropic shadows.

Concluding this section on the evolutionary necessity of recognizing the self-awareness of ultimate reality, I will offer the disclaimer that I am not trying to make an argument for God. In the context of our discussion of natural signs of spirit at the end of chapter 3, we saw how all such arguments are easily resistible. These reflections, however, do testify to my firm conviction regarding the reality of God's will and God's love. Indeed, by recognizing spirit's self-awareness through the concept of God, we may come to see that *as we experience spirit, spirit experiences us*. If the foregoing discussion of God's evolutionary necessity is too strong for some readers, perhaps we can at least agree that ultimate reality's self-awareness is highly likely from an evolutionary perspective.

My belief in a Creator with personal qualities is grounded in the direct experience of the love God has for me as an individual person. But although I experience God directly, I have also found that the truth of God's self-awareness is validated indirectly through my experience and creation of beauty, truth, and goodness. As we explored in chapter 4, the evolutionary practice of perfecting the universe through these intrinsic values leads to the conclusion that these comprehensible elements of divinity are, at their heart, messages of love.

Concluding this chapter's critique of nondual spirituality, it is important to acknowledge that at the traditional level of religious spirituality foreign teachings that tend to contradict the closely held convictions of a given tradition have little chance of being accepted or adopted. For instance, Buddhism cannot accept God, and Christianity cannot accept the idea of no-self. But beginning at the level of progressive spirituality we become less bound by traditional constraints. As we have seen, much of contemporary nondualism itself breaks out of strict compliance with tradition in its quest for a synthesis of Buddhism and Hinduism. And now through the emergence of evolutionary spirituality, not only can we amalgamate complementary truths, but we can actually begin to integrate truths that are essentially polar opposites. Accordingly, in the next chapter we explore the potential for a future evolutionary synthesis of nonduality and theism.

Chapter Seven

TOWARD THE FURTHER EVOLUTION
OF SPIRITUALITY

Beginning in chapter 5 we identified and explored the existential polarity of nonduality and theism, which has been discovered through humanity's historical quest to discern and understand the nature of ultimate reality. Our examination showed how this dialectical structure is not just a matter of doctrinal differences; it appears to be a relatively permanent feature of the inner landscape of human spiritual experience itself. Then in the last chapter we considered some of the enduring, or "necessary," elements of spiritual truth that are encountered primarily through theistic spiritual experience and confirmed by the spiritual teachings of evolution. And we also contrasted these truths with some of the enduring yet opposing truths of nonduality currently holding sway within progressive spirituality.

This analysis has set the stage for a consideration of the potential synthesis implied by the existence of this polarity. In other words, our understanding of evolution's dialectical method of development leads us to anticipate an impending new emergence, which is strongly suggested by the presence of the inherent tension energy of this polar structure. So now we are ready to turn toward the work of bringing about a higher-level integration of nondual and theistic truth teachings that can serve as a foundation for evolutionary spirituality in the time ahead. Accordingly, in this chapter we examine what form such a potential synthesis could take in the context of both teaching and practice.

First we revisit the importance of concepts of ultimate reality and why all forms of spirituality inevitably rely on such conceptions. Then we consider previous attempts by both nondualist and theistic authors to fashion a working synthesis of these two fundamental poles. Next we examine the idea that the practice of each of these poles in its fullness ultimately requires reference to its opposing pole, leading to a consideration of the cultural conditions that will be required to foster the emergence of such a transcendent synthesis. The chapter concludes with a brief exploration of the more developed understanding of ultimate reality beginning to appear through the emergence of evolutionary spirituality.

In Search of an Evolutionary Synthesis of Nondual and Theistic Truth

Evolutionary spirituality's synthetic ambitions necessarily focus on the teachings of truth about ultimate reality found at the heart of these contrasting forms of spirituality. As we discussed toward the end of chapter 5, these respective notions of ultimacy transcend mere belief or idle cosmological speculation in the way they are each grounded in direct spiritual experience of either undifferentiated unity or the love of God.

Some nondualists may object to this focus on alternative truth teachings about ultimate reality by contending that such a framing is biased toward theism from its very start. Potential objectors may claim that nondual spirituality is concerned much more with practice than with concepts of ultimate reality. And I agree that it would be a mistake to try to interpret one form of spirituality by using the concepts and symbols of a completely different or competing form. However, as I have argued, despite all claims to the contrary, progressive nondualism clearly employs concepts of ultimate reality in the course of its work in the world. Indeed, nondual spirituality teaches that the realization of unqualified oneness or formless emptiness is the goal of enlightenment and thus the ultimate reason for the practices it recommends.

Even practitioners who evince little interest in conceptual teachings are nevertheless relying on such teachings by participating in the spiritual-agreement structures that serve as the foundation of their practices. Stated differently, every significant form of spirituality uses its understanding of the truth about ultimate reality as the cornerstone of its worldview. And in the same way that one can use the foundations of a building without giving much thought to its structure or function, practitioners of progressive spirituality may be similarly unaware of how every spiritual path inevitably uses a specific set of truth teachings as its indispensible foundation.

In fact, at the center of practically every spiritual teaching is a concept or symbol of what is ultimately real. Ideas and ideals about ultimate reality thus serve as the source, or headwaters, for the watershed of values a given form of spirituality brings to society. Consider these examples: Thinking that ultimate reality is a stern judge may lead to both social order and oppression. Thinking that ultimate reality is merely physical energy and matter may lead to both scientific progress and nihilism. Thinking that ultimate reality is a formless void may lead to both peaceful equanimity and ambivalence toward progress. And approaching ultimate reality through a sophisticated conception that integrates absolute unified oneness with an unconditionally loving Creator may lead to both increasing social solidarity and a hunger for further spiritual evolution.

It is important to reiterate that teachings of spiritual truth and spiritual experience are tied together. So the evolution of spiritual teachings results in the evolution of our ability to experience spirit, which in turn expands our hold on spiritual truth. And, as we are coming to see, teachings of spiritual truth are almost always bound up with concepts of ultimate reality. So even as we discount the spiritual value of mere concepts, we must also recognize that it is through such concepts that the spiritual value of truth itself enters into our minds and thus into our work in the world. Therefore, because concepts of ultimate reality are central to every form of spirituality, the task of further evolving our spirituality inevitably entails the further development of our concepts of ultimacy.

Simply put, the goodness of any form of spirituality (in terms of its service value and leadership potential) goes hand in hand with the quality of its truth teachings regarding the nature of spirit. It is thus my contention that the spiritual leadership our society needs can be found through the realization of the enlarged understanding of ultimate reality that will emerge from a synthesis of nondual and theistic truth teachings.

PREVIOUS MOVES TOWARD SYNTHESIS

We can identify a number of notable spiritual teachers who have previously explored such a potential synthesis. As noted, as early as the twelfth century the Hindu sage Ramanuja taught a qualified version of nondualism, which was essentially panentheistic. Ramanuja, however, effectively rejected Shankara's prior teachings of the absolute undifferentiated oneness of ultimate reality. And although Ramanuja's teachings garnered a large following, his conflicts with the followers of Shankara were never resolved, and he failed to produce an agreeable synthesis that could unite the opposing schools of Hinduism.

More recent attempts to fashion a synthesis of theistic and nondual truth teachings within Hinduism can be seen in the work of Sri Aurobindo, who taught a sophisticated form of nondual panentheism. Yet, like Ramanuja's before him, Aurobindo's teachings were rejected by the Advaitan followers of Shankara, as exemplified by Ramana Maharshi's repudiation of Aurobindo's evolutionary premises.[1]

Similarly, within Buddhism many of Thich Nhat Hanh's teachings can be recognized as partially synthetic in character, as discussed in the last chapter in the context of free will. And his promotion of "Engaged Buddhism" has many affinities with evolutionary spirituality's focus on perfecting the universe. But he too has been criticized from within his own tradition for trying to smuggle non-Buddhist notions of a human soul into Buddhism.[2] Yet regardless of such criticisms, Nhat Hanh's sophisticated spiritual teachings are aligned with the synthetic ambitions of evolutionary spirituality, and he must thus be recognized as an important ally in this project.

Also starting from the nondual side of the polarity but moving toward a more synthetic position is integral philosopher Ken Wilber's recent writing about the "three faces of spirit."[3] Through this teaching, Wilber has tried to better integrate theistic notions of God into his nondual conception of ultimate reality by incorporating the devotional practices of Bhakti yoga. According to Wilber, a truly integral spiritual practice should include the recognition of a "second-person" aspect of spirit that can result in an authentic "I-thou" relation between humans and spiritual reality. Wilber's recent efforts to more fully acknowledge and include theistic conceptions of ultimacy within his work have been welcomed by integral theists, and I too applaud this addition to his position. His teaching about spirit's three faces contributes to evolutionary spirituality's attempts to integrate and synthesize nondual and theistic conceptions of ultimate reality.

From my perspective, however, Wilber's notion of "God in the second person" does not adequately express or connect with the spiritual experience of the personal love of the Creator that is the foundation of the theistic pole. Although his teaching about ultimate reality continues to evolve, he has not modified or corrected his long-held position that "nondual realization is the single ultimate summit of spiritual growth" and that "theistic traditions rank lower than nondual ones."[4] Therefore, because his overall writing reflects a strong preference for nonduality over theism and because his published explorations of "the second face of spirit" have been very minimal, his teaching in this area will need further development before it constitutes an authentic synthesis.

By contrast, another relatively recent example of an attempted synthesis that starts instead from the theistic side and moves toward the nondual can be found in the writings of German theologian Hans Küng. According to Küng, the development of a synthetic "Eastern-Western understanding of God" requires that Western religions respond to the "the challenge of the East" and vice versa.

Küng contends that Eastern religious-truth teachings challenge the West to demonstrate

> More respect in the face of the Ineffable, more reverence before the Mystery, in brief more awe in the presence of that Absolute that Jews, Christians, and Muslims call the one true God. The concept of the "void" could then be adopted in a Christian sense, as an expression of the ineffability of God. . . . His essence cannot even be fully disclosed from the standpoint of *being*: God is nothing of what is. He is no being, he transcends all beings. . . . Human thought here enters a realm where all positive statements (e.g., "God is good") prove inadequate. In order to be true, they must be immediately negated ('God is not good'—in a finite, human way) so as finally to be translated into the infinite: "God is ineffably, immeasurably, infinitely good, absolute goodness."[5]

Regarding the "Western challenge to the East," Küng calls for Hindus and Buddhists to better appreciate how "the Ultimate is not something indifferent to us. . . . The Absolute can be heard and spoken to, . . . it is a mysteriously communicative and responsive *Thou*."[6] As a panentheist, of course I find Küng's attempted synthesis appealing. But although he brings the theistic and nondual poles closer together, his analysis effectively leaves the poles lying side by side in an unintegrated relationship. His attempted synthesis has accordingly failed to satisfy nondualists, as demonstrated by the critique made by Kyoto school philosopher Masao Abe, who dismissed Küng's synthetic argument as "a misunderstanding."[7]

As a final example, evolutionary spiritual teacher Andrew Cohen's 2011 book, *Evolutionary Enlightenment,* presents an essentially synthetic conception of ultimate reality that acknowledges both poles within a nondual frame of reference. For Cohen, the nondual pole represents the

Absolute at rest in a state of pure being, and the theistic pole represents the Absolute in a state of becoming. Yet how the pure being of the Absolute at rest, which he describes as "formless" and as an "empty no-place," can give rise to our universe of becoming, which he characterizes as godlike "energy or intelligence," is not explained.[8]

Unlike the other authors discussed above, Cohen is a friend of mine and we have had several fruitful conversations about the character of ultimate reality. When I brought up the problem of how Absolute being creates our universe of becoming, he responded by pointing to the widespread agreement among religionists regarding the "oneness of God." We agreed that the idea of divine oneness provides an approach to ultimate reality that might lead to further integration between the nondual and theistic poles. But I contended that nondual spirituality needs a more "roomy oneness" that can better account for a panentheistic relationship between Creator and creature. Perhaps needless to say, our conversations have not resolved the tensions, but we continue to discuss the matter whenever we have a chance.

A variety of other spiritual teachers and academic thinkers could also be recognized for their explorations of a synthetic understanding of the theistic and nondual polarity. As examples, process theologian John Cobb, Benedictine monk Bede Griffiths, and religious philosophers Ninian Smart, John Hick, Raimon Panikkar, John Robinson, and Stuart Hackett have all produced noteworthy work in this area. Overall, I think all of these attempts at synthesis are commendable, and I am not sure I can do any better. However, I hope this brief discussion of some of these previous moves toward integration provides a sufficient background for the following exploration of my own approach to a potential synthesis of theistic and nondual spirituality.

Practicing Each Pole with Reference to the Other

If, as I have argued, there really is an authentic, existential, indestructible dialectical polarity not only in the overall body of the world's spiritual teachings but also in the inner landscape of human spiritual experience itself, then this fact presents a golden opportunity. As a result of the freshly emerging insights of evolutionary spirituality it is now becoming possible to bring the impending synthesis of theism and nonduality further into being. Now that we are beginning to see this polarity more clearly than ever before, we can more effectively harness the power of this evolutionary structure to deepen our realization of both poles of spiritual experience through a process that better integrates the wisdom of each pole with its opposite.

The way each pole can true up the other can be understood by reference to Taoism's well-respected yin-yang symbol. As shown in figure 7.1, at the heart or center of the black side is a small circle of white, and vice versa. And to the extent this symbol illustrates a principle of all existential polarities, it can be seen as pointing to the truth that practicing either pole in its fullness ultimately requires use of the other pole.[9] In other words, in their quest to know God and do God's will, theists would do well to reckon with the truths of nonduality—the truths of formless oneness and the truths of emptiness. Likewise, in their journey toward enlightenment, nondualists would do well to let the personal love of God shine into their hearts and feel the everlasting affection of our

Figure 7.1. Yin-yang symbol

universe's Creator. Put simply, getting to the heart of each of these essential forms of spirituality means partially embracing its opposing yet complementary pole.

Prior to the emergence of evolutionary spirituality, it may have been easy to conclude that the best approach to spiritual development was to find a tradition or spiritual path that seemed to resonate best and then practice that path in its fullness. That is, if Buddhism was one's chosen path, then one should go as deeply into this tradition as practicable and embrace its teachings as one's own truth. However, as evolutionary spirituality has emerged, moving further away from traditionalism and revealing an enlarged understanding of spiritual experience and the nature of ultimate reality, spiritual-path exclusivism, even at the postmodern level, becomes less tenable.

This is not to suggest that we should approach spiritual truth cafeteria style. Indeed, such a superficial approach can be seen as a shortcoming of progressive spirituality's relativistic pluralism. Rather, what I am suggesting is that at the evolutionary level of cultural evolution, practicing either theism or nondualism seriously and with rigor—going to the heart of one's chosen path—means acknowledging a place for the white dot within the black wave and vice versa. Stated otherwise, now that we are coming to discover this existential polarity within both spiritual experience and spiritual truth, we can no longer be satisfied with either strict nondualism or strict theism.

While we can certainly remain focused primarily on one of the poles, and while we can continue to have loyalty to our chosen path (as discussed below), insular traditionalism is no longer viable at the evolutionary level. To contend that the most advanced truth teachings of the pole that opposes our path are simply wrong or deluded or lower is to remain at the traditional level. Yet to contend that the two poles are essentially the same or to ignore the contradictions and claim that they are simply a matter of different preferences is to remain at the level of postmodern progressive spirituality. Thus, at the evolutionary level we have to reckon with this indestructible polarity in a way that engages the tension of the poles in the quest for higher levels of spiritual emergence.

However, this practice of working with both poles to further the enactment of each in our experience requires more than simply acknowledging the truth of both. It is not just a matter of seeing the importance of each pole for the other intellectually. The kind of practice now being made possible through evolutionary spirituality involves the *active use of the inherent contradiction energy*—the existential challenge—that each pole poses to the other. What this may look like in the personal life of each practitioner is explored in the subsections that follow.

Nonduality's Apophatic Character

As discussed in chapter 5, the rise of progressive spirituality over the last forty years has resulted in a still-partial yet ongoing merger of Western Buddhism and Advaita Vedanta Hinduism. This means that contemporary nondualism is itself largely a synthesis of these two great Asian traditions. And this shows how one level of synthetic emergence can lead to and make possible a next and even-higher level of synthesis. In other words, we can now use the recent synthesis of Buddhism and Hinduism to move toward the integration of nonduality and theism overall. But to do this we must appreciate how this first-level synthesis of Buddhism and Hinduism follows a primarily *apophatic* path to spiritual truth. Apophatic spiritual teachings approach truth through a negation or denial of what the truth is not. This idea was elegantly expressed by Meister Eckhart, who wrote, "Only the hand that erases can write the true thing."[10]

Nonduality's apophatic theme is found in Advaita Vedanta in its famous dictum *neti neti* (not this, not that), as well as in its exaltation of Brahman "without attributes" as the ultimate reality. This theme of negation can also be clearly recognized in Buddhism's focus on emptiness and its doctrine of no-self. Both of these spiritual traditions, of course, include abundant examples of positive and affirmative teachings, but most teachers of nonduality regularly employ the technique of negation to emphasize emptiness and dispel notions that "being" is an eternal "substance." Indeed, the word *nondual* itself is thoroughly apophatic.

Nonduality's focus on negation is explained by David Loy, who writes that in Buddhism, "Sunyata [emptiness] not only refers to the absence of a self but becomes the most fundamental 'characteristic' of reality. In function it is the category which corresponds most closely to the Vedantic concept of Brahman, serving as the standard by which the reality of phenomena is negated. . . . 'Essentially, there is only one thing . . . *not even one.*'"[11] In his attempt to reconcile Buddhism and Advaita Vedanta within an overarching and unified theology of nonduality, Loy observes that Buddhism's emphasis on no-self and Advaita's emphasis on all-self are two extremes that "in trying to eliminate duality, result in much the same description of nonduality—just as one may travel east or west around the world to arrive in the same place."[12]

Again, contemporary nondual spirituality is not a complete fusion of Western Buddhism and Advaita Vedanta Hinduism; it is only a partial amalgamation of these two paths within a progressive cultural context. But even though much of the distinctive character of these two great traditions is preserved in the current cultural agreement of nondual spirituality, the merger nevertheless shows more clearly than ever before the apophatic character of the nondual pole of spiritual experience. And, as we explore below, recognition of this negating function of nondual teachings is a key to their practice within the context of theism.

Nonduality and Emptiness

To the extent that nonduality is understood in the Advaita Vedanta sense as absolute oneness, it contrasts nicely with theism by holding up a polar opposite to the idea of a distinct and transcendent Creator. In other words, in this context the two poles are presenting opposing notions of an ultimate reality. But when nonduality is understood in the Buddhist sense as emptiness, it does not always refer to an ultimate or absolute reality. According to some teachers, the truth of emptiness empties itself of all totalizing or universalizing notions of ultimacy. And some may conclude that this interpretation of emptiness undermines my arguments for the existential polarity of theism and nonduality from the start, but I do not think this is the case. Indeed, I think the recognition of some kind of ultimate reality (even if it is conceived of more as an *ultimate process* than as an ultimate thing) is an evolutionary necessity for all forms of spirituality at the evolutionary level. The totality exists necessarily.

As we have seen, the spiritual experience of the infinite itself confirms the infinite's ultimacy, so my contention that the theistic and nondual poles are both fundamentally concerned with an authentic ultimate reality is not just theological speculation—spirit's ultimacy is confirmed by its very experience. Further, the idea of spirit's transcendental quality requires the recognition of ultimacy of one sort or another, and it cannot be forgotten that the concept of a transcendent ultimate is a cornerstone of panentheism in all its forms. While some Buddhist teachers of emptiness may feel obliged to deny the existence of an affirmative Absolute to be consistent with the apophatic implications of emptiness, many end up reclaiming spirit's transcendental and ultimate quality through other means. Buddhist teachers have evoked the idea of an ultimate reality through a variety of alternative concepts, including the dharmakaya, nirvana, suchness, and even emptiness itself. Indeed, Buddhism's two truths doctrine clearly includes the concept of ultimacy by recognizing relative and absolute truth.[13] And while these doctrines might be interpreted so as to avoid acknowledging ultimacy, post-traditional nondual spirituality generally has little problem with the idea of an ultimate reality.

Notwithstanding the subtleties of these doctrinal distinctions, the significance of emptiness for nonduality cannot be underestimated. So the important task of discerning how theism's teachings of a transcendent Creator and nonduality's teachings of emptiness can be synthesized, or at least better harmonized, begins with an analysis such as this: Perhaps within human nature there exists what might be called an "original side" and a "whole side." The whole side lacks self-nature; it is co-arising with all other things and beings and is thus an undifferentiated aspect of the one unified reality—it partakes of nondual oneness while remaining impermanent. On this whole side of our nature we are empty of a separate existence—our true being is "interbeing," as Thich Nhat Hanh calls it. Our whole side thus shares the same identity of no-self (or all-self) that is the essence of nonduality.

The original side, by contrast, is the seat of our *individual personality*; it is the locus of our evolving soul and the ground of our free will. Indeed, our personal originality is confirmed by our direct experience of being one of a kind. And this personal originality can also be confirmed by our friends and associates, who know there is no one else exactly like us. Further, as noted, our originality and relative freedom as agents of evolution are evident in our ability to be creative. Recognizing the original side of our nature thus allows us to affirm our authentic status as sons and daughters of a living God—real beings in our own right who can love and be loved as individuals.

There are, of course, many models of the self. And this description of the whole side and the original side of human nature is not intended as a comprehensive theory of the human self/no-self.[14] Yet even as we hold this idea loosely, we may still ask, how can both be true at the same time without rupturing the unity of truth or otherwise defying logic? I think the answer, with respect to our human nature and with respect to ultimate reality overall, is that every existential polarity is itself a shadow of some higher unity that cannot be fully realized at our current level of evolution. And realizing this truth helps us recognize all such dialectical polarities as openings for further development—systems of transcendence and engines of evolution.

These two poles of human nature—whole-side emptiness and original-side fullness—tend to serve as the ground for the respective forms of spirituality with which they are associated. One side emphasizes our lack of self-nature, and the other emphasizes our individual agency and creativity. While most practitioners gravitate toward one pole or the other, some hover above both without committing to either. Still others may be pulled from their native pole toward the opposite pole in the course of their development. But to use the full potential of this existential polarity as a system of development, as I am arguing, our practice must seek synthesis. Yet it is important to reiterate that working toward such a synthesis inevitably entails a back-and-forth operation wherein contradicting affirmations are each held to be true alternatively through a recursive process that dynamically reincludes each by turns. So in this process we cannot expect to find a final stationary position, or a place of ideational rest. Nor can any single snapshot of this moving-back-and-forth process capture it or define its ultimate truth.

Nevertheless, bringing the truths of this existential polarity to bear so as to better understand our essential human nature helps show how relevant these truths can be for our personal spiritual growth. As an example, I will give a brief account of my own attempts to practice emptiness in a theistic context.

Nondualism for Theists

I have come a long way in my relationship to nondual spirituality. When I first encountered it forty years ago, I didn't really understand it. Later, as I became more familiar with it, I rejected it and was even slightly bothered by it. But now I am coming to accept it as "true but partial," which has helped me appreciate how it is essential for a deeper realization of my own panentheistic spiritual path. And recently, through the practice of evolutionary spirituality, I have been working with it in a way that surpasses my previous approach of simply holding it in my mind as an incongruent truth I must nevertheless accept. This "truth practice" involves going beyond tentative philosophical reconciliation by using the truth of nonduality to actually advance my knowledge and experience of God.

In this practice the apophatic nature of nonduality serves as a humbling critique of all my beliefs, reminding me never to be satisfied with the spiritual knowledge I have attained. The deep truths of nonduality help me appreciate how almost all teachings of spiritual truth, no matter how dazzling, are finite constructs that are merely rungs on a ladder, which I will eventually step over in my ascent. Stated differently, nondual spiritual truth helps chasten theistic spiritual truth by relentlessly pointing to the finite content of almost all positive spiritual propositions. Nonduality constantly reminds me that my human ego-self, my mind, and the phenomenal universe are only partially real. This finite realm of time is like a womb wherein I am still unborn—my spiritual reality is far from complete. My experience of this finite life is thus like a shell in which the "chick" of my soul is developing. But once the chick is hatched, the shell will be of little use.

By teaching me to hold my spiritual convictions lightly and not take myself too seriously, nondual truth helps "rinse the glass" of my mind, washing away any constructs and concepts that have lost their dynamism or vitality. These attempts to include the truths of nonduality in my understanding of what is spiritually real have helped me to continually start fresh with God, approaching our Creator with a "beginner's mind" free of expectations or preconceptions.

Even at the evolutionary level, theistic spirituality is in constant need of restraint to prevent the house of conceptual cards it often builds from distracting our attention from the unmediated experience of the infinite. This restraining is at least one way the integration of nonduality's apophatic teachings can help all those who seek to know God by continuously reminding us to remain circumspect in the face of the aspects of ultimate reality that will always remain an unknowable mystery to humans.

Conversely, not only does the truth of nonduality chasten and restrain my understanding of God, but it also expands and enriches my conception of our Creator's personal qualities. How the nondual pole helps to enact and vivify the theistic pole can be seen in nondual depictions of ultimate reality as essentially formless or empty. By fully expressing the completely formless character of the nondual pole, the teaching of emptiness serves to illuminate the full expression of the opposing theistic pole. In other words, when the nondual pole is understood in its extreme sense as the void, or as Absolute Nothingness (as Nishida called it), the thoroughgoing absence behind this conception simultaneously provides a kind of inverse teaching that reveals God as an unconditionally loving parent, which (as discussed below) represents the contrasting expression of the theistic pole in its fullness. Simply put, the extremity of each pole helps enact the fullness of its opposing pole by symmetrical comparison.

By contrast, some teachers, perhaps sensing the partiality of either pole by itself, have moved toward the middle in their conception of ultimate reality in an effort to avoid either Absolute Nothingness on one side or a personal God on the other. This can be seen for example in nondual depictions of sunyata as interbeing, or in nominally theistic depictions of God as an impersonal creative force or as merely a "self-organizing tendency." While these attempts to partially depolarize ultimate reality are not all wrong, they do tend to mute the expression of each pole in its abundance. However, when I allow myself to embrace the depths of the nondual teaching that ultimate reality is void-like and thus feel the sinking sense of cosmic vertigo this produces, then I am better able to feel the contrasting fullness of God's everlasting love for me as an individual, which is nonduality's complementary antipode.

Beyond this subjective level of truth practice, integrating nonduality into my theistic path has also borne fruit at the intersubjective, or cultural, level. Reckoning with the teachings of nonduality has led to a deeper affinity with my friends and associates who are nondualists. By working with the theistic and nondual polarity—by attempting to discern the black dot in the white wave—I have become more curious about and less resistant to teachings that seem to negate my most closely held convictions. Again, this is not relativism; I am not giving up on God or concluding that God is essentially nondual. But I am finding a deeper level of sympathy for my fellow religionists—even for those who think my convictions are deluded.

The Love of God for Nondualists

Although I do not identify myself as a Christian, in my experience the high-water mark of theism remains the life and teachings of Jesus of Nazareth. Jesus's teaching even transcends Christianity in the way it speaks of eternal truths that are relevant for every spiritual practitioner. And at the heart of Jesus's message was the revelation of our Creator's unconditional parental affection for each creature. Jesus taught that God's "fatherly" love for each of us enacts a universal family—the "brotherhood of man"—that naturally follows from the fact that we each share the same universal Father/Mother. This is what makes his teachings so deeply moral. Ultimate reality's parental love creates both the reason and the duty to love one another, to "love our neighbor as our self." However, the teaching that the source of the universe cares about us as persons—that God knows us and loves us as individuals—discloses an aspect of ultimate reality that is undeveloped in nondualism. And this is the *goodness* of the Absolute—not just its excellence or even perfection, but its *caring morality*, which is really the highest kind of goodness. As I argued in the last chapter, nondualists may point to compassion as a cornerstone of their creed, but this essentially *personal quality* of compassion cannot find its source in an ultimate reality that is understood either as lacking personal qualities or as being completely *unqualified*.

For nondualists, acknowledging that, somehow, the universe is loving does not mean becoming Christian or even theistic. Although like Buddhism and Hinduism, Christianity is a beautiful religion for the most part, one need not accept its teachings as a whole to benefit from the practice of feeling God's love. Even though I am not a Christian, I have been greatly inspired by Jesus, so I know from my own experience that one can receive the spiritual benefits of Jesus's message without assenting to the doctrines of Christianity.

Nevertheless, for those committed to a nondual path, the practice of experiencing the love that comes from the creative Source of the universe involves allowing for the truth that there is more to ultimate reality than a formless void or an impersonal oneness. Admittedly, coming to terms with the goodness, morality, and loving-kindness of ultimate reality may require reflection and contemplation on the part of nondualists, and reconciling this perfect love with the imperfection, suffering, and evil that remains in the finite universe is inevitably part of this task. But at the evolutionary level, the dialectical practice of integrating opposing forms of spiritual truth becomes desirable, achievable, and inevitable.

Regarding the existence of suffering and evil in a "universe that cares," there have been numerous philosophical attempts to reconcile this seeming contradiction, with my favorite being that the potential for evil is the shadow of free will. But I think the best response to this concern is more spiritual than philosophical. And this spiritual response is found in the faith conviction that *all things ultimately work together for good.* This proposition of faith, however, can be completely true only if there is an afterlife in which innocent suffering can be redeemed. Indeed, from this perspective our earthly suffering might be seen as the inventory of our comparative joy in the future. Perhaps the greatest affliction a person could suffer would be to go through life without ever having been afflicted. Yet this is not meant to imply that evil or suffering should be tolerated; the ongoing presence of these horrors creates an urgent obligation to work for a better world. Nevertheless, faith in ultimate reality's essential goodness helps keep the pathologies of our world in perspective.

On the subjective level, the practice of receiving the love of God also involves loving our Creator in return. This practice may include acknowledging God's presence, being thankful, or even worshiping God in a post-traditional manner. In the same way that "spirit experiences us as we experience spirit," the more we love God the more we establish the channels of faith through which we can increasingly experience God's love for us. As Blaise Pascal wrote, "Human things must be known to be loved, but Divine things must be loved to be known."[15]

Further, on the intersubjective, or cultural, level, the practice of experiencing the love of God in a nondual context may also result in greater sympathy for the theistic foundations of Western civilization. And this sympathy may in turn help lessen some of the antimodernist and antitraditional sentiments that tie many progressive spiritual practitioners to the postmodern level of cultural evolution.

However, given my limited experience with nonduality, it is undoubtedly best that the further explication of this practice of experiencing the love of God in the context of a nondual spiritual path be left to those already committed to nondualism. I thus invite my nondualist sisters and brothers to give this a try and then share their experience with the rest of us. One need not accept any specific theological beliefs to experience this love. But actively denying our Creator's existence may tend to fog the glass through which such love shines.

The Enduring Value of Loyalty

Even so, it is important to add that the evolutionary practice of attempting to integrate these opposing poles of spiritual experience does not require us to become uprooted from either the culture or the teachings of the spirituality we identify with most closely. In the process of attempting to synthesize the poles, we must avoid the mistake of simply substituting one pole for the other.

An example of this can be seen on the theistic side where a number of progressive Christian teachers have recently become strong advocates of nondual spirituality, partially forsaking the core teachings of their own tradition in the process. Many of these nondual Christians contend that "Jesus was a nondual teacher." While we can certainly identify a few Christian mystics who were in fact nondual teachers, such as Meister Eckhart, Jesus's emphasis on the love of God and the growth of the soul clearly contradicts many nondual doctrines. In the Bible Jesus does occasionally refer to truths that can be interpreted as nondual. And his teachings as I understand them instruct us to follow the truth wherever it may lead, even into the truths of nonduality. But when nondual Christian teachers ignore the contradictions and the dialectical tension by claiming that one pole is simply the other, they misunderstand both theism and nonduality.

This observation begins to illustrate the point, discussed further in the next section, that we cannot effectively synthesize or integrate these existential poles by simply abandoning one of them. "Suicide is no way of cementing a relationship." Therefore, on the one hand, we must avoid overidentifying with a given form of spirituality to the exclusion of all others because this inevitably limits our growth and results in unnecessary conflict. But, on the other hand, a certain amount of loyalty and identity must be invested in our chosen spiritual path if we are to receive its full benefits. That is, if we expect our spirituality to benefit us, we have to be willing to benefit it by advancing its teachings and practices in a way that contributes to our larger pluralistic spiritual culture.

With the rise of evolutionary spirituality, however, we can now begin to have it both ways. We can continue to identify ourselves (albeit somewhat loosely) as Buddhists or Christians or as followers of almost any kind of spirituality, while at the same time avoiding both absolutism and relativism in our quest for ever-deeper experiences of spirit.

Gardening for Synthetic Emergence

The spiritual teachings of evolution make clear that historically significant events of evolutionary emergence cannot be engineered or otherwise produced formulaically by human efforts alone. The work of promoting emergence is better compared to gardening than to building. According to this understanding of emergence, the best way to nurture the rise of a more evolved form of spirituality is to work to create conditions that will foster the emergence of an authentic synthesis and then trust that a new form of life will sprout up. Based on what we have discussed, I believe these prerequisite conditions for synthetic emergence include the following five elements of cultural understanding or agreement:

1. a sophisticated and respectful appreciation of the nondual pole of spiritual experience and the forms of spirituality that hold nonduality to be the ultimate reality;

2. a renewed appreciation of the panentheistic forms of spirituality that have brought forward a vision of a loving Creator that overcomes the limitations of traditional theistic religion;

3. a clearer collective recognition of the dialectical polarity between the nondual and theistic poles and how these essential modes of spiritual experience simultaneously conflict with and also complement each other;

4. a willingness to use the evolutionary method of dialectical epistemology to perform the ongoing back-and-forth work of debate and reconciliation—the inevitable wrestling with tensions and contradictions through which a deeper understanding may appear;

5. a resolute intention to integrate nonduality's insights regarding the apophatic nature of the Absolute, theism's contrasting insights regarding the personal nature of the Absolute, science's stupendous discoveries of the empirical facts of evolution, and the confirming evidence of direct spiritual experience itself.

Although progressive spiritual culture may still be far from realizing these elements of cultural understanding, the work of developing these agreements involves teaching and practicing the exciting new truths of evolutionary spirituality. And this work can be done on many fronts and in many contexts.

Of course, the natural tendency is to approach this gardening for synthesis at a superficial level by declaring that it is just a matter of both/and thinking. We may be tempted to conclude that theism and nonduality are simply different sides of the same coin and that the contradictions they seem to present stem from the limits of finite human comprehension—that they are both true despite the disagreements and that's that. But according to the method of dialectical epistemology, such a conclusion would amount to a "compromise fallacy," as explained in chapter 2. In other words, ignoring the conflicts or settling for the acceptance of paradox as a final answer would only provide a kind of false rest.

Rather than trying to make a polite pluralistic peace between these contrasting poles, the practice of evolutionary spirituality involves seeing how the dialectical currents of history are now bringing back the truth of our loving Creator—but bringing it back at a higher level that transcends the relatively immature and mythic conceptions of God found in traditional forms of spirituality.

Those privileged to participate in the birth of evolutionary spirituality can see that we live in a time of movement not equipoise. Emergence is on the march, and we do well not to try to quash this dynamic movement of history by clinging to progressive spirituality's habit of superficially declaring both/and in the face of most conflicts. Therefore, as described in the last chapter, working toward such a higher synthesis involves a partial negation of the negation that reaffirms the evolutionary necessities now being rediscovered by evolutionary spirituality, despite the challenges such necessities imply.

However, nondualists need not feel threatened by such a renewed affirmation of the theistic pole. Nondualists who have an evolutionary perspective understand how existential polarities mutually enact one another, even if by dialectical turns. So they can be assured that the reaffirmation of the theistic pole in the context of the emergence of evolutionary spirituality will eventually lead to an even deeper realization of the nondual pole of spiritual experience.

Further, as affirmed by the first element of cultural understanding listed above, evolutionary spirituality validates and confirms that nonduality is an authentic and important mode of spiritual experience. Therefore, the full potential of evolutionary spirituality can be realized only through an approach that includes practices leading to nondual experience—practices that produce "a change in the very texture of life itself."[16]

It thus bears repeating that the flowering of nondual spirituality within postmodern American culture is an important historical development, without which the emergence of evolutionary spirituality would not be possible. And the fulfillment of evolutionary spirituality's promise of more inclusive spiritual leadership for our society requires that the continuously developing gifts of nondual spirituality be honored and included within evolutionary spirituality's emerging cultural agreement.

GLIMMERS OF INTEGRATION

As I have argued, the experiential polarity I am labeling "nonduality and theism" is an indelible feature of the fabric of our finite reality that will never be completely resolved or rendered into a static thesis or a tidy belief system. Although both nondual and theistic spirituality will inevitably be transfigured in the course of future history, the existential polarity from which their differences arise is a permanent feature of human spiritual experience.

Progress, however, is still possible. Humanity's understanding of what is ultimately real has clearly evolved over the course of our history. And this evolutionary progress has been possible because humans can make authentic contact with ultimate reality. As first discussed in chapter 3, because that which is ultimate is both the center and circumference of reality, and because it lives within us as the foundational essence of who we really are, we can experience it directly. Our deepest experiences of spirit thus provide limited yet nevertheless veridical testimony to the nature of the Absolute. However, while most spiritual paths claim to provide authentic access to ultimate reality, their descriptions of the nature of the Absolute vary widely. So is this simply a matter of the proverbial blind men feeling different parts of the elephant? Of course. But now, through the insights of evolutionary spirituality we are beginning to get a clearer picture of the elephant as a whole.

We can now glimpse the Absolute with new clarity because (1) it is only recently that we have gained access to the wisdom teachings of the ages within a global context; (2) it is only recently that we have come to understand spiritual experience in the context of integral philosophy; and (3) it is only recently that we have had access to the dialectical epistemology made available by the evolutionary perspective. The use of this dialectical way of knowing can now help us grow beyond the unintegrated and unchallenged plethora of spiritual teachings that constitute progressive spirituality's "anything goes" pluralism. In other words, evolutionary spirituality reveals a clearer picture of ultimate reality because it can better evaluate diverse spiritual teachings and can thus perceive such teachings more accurately and integrate them more effectively.

Yet, at the same time, most of the challenges to achieving a higher level of integration remain. As examples, is it possible to hold the teachings of no-self and emptiness as ultimately true in the face of our experience of free will and creative progress? Is it possible to work toward the evolutionary perfection of self, culture, and nature in the context of the teaching that desire is the cause of suffering? Is it possible to maintain the conviction of undifferentiated oneness in the light of a transcendent and loving Creator? Even though our emerging understanding of the dialectical nature of humanity's experience of ultimate reality helps us transcend progressive spirituality, cognitive dissonance remains. But, at the very least, coming to know the substance of these differences is part of the spiritual education required for practitioners of evolutionary spirituality.

However, even as we acknowledge the persistence of these challenges, by deepening the practice of each pole by engaging its opposite as described above, we might be able to dimly discern the future state of development of this synthesis.

SPECULATING ON A FUTURE SYNTHESIS

Although the spiritual experiences imparted by nondualism and theism both provide partial access to ultimate reality, my intuition tells me that this reality is more than a polarity. While it may manifest as a polarity in the finite realm of time, it must be more than this. Yet as we have seen, to conceive of it as simply oneness is to effectively side with one of the poles (confusing oneness with wholeness). But conceiving of it alternatively as simply twoness is not satisfactory either. So rather than falling back on earlier arguments from both sides that contend one pole is ultimate and the other penultimate, or rather than settling for a conception of a polar ultimate reality, we might entertain the notion that the Absolute is not merely dipolar, but is actually *tripolar*. In contrast to the familiar yin-yang polarity shown in figure 7.1, this triune relationship is suggested by figure 7.2, the "diagram of the supreme ultimate" of Lai Zhide, who introduced the original yin-yang symbol into Chinese philosophy in the sixteenth century.[17]

Figure 7.2 shows how two opposing poles can enact a third central element through their integration. This symbol thus depicts a unified trinity of three interactive elements. Although speculative, this analysis suggests that perhaps ultimate reality has a triune structure or essence consisting of a loving Creator, an unqualified Absolute, and a third binding element that is at once both and neither. Although this idea is largely

217

Figure 7.2. The *taijitu* of Lai Zhide, "diagram of the supreme ultimate"

beyond experience and is merely a conceptual theological conjecture, it is bolstered by both reason and faith.

This evolutionary theological hypothesis that ultimate reality is a *tri-unity*—"the three, that are two, that are one"—could at least help us avoid the inelegant notion of plural ultimates. While the idea of a trinity may sound too Christian for some, we can observe that triadic concepts of deity can be found in many ancient religions from both the East and West. And we should also not ignore the fact that the beautiful, the true, and the good form a unified triadic system in themselves, which certainly suggests their connection to some kind of triune source within the nature of the ultimate. In fact, even the dialectical process of evolution itself demonstrates a kind of threeness in the way it overcomes polarity in its ongoing advance into the new.

While the synthetic cultural progress promised by evolutionary spirituality will certainly require more than mere theological speculation about the trinity of divinity, it seems to me that further contemplation of the nature of ultimate reality will be a necessary part of this historical process. And as we come to increasingly understand that in the human experience of spirit we are literally encountering the presence of the

Figure 7.3. Fractal yin-yang

infinite in the finite, we may begin to reinterpret and even play with traditional symbols, as shown in the fractal depiction of the yin-yang symbol illustrated by figure 7.3.

This synthetic process of emergence will of course take time, like all forms of evolution. Indeed, it is only just now that we are beginning to see the polarity of nondual and theistic spiritual experience with the requisite clarity needed to recognize this polarity's potential to give rise to a higher synthesis. So here at the inception of this emergence we cannot expect a mature expression of the synthesis that we are only beginning to sense may actually be possible.

Further, and notwithstanding the above, I trust it is clear that I am not capable of framing an evolutionary synthesis of nonduality and theism by myself. Faced with the awesome spiritual truth of these polar veils of ultimate reality, I am like a candle trying to illuminate the sun. Moreover, my loyalties to a panentheistic vision of a loving Creator, together with my limited experience of the nondual pole, render me unable to frame a satisfactory or otherwise workable synthesis. So the best I can do is suggest the prerequisites for emergence as set out above and then join with other evolutionaries in the work of helping to bring about these cultural conditions. The achievement of an authentic evolutionary synthesis of nonduality and theism will require many religionists and spiritual practitioners working on it over decades, so that the glacial polish that occurs as ideas move through history can take place.

By way of conclusion, I can affirm that in its essence, the evolutionary impulse is the desire for the transcendent itself. As we have seen, it is a kind of perfection hunger whose satisfaction seeks an ultimate reality. Satisfying this hunger involves cultivating a life of spiritual experience—a life of beauty, truth, and goodness—which inevitably involves the ongoing work of creating perfection within our midst. So, following this insight, in the next and final chapter we will further explore some of the methods and strategies that evolutionaries can use to make our world more beautiful, true, and good.

Chapter Eight

TOWARD A METHOD FOR
EVOLVING CONSCIOUSNESS

Evolutionary spirituality is now emerging as part of the larger but still relatively obscure evolutionary worldview. Yet even though the evolutionary worldview itself is only in its infancy, it is evolutionary spirituality's connection to this larger and potentially historically significant new worldview that gives evolutionary spirituality much of its potential to bring about a spiritual renaissance in America and beyond. However, while the evolutionary worldview gives evolutionary spirituality the *power* of an enlarged frame of reality, evolutionary spirituality can in turn give the evolutionary worldview a *method* for accomplishing its goals. This method can be found through the insight that the evolution of human consciousness and culture is fostered most effectively through the experience and creation of spiritual realities.

As mentioned in the introduction, history reveals that when the quantity and quality of spiritual experience are increased in a given social context, evolution usually results. Simply put, spiritual experience evolves consciousness. And as we have explored throughout this book, evolutionary spirituality expands our understanding of what spiritual experience is and how it works. Therefore, by combining evolutionary spirituality's fresh insights about the spiritual experience of beauty, truth, and goodness with the observation that such experiences actually cause consciousness to evolve, we may well be able to discover a new approach to solving some of our most pressing social problems. In this final chapter, we will explore how this new approach or method involves raising consciousness by increasing the scope of what people are able to value.

The quest for this promising new method for evolving consciousness is only just beginning. It may be decades before the evolutionary worldview is able to fully describe or effectively employ such a method in a way that achieves measurable results. Nevertheless, this chapter begins the search for such a method by examining both the need and the opportunity that are creating the current conditions for its potential emergence.

So far I have argued for my interpretation of evolutionary spirituality with relative confidence, but now I have to take a more circumspect approach. At this point much remains unclear about exactly what such a method would entail and how it would work, so the best I can do is speculate about its operational details. Yet even though this discussion falls short of a full-blown manifesto of the method for a second Enlightenment, it does explore the underlying premises and illustrative examples that make the future emergence of such a method seem possible.

The Emergence of a New Stage of Culture— From Antithesis to Synthesis

The idea of a new worldview or new paradigm has become somewhat hackneyed within progressive discourse. Some readers may therefore have a sense of new paradigm fatigue, which is understandable given that proponents of the progressive postmodern worldview have been proclaiming its emergent virtues for close to fifty years now. As discussed in the introduction, the postmodern worldview *is* an authentic "new" paradigm—its inclusive, sensitive, and environmentally conscious values represent an authentic advance over the more individualistic values of the modernist worldview. Yet, while postmodernism is more evolved than modernism in many important respects, it is not evolved enough to serve as a model for the future of our civilization. While postmodern culture has attracted many people in the developed world who are dissatisfied with modernism, postmodernism has not been able to recruit a politically significant number of modernists to its ranks, as evidenced by its ongoing countercultural status.

The main reason why the growth of the postmodern worldview remains seemingly stalled at approximately 20 percent of the US population is that contemporary postmodernism rejects much of what modernism and traditionalism have achieved. The postmodern worldview thus stands in antithesis to the globalizing culture of modernism. While this rejection of mainstream culture may be evolutionarily appropriate—while postmodernism's dialectical move toward antithesis may have been the way forward at the time of its original emergence in the sixties and seventies—the gravity of its values by themselves is not strong enough to pull the rest of the developed world into a more sustainable and compassionate form of civilization.

Nevertheless, the increasingly urgent problems we face in the twenty-first century call for further cultural evolution. And these problematic conditions are creating the evolutionary pressure that is providing the energy for further emergence. In other words, postmodernism's cultural maturation and consolidation into a clear position of antithesis with respect to the thesis of our larger society now presages the emergence of a synthesis. This synthesis, of course, is represented by the evolutionary worldview, which holds the promise of a future form of culture that will be attractive enough to entice politically significant numbers of people in the developed world to adopt the more evolved perspectives we need to meet the challenges of our age.

The evolutionary worldview is a post-postmodern frame of reality that effectively transcends previous worldviews by better appreciating and integrating the values of every previous historically significant worldview—including pretraditional, traditional, modernist, and postmodern worldviews. Although this new worldview honors and includes the values of previous worldviews, it avoids value relativism by recognizing a vertical dimension of cultural development through which the more evolved and the less evolved can be clearly distinguished. This ability to see "which way is up" provides a kind of depth perception that makes cultural evolution easier to recognize and understand.

The evolutionary worldview, however, is able to make firm value judgments without falling into the ethnocentrism and chauvinism that characterized the cultural assessments of previous generations because it sees how the positive values of each worldview are working within the larger structure of cultural evolution overall. Through the guidance provided by the spiritual teachings of evolution, this emerging worldview is able to recognize a natural scale of human development that provides a new kind of moral compass. In short, the evolutionary worldview illuminates the directions of evolution in consciousness and culture through its enlarged understanding of goodness, truth, and beauty.

A comprehensive description of the emerging evolutionary worldview is beyond the scope of this chapter, but I can refer readers to my two previous books, *Integral Consciousness* and *Evolution's Purpose*, which are both largely devoted to the explication of this worldview.[1]

Nevertheless, the proposition that a post-postmodern worldview is emerging in our time serves as the basis for my hope that we can discover a new method for evolving consciousness. If the evolutionary perspective ends up fulfilling its potential of becoming a historically significant new stage of culture, then the history of the emergence of previous stages will prove instructive about what we can expect. And among the historically significant stages of culture recognized by integral philosophy, the rise of the modernist worldview during the Enlightenment is the most relevant in our search for an evolutionary method.[2] Although the Enlightenment was brought about by a host of influences, the rise of science was undoubtedly paramount. Indeed, modern science itself arose as a result of a new method of investigating the natural world that involved the careful measurement of empirical evidence using specific principles of reasoning. While less developed forms of the scientific method were employed by the ancient

Greeks and Muslims prior to the Enlightenment, this empirical approach reached its full potential in the context of early European modernism, leading to the Industrial Revolution and eventually to our increasingly globalized civilization.

The scientific method was not modernism's only foundational method; the advent of the free enterprise system was also essential to the success of the modernist worldview. But this does not diminish the central significance of the scientific method in the global ascent of modernism. And it is also worth noting in this context that the traditional worldview originally emerged thousands of years ago through the advent of a similarly ground-breaking new method that served as a foundation for its ascension. This new method was *writing*, which helped consolidate civilization beyond previous tribal boundaries through written law, history, and scripture.

This analysis suggests that if the emergence of the evolutionary worldview is to achieve a kind of second Enlightenment, it will need something akin to the scientific method—a new approach and technique that gives it the power to see more deeply into reality and to use these insights to benefit humanity. Indeed, the most significant accomplishment of modernism's scientific method can be seen in its application in medicine. The advent of scientific medicine has improved the quality of human life more than, perhaps, any other single factor in history.

ALMOST EVERY HUMAN PROBLEM IS A PROBLEM OF CONSCIOUSNESS

Practically all human problems (except natural disasters) can be understood, at least partially, as problems of consciousness. For example, among the myriad problems faced by humanity in the twenty-first century, the challenges of a changing climate are likely to be among the most significant. Our warming globe is an emergent condition of modernism, so the key to ameliorating carbon pollution involves persuading modernists to vote and consume in ways that take the costs of carbon into account. Yet, as of the time of this writing there is insufficient political will to tackle this problem effectively. Despite the merits of proposed policy solutions (such as a carbon tax) and potential engineering solutions (such as increased renewables and carbon sequestering), America has yet to respond to the problem in ways that can lead to a permanent solution. This lack of political will is primarily the result of deep levels of disagreement among the major segments of American society. The disagreements are not really about the right policy solutions; they are more about the foundational values by which these different groups frame reality and define their identity, as evidenced by America's ongoing culture war. Hence, if the consciousness of America's voters could be raised at the level of values, the conflicts preventing meaningful action on climate change could be reduced.

As another example, consider the problem of poverty. Like climate change, poverty is a complex problem caused by a variety of factors. But within the developed world where opportunities for upward economic mobility exist, poverty can usually be reduced through education. Education raises consciousness, and this provides a straightforward illustration of how the problem of poverty in America is, for the most part, a problem of consciousness.

In the developing world, however, education alone cannot solve the problem of poverty because even those who have become educated cannot get ahead due to the lack of decent jobs. Poverty in the developing world is still a problem of consciousness, but the solution requires more than just raising the consciousness of the impoverished through education. In this case the solution requires the evolution of the overall culture from the premodern level to the modernist level of economic development, which will help create middle-class jobs. And cultural evolution of this kind is in fact happening in places like China, India, and Brazil. Yet, despite ongoing progress, the transition from traditional culture into modernist culture (and beyond) throughout the developing world could be accomplished more quickly and less painfully if we were as effective at raising consciousness as we are at curing disease. While the scientific method has led to tremendous strides in medicine, we now need a similarly powerful method that can help us make strides in the development of culture and consciousness. And this need for more effective methods of fostering cultural evolution is particularly urgent in the case of the challenges faced by the Islamic world.

However, although the worldwide development of modernist culture is gradually reducing the problem of poverty, it is only exacerbating the problem of climate change. And this illustrates how the existential problems of each stage of cultural evolution call for evolution into the next emergent stage for their solution. Just as the impoverished conditions of premodern culture call for evolution toward modernist consciousness, the polluted conditions of modernist culture in turn call for evolution toward postmodern consciousness, where the political will to combat the problem can be found.

This idea that solving existential challenges requires new levels of consciousness is well expressed in a popular idea from Albert Einstein: "Problems cannot be solved at the same level of thinking that created them."[3] This insight stresses the need for a new methodology that can ameliorate humanity's most pressing problems by actually evolving consciousness and culture to "higher levels of awareness."

Underlying Premises for an Evolutionary Method

As I lamented at the beginning of this chapter, while I can sense that the development of a powerful new approach to cultivating cultural emergence is possible, and indeed necessary, I have yet to find a step-by-step procedure that can be appropriately compared to the scientific method. And it may turn out that the search for a methodological approach to evolving consciousness and culture is misguided. But even if no reliable technique can ultimately be found, advancing our civilization through the cultivation of evolution is certainly a subject worth exploring.

Based on what we have considered so far, I can begin to sketch the premises that point to the possibility of a method. These premises do not constitute a recipe for raising consciousness in themselves, but I believe their articulation can bring us one step closer to the discovery and refinement of a methodological "social medicine" that has the power to solve problems by evolving consciousness. Stated below are eight premises that can serve as the foundation of this promising new evolutionary method. These premises are discussed and elucidated in the following subsection. Once we have gained a basic grasp of these premises, we will be ready to consider some examples that indicate how such a potential method might operate.

1. Human consciousness can evolve independently from biological evolution.

2. Human consciousness and culture coevolve as people try to solve problems and improve conditions.

3. Evolutionary emergence in consciousness and culture occurs when people adopt more inclusive frames of value and improve their definition of improvement itself.

4. More evolved frames of value—higher-level worldviews—attract evolutionary emergence by illuminating the intrinsic values that help solve the existential problems that cannot be solved at the level that created them.

5. The power of intrinsic values to raise consciousness is found in the spiritual energy of goodness, truth, and beauty—the spiritual experience of these values evolves consciousness.

6. Works of culture having the most potential to attract evolutionary emergence—works providing the spiritual experience of intrinsic value—are those produced with the primary intention of sharing their creators' own spiritual experience.

7. Spiritually fragrant works with the most potential to evolve the consciousness of their audience are those that also help self-actualize the creator of the work and are thus undertaken partially for their own sake as ends in themselves.

8. The project of evolving consciousness through services of goodness, teachings of truth, and creations of beauty is facilitated and empowered through the use of evolution's own method of development—the ongoing dialectical synthesis of existential polarities.

Discussion of the Eight Premises

Premise 1: Human consciousness can evolve independently from biological evolution. The fact that a person's consciousness can evolve in ways that do not depend on the corresponding evolution of the biological brain provides the starting point for the evolutionary method. While the evolution of consciousness inevitably results in physical changes in the brain, such neurological "rewiring" is more like the strengthening of a muscle than physiological evolution per se. This can be seen in the fact that human anatomy has remained relatively unchanged over the last fifty thousand years, even while human consciousness has evolved in dramatic ways over this same time period. While the consciousness of animals generally evolves in lockstep with the evolution of their bodies, human consciousness is able to transcend biological determinism through its ability to undergo authentic evolution within the lifetime of a single individual. With the emergence of humanity comes a new kind of freedom to continuously envision new and better ways of living. And it is this freedom to imagine a more perfect state of affairs that results in the ongoing improvement of the human condition.

Again, the development of human consciousness and culture is not just analogous to evolution; it is real evolution because it builds on and extends the structure of emergence that can be traced all the way back to the big bang. It is thus in the phenomenon of emergence that we find the most authentic instances of evolution in the consciousness of individuals. But to understand the evolution of consciousness in terms of emergence, we need to distinguish between the normal growth in awareness that comes from the accumulation of knowledge and experience over one's lifetime and the less frequent but more profound events of emergence that constitute evolution proper. While it may be difficult to draw hard lines between the different ways our minds can grow, as I argue in *Evolution's Purpose* human consciousness undergoes authentic evolution most clearly when it develops in ways that roughly recapitulate the larger cultural emergences that have marked the course of humanity's historical evolution. Even though individual development and cultural evolution are not identical, the developing mind does reveal patterns in its unfolding, and those patterns resonate with the historical unfolding of culture that occurs on an evolutionary time scale.[4]

For example, if through religious conversion individuals raised in a tribal setting exchange a pretraditional worldview for a traditional worldview, they are reenacting a form of evolutionary emergence that first occurred several thousand years ago. Continuing the example, if as a result of higher education, individuals raised in a conservative religious culture exchange their traditional worldview for a modernist worldview, this too is a form of emergence that represents the authentic evolution of consciousness. However, evolving one's consciousness by participating in a larger form of cultural emergence need not be limited to reenacting the already-existing advances of history. As we are coming to see, a significant new form of culture is appearing in our own time—one that provides a real opportunity for further evolutionary emergence.

Premise 2: Human consciousness and culture coevolve as people try to solve problems and improve conditions. Human consciousness does not evolve by itself; it coevolves with the culture in which it lives. Through the network effect of cultural transmission, when one person has a conceptual breakthrough or new realization, this advance can be shared with others.

And as new discoveries or new skills are adopted within a larger social context, such advances become refined and reinforced and eventually result in the elevation of the average level of overall consciousness in a given culture. Yet the coevolution of human consciousness and culture proceeds by more than the simple accumulation of greater knowledge or more learned skills; the development of civilization also depends on the evolution of values. Over the course of recorded history, *human nature itself* has evolved through the series of values-based worldview stages we have been discussing throughout this book. For example, as a result of the emergence of new value systems, the human value of morality has evolved to encompass larger and larger estimates of the scope of those worthy of moral consideration—from the tribe to the nation to the world and eventually to all sentient beings.

This second premise serves as the basis for the focus of the method, which is generally more cultural than psychological. As discussed below in premise 5 and the examples that follow, the basic idea is that the spiritual energy and gravity of beauty, truth, and goodness can be harnessed in ways that can reliably cause consciousness to evolve. And these essential qualities are harnessed and transmitted through the cultural works or cultural institutions that communicate or demonstrate these intrinsic values within a given culture. Therefore, because consciousness and culture almost always coevolve, the evolution of consciousness cannot be effectively cultivated outside of the cultural context in which it is situated.

Premise 3: Evolutionary emergence in consciousness and culture occurs when people adopt more inclusive frames of value and improve their definition of improvement itself. This premise points to the insight that values are the leading line of development within consciousness and culture. Although human consciousness can grow and evolve along a wide variety of relatively independent cognitive and emotional lines of development, the evolution of values is the most significant factor in the process. This can be seen in the way consciousness and culture evolve as a result of both the *push* of unsatisfactory life conditions and the *pull* of values. Values are accordingly defined and animated by their relation to the real and pressing problems faced by people as they struggle to improve their lives.

And the reason why the development of values is the single most important factor in understanding the evolution of consciousness and culture overall is that it is through the gravity of values—the pull resulting from the intuition that a better way is possible—that consciousness and culture are drawn toward ever-higher levels of evolutionary development. Recognizing how the gravity of values pulls evolution forward from the inside through its influence on consciousness clarifies our understanding of cultural evolution by showing where evolution is headed and how we can best align ourselves with its positive trajectory of growth. This third premise thus goes to the heart of the method's essential technique, which involves harnessing the gravity of values. Values come alive with the power to motivate and mobilize people when those values appear to offer solutions to the existential problems people care deeply about.

The operation of this third premise was initially illustrated in the previous section's examples of poverty and climate change. In the case of poverty, we can see that as the prosperous modernist lifestyle becomes increasingly visible in the developing world, this perceived value contrasts with the prevailing conditions of poverty and provides a powerful stimulus to pursue the upward mobility that eventually results in a modernist society. Similarly, in the case of climate change, the specter of a warming globe threatening to degrade our natural environment illuminates the value of sustainability and a lifestyle that is more conscious of modernism's environmental impact. And this in turn draws people's consciousness into postmodern value frames where material possessions and personal status are valued less and overall quality of life is valued more.

This process begins to show why values are usually location specific. Each of the major worldviews we have examined has arisen along the timeline of human history in response to a specific set of problematic life conditions. The values of each worldview have thus been specifically tailored to overcome the problems that prevailed during the time in history when that worldview originally emerged. And most of these specific problem sets continue to prevail in different parts of the world and different sectors of society. Even though we are all alive here in the present, not all of us live in "the same time in history."

Working to solve the different problems that continue to plague humanity certainly helps perfect the universe. But according to premise 3, the most potent problems for producing authentic evolution are those that require the evolutionary emergence of new stages of consciousness and culture for their solution.

Premise 4: More evolved frames of value—higher-level worldviews— attract evolutionary emergence by illuminating the intrinsic values that help solve the existential problems which cannot be solved at the level that created them. This premise brings us back to the truism that problems cannot be solved at the same level of awareness that created them. While this is not true of every problem, it is the case with the existential problems that require evolutionary emergence for their solution. Existential problems provide openings for evolutionary emergence. These are the pressure points upon which the method can operate to nurture cultural evolution along its entire spectrum of development. Identifying these problems, together with the value solutions to which they point, can accordingly lead to a methodological technique for "gardening for emergence." The application of this technique is illustrated by the examples discussed in the next section. But before getting to these examples, we need to consider the four additional premises upon which the effectiveness of this evolutionary method depends.

Premise 5: The power of intrinsic values to raise consciousness is found in the spiritual energy of goodness, truth, and beauty—the spiritual experience of these values evolves consciousness. This premise is based on a simple proposition: spiritual experience raises consciousness. While this may seem fairly obvious at this point, it is a crucial aspect of the method, so it is worth unpacking a bit here. This fifth premise is derived directly from the spiritual teachings of evolution, which help us recognize that the development of the finite universe overall is essentially a process of spiritual growth. It thus follows that if evolution is essentially spiritual growth, then an effective technique for promoting the evolution of consciousness can be found in that which delivers authentic experiences of spirit. And as we have seen, the most useful and important kinds of spiritual experience are experiences of goodness, truth, beauty, and their value derivatives.

Again, these most intrinsic values are forms of spiritual energy that can be harnessed in the service of evolution. Through their inherent power to attract the attention and desire of our evolutionary impulses, these values provide the energy that pulls cultural evolution upward, illuminating the way forward and supplying the motivation necessary to break the inertia of the status quo. Examples of the power of beauty, truth, and goodness to stimulate cultural evolution can be abundantly found in history, such as in Thomas Paine's revolutionary pamphlet *Common Sense*, which contributed to the emergence of modernism, and Bob Dylan's song "The Times They Are a-Changin," which helped bring about the emergence of postmodernism. These significant works of truth and beauty produced cultural evolution by providing a kind of spiritual experience perfectly in tune with the zeitgeist of their time.

Premise 6: Works of culture having the most potential to attract evolutionary emergence—works providing the spiritual experience of intrinsic value—are those produced with the primary intention of sharing their creators' own spiritual experience. This premise emphasizes the role of intention in the methodological approach to raising consciousness. Through our heart-felt intention to share the spiritual experience that we ourselves have already found, our work becomes infused with the spiritual quality necessary to reproduce this experience in others. In other words, by focusing on the essence of the intrinsic value we are endeavoring to communicate or demonstrate in our work, we may bear the spiritual fruits that can provide spiritual experience for others. Stated yet another way, as explored in chapter 2 in the discussion of the practice of value metabolism, the spiritual energy of intrinsic value is most effectively engaged in a *circuit of practice*. When our sincere intention is to allow the spiritual experience we have received to pass through us into the experience of our fellows, our work's potential for raising consciousness is greatly enhanced.

This aspect of the evolutionary method is guided by the understanding of the spiritual messages of beauty, truth, and goodness described in chapter 4. There we explored how the pleasure and delight found in the aesthetic dimension of beauty communicates the message, "Feel loved." Similarly, in the intellectual dimension of truth we find assurance that the universe is intelligible and that the way is open for us increasingly to discover reality and become more real in the process. The experience of truth thus subtly communicates the message, "Grow." And finally, in the realm of goodness, and particularly within the moral domain of value, we may hear the message, "Love others." When we endeavor to communicate explicitly or implicitly these messages to those we wish to serve or teach—when our underlying intention is to share these spiritual messages through our work—we become partners with spirit in the grand adventure of perfecting the universe.

Premise 7: Spiritually fragrant works with the most potential to evolve the consciousness of their audience are those that also help self-actualize the creator of the work and are thus undertaken partially for their own sake as ends in themselves. This premise concerns the intention to achieve our own self-actualization through our work. The underlying idea is that our creations of beauty, truth, or goodness become most effective at raising consciousness when we undertake such work with the aim of giving our gift and living up to our potential to bear spiritual fruit in our lives. That is, to maximize the consciousness-raising potential of our work, not only must we intend to create spiritual experience in others (premise 6), we must also undertake such work with the intention of creating spiritual growth in ourselves. Again, the insights of evolutionary spirituality make clear that the fruits of the spirit we bring into the world actually serve as the rungs of the ladder of our own ascent. And when we are motivated to create these primary values both for the benefit of others and for our own self-actualization, the evolutionary potential of our work is maximized.

Premise 8: The project of evolving consciousness through services of goodness, teachings of truth, and creations of beauty is facilitated and empowered through the use of evolution's own method of development—the ongoing dialectical synthesis of existential polarities. The arguments and explanations that support this final premise have been developed throughout this book. Beginning in chapter 2, we saw how the evolutionary practice of dialectical epistemology involves the ability to hold two or more opposing perspectives at once, recognizing how these opposing positions tend to mutually cocreate each other through their developmental tension. Then in chapter 4 we discussed how existential polarities are actually systems of development—localized engines of evolution—mirroring the dialectical structure and function of the evolving universe as a whole. Then in chapter 7 we explored the application of this dialectical method in the attempt to advance a synthesis between the existential polarity of nondualism and theism that appears in spiritual experience itself.

This final premise thus serves as a kind of capstone for these eight methodological premises by affirming that evolutionary spirituality's method for evolving consciousness is essentially the same method employed by the evolving universe itself.

These, then, are the initial premises that point to the promise of a new method for evolving consciousness and culture. But, again, our search for an evolutionary method is only just beginning, and these early premises are bound to be expanded and refined as the potential for such a method is explored further. Moreover, the primarily cultural focus of the method as I have described it needs to be supplemented by and better integrated with the psychological focus of the social sciences, as discussed later in this chapter. But before getting to that, we will consider some examples suggesting that the development of an evolutionary method is a real possibility.

EXAMPLES OF EMERGENCE IN CONSCIOUSNESS AND CULTURE

Some academics have questioned the idea that scientists actually follow a procedural method in their investigations. These critics claim that, in practice, the scientific method is simply a matter of whatever scientists do, and that the real method is "anything goes."[5] So it may turn out that our search for an evolutionary method for evolving consciousness and culture will boil down to whatever successful creators of transformative culture actually do.

Indeed, all those who create beauty, truth, or goodness through their work are adding to the corpus of human culture and thus advancing its evolutionary development, even if in small and incremental ways. At the level of individual consciousness, anything that elevates our thoughts by helping us to be more loving, forgiving, wise, or mindful can be said to raise our consciousness. As explained in chapter 4, even the most commonplace expressions of these intrinsic values can create spiritual experience under the right circumstances.

Yet, there is an important difference between the incremental growth of consciousness and culture and the kind of development that actually extends the structure of emergence itself. As discussed in premise 1 above, human consciousness undergoes authentic evolution most clearly when it develops in ways that roughly recapitulate the larger cultural emergences marking the course of humanity's historical evolution. In other words, the difference between evolutionary emergence and mere incremental growth is that authentic evolution usually involves the move from one stage of development to the next higher stage—"a new level of awareness." Therefore, the best examples of the evolutionary method in action are found in the specific works of goodness, truth, or beauty that have helped bring about historically significant new worldviews. In addition to highly influential books or liberating forms of music such as those already cited, we can also identify a wide variety of other cultural works that have been instrumental in the emergence of new levels of awareness. For instance, emergence-producing works of culture can be recognized in the creation of movements or transformative organizations, such as the civil rights movement of the 1960s or the founding of the Sierra Club in the 1890s. Transformative cultural works can also include architecture, such as the Parthenon in the fifth century BC, or St. Peter's Basilica in Vatican City during the Renaissance. Indeed, hundreds of similar examples could be cited.

These examples, however, also illustrate how the evolutionary potential of a given work of culture, whether it be artistic, political, scientific, philosophical, or spiritual, usually depends as much on the historical timing and cultural readiness for such work as it does on the talent and motivational intention of the creators. And the fact that the evolutionary potential of a given work of culture depends largely on the historically situated receptivity of the audience suggests that such works may be drawn into existence by the aspirations of collective culture as much as they are created by their individual authors or founders. As Virginia Woolf wrote, "Masterpieces are not single and solitary births; they are the outcome of many years' thinking in common, by the body of people, so that the experience of the mass is behind a single voice."[6]

But while the emergence-producing masterpieces of beauty, truth, and goodness that we find in history may remain culturally potent for many, most are no longer producing the kind of fresh emergence for which they originally became famous. Nevertheless, beyond specific, historically situated works of transformative culture, there are also larger social institutions that do manage to continuously produce the evolution of consciousness and culture in an ongoing way. These forms of culture serve as "conveyor belts," as Ken Wilber calls them, which work continuously across generations to advance consciousness from one stage to another.

The best examples of these consciousness-raising institutions are found in the field of education and in spiritual teaching and practice. For instance, primary education serves to move children up through the cognitive and moral stages of development identified by developmental psychologists. And higher education, as noted, often results in the emergence of modernist and even postmodern consciousness in young adults. Similarly, emergence into new stages of consciousness is being continuously facilitated worldwide by the forms of spiritual culture we have identified as religious spirituality, secular spirituality, and progressive spirituality. As examples, religious spirituality continues to function as an effective conveyor belt from pretraditional to traditional levels of consciousness, as currently seen in sub-Saharan Africa and also in gang and prison cultures. Secular spirituality seems to help some people in transcending religious fundamentalism. And progressive spirituality is playing a similar role in the contemporary emergence of consciousness beyond modernism into the postmodern worldview, and even occasionally beyond that.

These examples of the ongoing success of spirituality in the work of evolving consciousness by promoting emergence into higher-level worldviews are particularly relevant in our search for a method because they well illustrate the operation of methodological premise 5: consciousness can be evolved most reliably and effectively through the provision of spiritual experience. And the fact that spirituality in general appears to be one of the most powerful ways of furthering emergence reinforces my hope that evolutionary spirituality in particular will come to serve as the primary catalyst for the emergence of the next great stage of human history.

In this chapter so far we have examined the potential for the discovery of a reliable method for evolving consciousness and culture from inside the perspective of the evolutionary worldview itself. The subject of cultural change, however, has already been carefully investigated for over a century by mainstream academic social science. The process through which people are persuaded to adopt new perspectives—the process through which large-scale social changes come about—has been studied within the fields of sociology, anthropology, history, political science, behavioral economics, social movement theory, and perhaps most directly in the interdisciplinary domain known as social psychology. So we now turn to a brief discussion of this field.

SOCIAL PSYCHOLOGY AND THE EVOLUTION OF CONSCIOUSNESS

The Relevance of Social Science for an Evolutionary Method

The interdisciplinary field of social psychology encompasses a broad range of investigations, but the aspect of the field most relevant for understanding the evolution of consciousness and culture is found in its study of social influence. This study encompasses all the ways that human perspectives and behaviors can be effectively changed through persuasive communications in the public sphere.

Like most forms of social science, social psychology prefers narrowly focused empirical studies and controlled experiments. This understandable preference for what can be clearly measured results in a focus on changes in perspectives or behaviors that are small and incremental and thus easier to reproduce in an experimental setting. However, changes in perspectives that actually constitute evolutionary emergence into higher levels of consciousness are much harder to find or measure in a social-science experiment. Therefore, although the findings of social psychology are relevant for our larger search for an evolutionary method, this academic field has not really addressed the deeper issues that concern the evolutionary method, such as the role of spiritual experience in the evolution of consciousness or the function of intrinsic value in the evolution of culture. Further, as a result of its empirical constraints, the social psychology literature tends to be rather tedious, stating in excruciating detail what is already fairly obvious to even a casual observer.

That being said, the research of social psychology most useful in our search for an evolutionary method for raising consciousness is found in what the field has discovered about the process of *persuasion*. Again, as Alfred North Whitehead understood, all evolution can be broadly conceived of as "gentle persuasion through love." While the method we are searching for cannot be reduced merely to clever persuasion techniques, what the social sciences have learned about persuasion is nevertheless important. Beginning with Freud, psychology's most important breakthrough was its identification of the influence of the subconscious mind on our overall consciousness. Psychology's study of the subconscious has shown how people often form opinions or make decisions for reasons they may not be fully aware of. For example, psychologists have found that political activists are mobilized more by loyalty to their group identity than by a rational choice to fight for a given political cause. Loyalty to one's tribe, which includes both conscious and unconscious factors, is the main value supplying the motivational energy to "take to the streets."[7] And the fact that loyalties can lead to either positive or negative behaviors underscores how the subconscious mind plays a significant role in the process of changing people's consciousness.

Social psychology's study of persuasion began with research into political propaganda during World War II. Then in the 1950s researchers began focusing on the persuasive influence of advertising in an attempt to discover an empirical rhetoric that could be used by marketers to sell products. Although these efforts ultimately proved unsuccessful, with no magical key to persuasion being found, this line of inquiry did expose the dark side of social influence, which includes deception and manipulation through dubious tactics such as fear-based advertising or appeals to prejudice. This potential for abuse can still be found in books and workshops that tout sales techniques and negotiation strategies that approach persuasion as a zero-sum game of winners and losers. And this abiding potential for unethical manipulation means that the evolutionary method's techniques of persuasion must be scrupulously transparent and exclusively focused on gentle persuasion through genuine truth, goodness, and beauty.

Social Psychology and the Art of Rhetoric

Recently, contemporary academic social psychology has begun to rediscover the relevance of the ancient art of rhetoric, as originally conceived by Greek philosophers such as Aristotle. In fact, Aristotle's fourth-century-BC treatise on rhetoric identifies the three basic categories of persuasion, which remain influential to this day. For example, following philosopher Jürgen Habermas's model of communicative action, social psychologists have identified three essential "appeals" that give communications the power to convince people or otherwise reconcile their oppositions. According to this understanding, the appeal of any communicative truth claim is inevitably tested or evaluated (consciously or subconsciously) according to three criteria: objective truth, expressive authenticity, and moral rightness.[8] And it turns out that Habermas's three avenues of appeal strongly resemble the three primary means of persuasion originally described by Aristotle's work on rhetoric.

Aristotle identified the three essential modes of persuasion as ethos, pathos, and logos. *Ethos* is understood as the method of persuasion that relies on the credibility of the speaker to establish trust. Communications that persuade through ethos are those perceived to be the most sincere or pure, or those coming from a wise source that is "without guile." *Pathos* is the method that stirs the emotions of the audience, moving them through appeals to their passions or fears. Communications that persuade through pathos are those that fire up the audience or inspire them to act by appealing to their deepest loyalties. And, finally, *logos* refers to the actual message of the communication, which usually takes the form of a good argument or a compelling reason that has the power to convince or otherwise entice the audience into agreement. Logos was the preferred form of rhetoric for Aristotle, who saw it as the most honest, ethical, and ultimately most effective form of persuasive communication.

Comparing Aristotle's three modes of persuasion with the premises of the evolutionary method, we can detect the influence of goodness, beauty, and truth on his overall categorical scheme. Specifically, ethos is most closely connected to the virtue or goodness of the speaker; pathos employs style or beauty to move the audience; and logos is about the actual message content or truth of the communication itself. Each of these modes is thus focused on delivering a distinct kind of persuasive spiritual energy. And the most successful communications almost always include all three elements of persuasion to some extent.

Effectively employing the lessons of Aristotle's rhetoric, however, involves more than just working to maximize all three value categories in our communications. The art of using these modes of persuasion also involves working with the specific primary value underlying each mode in a way that allows that value to modify and refine the values behind the other two modes. For example, the rational mode of logos ideally needs the aesthetic touch of pathos, or an entertaining style, to make the truth of the message easy to hear and appreciate. And likewise, to be truly artful, communications of beauty need an underlying message, or essential truth, to make them meaningful.

While this may seem fairly obvious, it begins to appear more methodological when we bring in the vertical dimension of evolution in which different worldviews perceive the beautiful, the true, and the good within their own frame and at their own level of development.

This means we need to tune our communications of value to the "octave" of truth, goodness, and beauty used by our audience to make meaning. By speaking to our audience's most deeply held values, our work may become charged with the spiritual energy that can produce spiritual experience. Indeed, it is the spiritual experience that does the persuading. Thus, by identifying and emphasizing the core or essence of truth, goodness, and beauty within our work and by skillfully tailoring these intrinsic values to connect with the values of our audience, we can reveal the *message within the message*, which is ultimately the *infinite within the finite*.

But, again, this process of infusing our cultural works with the spiritual energy of intrinsic value cannot be easily reduced to a simple formula or procedure. Communicating the infinite within the finite is more a matter of inspiration than analysis, and this is why comparisons between the scientific method and the evolutionary method can be taken only so far. Unlike the analytical method of science, the evolutionary method of raising consciousness through spiritual experience is discovered experientially and intentionally in our attempts to give our gifts, as described in the methodological premises set out above.

Obviously, this discussion of how the findings of social science can inform the evolutionary method is only a preliminary investigation of a subject that I hope will become the focus of numerous books and even entire academic departments. Much work remains to be done before we will have found a reliable method for evolving consciousness into new levels of awareness. So my wish is that this chapter's brief exploration of the potential for such a new method will stimulate further thinking and research on the subject.

When all is said and done, our efforts to bring beauty, truth, and goodness into the experience of our fellows is best understood through the concept of service and leadership. And this brings us back to the subject of spiritual leadership, which is where we started in this book.

Spiritual Leadership Revisited

As discussed in chapter 1, evolutionary spirituality conceives of spiritual leadership broadly as practically anything that creates spiritual experience in others. Yet the most effective and transformative spiritual leaders do not just give people experiences of the beautiful, the true, and the good; they also empower people to create these values for themselves. It is in this way that spiritual leadership becomes contagious. That is, all practitioners of evolutionary spirituality can become spiritual leaders in their own right through the practice of bearing the spiritual fruits of intrinsic value—the practice of value metabolism.

Authentic leadership means giving people what they really need. And leadership becomes truly spiritual when it fulfills people's existential needs, such as the need for self-actualization. According to the spiritual teachings of evolution, we satisfy this existential need most completely when we work to fulfill our purpose in the cosmic economy, which is to help make ourselves and our world more beautiful, true, and good. So the most effective spiritual leaders—those who employ the evolutionary method most skillfully—will be those who show people how to bring these values into the world by their own efforts. At the individual level, the need for self-actualization is accordingly fulfilled through the practice of perfecting the universe. And when self-actualization occurs, consciousness evolves.

However, at the larger cultural level, our collective existential need is for a truer and more inclusive form of spirituality. As we have discussed, the developed world now needs a form of spiritual teaching and practice that can transcend the limitations of the religious, secular, and progressive versions of spirituality currently on offer in our culture. And this truer form of spirituality is found in evolutionary spirituality, which provides a clearer view of ultimate reality and our purpose in life. Through its power to overcome the pathologies and weaknesses of religious, secular, and progressive spirituality while at the same time preserving and

245

carrying forward the important accomplishments of these earlier forms, evolutionary spirituality can help unite our increasingly fragmented society. Indeed, evolutionary spirituality holds the promise of building the greater solidarity we need to address the pressing challenges we face and thus to grow into the next phase of our development as a civilization.

Moreover, the greater sense of spiritual solidarity that will result from the growing recognition of the powerful new truths revealed by the spiritual teachings of evolution can lead to what we really need deep down—a spiritual renaissance. This is what I have longed for since I was twelve years old—a historically significant renaissance brought about by the deepening recognition of the spiritual reality of beauty, truth, and goodness. And just as the original Renaissance in Europe paved the way for the subsequent Enlightenment, the coming renaissance promised by the rise of evolutionary spirituality can similarly lead to the second Enlightenment we now so urgently require.

Everyone who is moved to participate in the emergence of evolutionary spirituality is therefore called to be a spiritual leader. The new truth, beauty, and goodness now becoming available through the emergence of this expanded frame of reality offers us a tantalizing opportunity for self-actualization—a chance to participate in the emergence of a new level of evolution. Evolutionary spirituality can help make spiritual leaders out of each of us by giving us the power to fulfill the existential needs of our society and further our own self-actualization in the process. The rise of evolutionary spirituality thus promises to create more spiritual experience than the world has ever seen and thereby evolve the universe of self, culture, and nature in unprecedented ways.

Notes

Introduction

1. The discussion in this section of the introduction is adapted from my book *Evolution's Purpose* (New York: SelectBooks, 2012), xxiv–xxix. A more thorough and complete description of the worldview stages recognized by integral philosophy can be found in my 2007 book, *Integral Consciousness and the Future of Evolution* (St. Paul, MN: Paragon House, 2007).

2. See, e.g., Ronald Inglehart, ed., *Human Values and Social Change* (New York: Brill, 2003); Paul Ray and Sherry Anderson, *The Cultural Creatives: How 50 Million People Are Changing the World* (New York: Harmony Books, 2000). See also, Jean Piaget, *The Child's Conception of the World* (New York: Routledge, 1928); Lawrence Kohlberg, *From Is to Ought* (New York: Academic Press, 1971); Clare W. Graves, "Levels of Existence: An Open System Theory of Values," *Journal of Humanistic Psychology* (November 1970); Don Beck and Chris Cowan, *Spiral Dynamics* (New York: Blackwell, 1995); Jenny Wade, *Changes of Mind: A Holonomic Theory of the Evolution of Consciousness* (Albany, NY: SUNY Press, 1996); and Jeremy Rifkin, *The Empathic Civilization* (New York: Tarcher Putnam, 2009).

3. Retrieved from: http://plato.stanford.edu/entries/panentheism, August 2014.

Chapter 1

1. Robert Wuthnow, *After Heaven: Spirituality in America Since the 1950s* (Berkeley: University of California Press, 1998), viii.

2. Charles Taylor, *A Secular Age* (Cambridge, MA: Belknap Press, 2007), 562.

CHAPTER 2

1. See chapter 8, premise 1 (p. 228), which explains the distinction between mental growth and the evolution of consciousness.

2. Wilber's four-quadrant model is an important conceptual framework for understanding the individual and collective aspects of evolution, including the interior and exterior dimensions of evolutionary emergence. However, I have some reservations about this model, which are explained in *Integral Consciousness* (pp. 324–42) and developed further in the article "Problematizing Interobjectivity: A Response to Edwards," originally published in *The Journal of Integral Theory and Practice* 3, no. 4 (Winter 2008), available online at: http://www.stevemcintosh.com.

3. Terrence Deacon, "The Hierarchic Logic of Emergence," in Bruce H. Weber and David J. Depew, eds., *Evolution and Learning: The Baldwin Effect Reconsidered* (Cambridge, MA: MIT Press, 2003), 306.

4. This italicized phrase is not a direct quote from Whitehead. However, that it is in fact Whitehead's view is well documented by one of his most able interpreters, David Ray Griffin, who writes: "This Whiteheadian criterion for judging evolutionary progress—greater capacity for experience that is intrinsically valuable—is positively correlated with greater capacity to include more feelings and objective data from the environment in one's experience" (*Religion and Scientific Naturalism: Overcoming the Conflicts* [Albany, NY: State University of New York Press, 2000], 301). In other words, evolutionary development involves increasing awareness of value. Thanks to Mary C. Coelho for the correction.

5. See, e.g., Michael W. Brierley, "The Potential of Panentheism for Dialogue Between Science and Religion," in Philip Clayton, ed., *Oxford Handbook of Religion and Science* (New York: Oxford University Press, 2008), 635–51.

6. Cosmologists and astronomers do not know whether the physical universe is straightforwardly "finite," or whether it expands into infinity. But unlike the existential, eternal, "metaphysical infinite" we are considering in this book, our physical universe of time definitely had a distinct beginning, which certainly makes it finite for purposes of our analysis of spiritual experience.

7. Barry Johnson, *Polarity Management* (Amherst, MA: HRD Press, 1996), xviii.

8. Charles Johnston, *Necessary Wisdom: Meeting the Challenge of a New Cultural Maturity* (Berkeley: Celestial Arts, 1991), 32.

9. Ibid., 35–36.

10. Ibid., 38.

Chapter 3

1. *Dictionary.com*, s.v. "experience," accessed August 2014, http://dictionary. reference.com/browse/experience?s=t.

2. *Integral Consciousness*, 9–12, 201–203 (see intro., n. 1).

3. Jorge Ferrer, *Revisioning Transpersonal Psychology* (Albany, NY: State University of New York Press, 2002), 93–94.

4. This point is well argued by Ferrer, who teaches a course in comparative mysticism at the California Institute of Integral Studies. See *Revisioning Transpersonal Psychology*, 51–70.

5. Jerome I. Gellman, "Mysticism and Religious Experience," in *The Oxford Handbook of Philosophy and Religion*, ed. William J. Wainright (New York: Oxford University Press, 2007), 140.

6. Ken Wilber, for example, claims a broadly empirical status for the metaphysical levels he identifies as "gross, subtle, causal, and nondual." While that may indeed be valid as a phenomenology of meditative experience, his teaching that these states of awareness represent a relatively complete and empirical description of what is ultimately spiritually real has its limitations. Wilber's contention that the ultimate form of reality is formless and nondual tends to contradict and partially invalidate the venerable spiritual teachings of theistic traditions. And even if true for nondual levels of spiritual experience, Wilber's Vedanta/Vajrayana hierarchy of levels is only half the story, as discussed in chapter 7. See also, endnote 4, chapter 7.

7. Paul Marshall, *Mystical Encounters with the Natural World* (New York: Oxford University Press, 2005), 227.

8. Paul's Epistle to the Hebrews, 11:1.

9. Father Thomas Keating, one of the leading proponents of centering prayer, explicitly says that the kind of contemplative prayer he

advocates is not meant as a replacement for other forms of prayer. Yet in practice, witness meditation is becoming a substitute for prayer within many forms of postmodern Christianity and Judaism. See: http://www.centeringprayer.com.

10. Western writers were, of course, well acquainted with mind-altering drugs prior to Huxley, as seen in William James's use of nitrous oxide, Samuel Taylor Coleridge's use of opium, and Sigmund Freud's use of cocaine. However, none of these drugs produce an authentic psychedelic experience.

11. See, e.g., Andrew B. Newberg and Eugene G. D'Aquili, *Why God Won't Go Away*, quoted in Marshall, *Mystical Encounters with the Natural World*, 229–32.

12. Integral philosophy's recognition of the correspondence that can be found between a person's interior consciousness and the activity in their exterior brain is explained by Wilber in *Sex, Ecology, Spirituality* (Boston: Shambhala, 1995), 127–39, and graphically illustrated in his four-quadrant model of evolution. However, my reservations about this model are cited in endnote 2 to chapter 2 above.

13. Quoted from "The Embodied Mind: An Interview with Philosopher Evan Thompson" in *Tricycle: The Buddhist Review* 24, no. 1 (Fall 2014), 40.

14. See Janice Miner Holden, Bruce Greyson, and Debbie James, eds., *The Handbook of Near-Death Experiences: Thirty Years of Investigation* (Santa Barbara, CA: Praeger, 2009), and Pim van Lommel, *Consciousness Beyond Life: The Science of Near-Death Experience* (New York: HarperOne, 2011).

15. The "chords on the keyboard" analogy is from Neal M. Goldsmith, *Psychedelic Healing: The Promise of Entheogens for Psychotherapy and Spiritual Development* (Rochester, VT: Healing Arts Press, 2011), 110.

16. For a recent discussion of the brain as an antenna for consciousness, see: Charles Foster, *Wired for God? The Biology of Spiritual Experience* (London: Hodder & Stroughton, 2011), 181–93.

17. In addition to the work of C. Stephen Evans in *Natural Signs and Knowledge of God: A New Look at Theistic Arguments* (Oxford: Oxford University Press, 2010), discussed in the remainder of this chapter, other recent books that have contributed to the reemergence of natural theology include Alister McGrath's *The Open Secret: A New Vision for Natural Theology* (Malden MA:

Blackwell, 2008) and Frederick Turner's *Natural Religion* (Edison, NJ: Transaction Publishers, 2006).

18. Blaise Pascal, *Pensées*, trans. W. F. Trotter (New York: E. P. Dutton, 1958), 118.

CHAPTER 4

1. Albert Einstein, quoted in Abdus Salam, *Unification of Fundamental Forces* (Cambridge, UK: Cambridge University Press, 1990), 99.

2. Quoted in Marcus Borg, *The Heart of Christianity* (New York: HarperOne, 2003), 155.

3. Although this dialectical pattern or process was first realized over two hundred years ago by idealist philosophers such as Hegel and Fichte, now in our time we can begin to see more deeply into this dynamic feature of the universe by using the emerging insights of the spiritual teachings of evolution. Of course, not all forms of emergence are straightforwardly dialectical. The Internet, for example, did not really emerge out of a dialectical interplay. But the modernist worldview overall, which has brought about technological breakthroughs such as the Internet, can definitely be recognized as having emerged dialectically from the traditional worldview that preceded it.

4. Iris Murdoch, *The Sovereignty of Good* (New York: Routledge, 1970), 103.

5. Bhagavad Gita, chapter 10, verse 36.

6. Pitirim Sorokin, quoted in "Integralism is My Philosophy," *in* Whit Burnett, ed., *This is My Philosophy* (New York: Harper and Brothers, 1957), 184.

7. Howard Gardner, *Truth, Beauty, and Goodness Reframed* (New York: Basic Books, 2011), 9.

8. Regarding the idea of levels of spiritual experience, I understand that the recognition of levels of realization in mystical experience is an important feature of some spiritual paths. This analysis, however, is specifically about beauty, truth, and goodness. And as I have said, these are like vectors of perfection. So of course there is a hierarchy of their realization, as illustrated by the notion of the highest truth, for example. Yet at the same time, what creates spiritual experience in a

given individual at a given time may be a lesser truth that is nevertheless tailored to the level of the experiencer. Therefore, the relative value of these things, as either experiences or as distinct aspects of the world, depends on the amount of perfecting they can do, and this in turn is relative to the consciousness of the persons involved. While this is not a thesis of relativism, it is also not an account that holds the hierarchy of levels to be fixed or pregiven.

9. This idea is developed in the discussion of shadow work in Ken Wilber et al., *Integral Life Practice: A 21st-Century Blueprint for Physical Health, Emotional Balance, Mental Clarity, and Spiritual Awakening* (Boston: Integral Books, 2008), 41–66.

10. In addition to *Integral Life Practice*, I can also point to *The Shadow Effect* by Deepak Chopra, Marianne Williamson, and Debbie Ford (New York: HarperOne, 2011).

11. These ideas are discussed in greater detail in *Evolution's Purpose*, 162–64 and 180–81 (see intro., n. 1). See also, chapter 7, p. 208.

12. John Cottingham, "Philosophers Are Finding Fresh Meanings in Truth, Beauty and Goodness," *The Sunday Times* (London), June 17, 2006.

CHAPTER 5

1. See, e.g., "American Nuns Stunned by Vatican Accusation of 'Radical Feminism,' Crackdown," *Washington Post*, April 20, 2012.

2. David Loy, *Nonduality: A Study in Comparative Philosophy* (New Haven, CT: Yale University Press, 1997), 7.

3. Alan Watts, *Buddhism: The Religion of No-Religion* (Boston: Tuttle Publishing, 1999), 6.

4. William James, *The Varieties of Religious Experience* (Seattle: CreateSpace, 2009), 218.

5. Developmental psychologists have now discovered a wide variety of "developmental lines" within the human mind. Within this branch of psychology, a line of development is defined as an aspect or capacity of consciousness with a distinct trajectory of growth that can develop with a degree of independence from other components of the mind.

For example, distinct developmental lines in consciousness include ego or self-sense, cognitive reasoning, moral reasoning, linguistic ability, and interpersonal skills.

6. A more theologically accurate label for this polarity might be "pantheism and panentheism," but these words are so close to each other that using this label would be potentially confusing. Further, although there are numerous forms of nonduality's polar alternative that cannot be accurately characterized as straightforwardly "theistic," I think "nondual and theistic" is perhaps the least objectionable and most generally descriptive label. And this label is broad enough to describe this polarity in both ancient and modern contexts.

7. For a description of this debate see *Maya and Avidya: The Shankara Ramanuja Debate*, by Darren Hackler, http://www.scribd.com/doc/73423856/Maya-Avidya-Shankara-Ramanuja-Debate, accessed August, 2014.

8. Nisargadatta Maharaj, Nonduality.com, "What Is Nonduality," http://www.nonduality.com/whatis.htm, accessed August 2014.

9. "Talk: Augustine of Hippo," *Wikiquote*, http://en.wikiquote.org/wiki/Talk:Augustine_of_Hippo, accessed August 2014.

10. Simone Weil, *Waiting for God*, trans. Emma Craufurd (New York: G. P. Putnam's Sons, 1951), 69.

11. Eric Reitan, *Is God a Delusion? A Reply to Religion's Cultured Despisers* (Malden, MA: Wiley-Blackwell, 2009), 163.

12. Hans Küng, *Christianity and World Religions: Paths to Dialogue* (New York: Orbis Books, 1993), 176–77.

13. Rose Drew, *Buddhist and Christian? An Exploration of Dual Belonging* (New York: Routledge, 2011), 136.

14. Aloysius Pieris, quoted by Drew, *Buddhist and Christian?*, 145. The source of the quote is *Love Meets Wisdom: A Christian Experience of Buddhism* (New Delhi: Intellectual Publications, 1988), 10.

CHAPTER 6

1. Loy, *Nonduality*, 287 (see chap. 5, n. 2).
2. Ibid., 290.

3. The Buddhist doctrine of dependent origination is certainly beautiful in the way it grounds our interdependence and interconnectedness in a cosmological theory, but it does not stand up well to the spiritual teachings revealed by the structure of evolutionary emergence.

4. See *The Stanford Encyclopedia of Philosophy*'s article on the Kyoto School, http://plato.stanford.edu/entries/kyoto-school, accessed August 2014.

5. See, for example, Mervyn Sprung, ed., *The Problem of Two Truths in Buddhism and Vedanta* (Dordrecht, Holland: D. Reidel Publishing, 1973).

6. Küng, *Christianity and World Religions*, 180 (see chap. 5, n. 12).

7. John A. T. Robinson, *Truth is Two-Eyed* (London: SCM Press, 1979), 39, 143.

8. Ramana Maharshi, "Be As You Are," *The Teachings of Sri Ramana Maharshi*, ed. David Godman, http://peacefulrivers.homestead.com/Maharshi.html, accessed August 2014.

9. Adyashanti, "Writings," http://www.adyashanti.org/index.php?file=writings_inner&writingid=24, accessed August 2014.

10. Loy, *Nonduality*, 128 (see chap. 5, n. 2).

11. Jay Michaelson, *Everything Is God: The Radical Path of Nondual Judaism* (Boston: Trumpeter, 2009), 209.

12. A. H. Almaas, Facets of Unity, http://www.ahalmaas.com/glossary/free-will, accessed August, 2014.

13. Thich Nhat Hanh, "Dharma Talk: The Buddhist Understanding of Reality," June 21, 2009, *The Mindfulness Bell*, http://www.mindfulnessbell.org/wp/tag/free-will, accessed August 2014.

14. See, e.g., Glenn Wallis, "Thich Nhat Hanh's Imaginary Soul," October 12, 2012, *Speculative Non-Buddhism*, http://speculativenonbuddhism.com/2012/10/12/thich-nhat-hanhs-imaginary-soul, accessed August 2014.

15. Riccardo Repetti, "Buddhist Theories of Free Will," *Journal of Buddhist Ethics* 17 (2010), http://blogs.dickinson.edu/buddhistethics/2010/12/21/buddhist-theories-of-free-will-compatiblism-2, accessed January 2014.

16. Ibid.

17. T. R. V. Murti, "Samvrti and Paramartha in Madhyamika and Adaita Vedanta," in *The Problem of Two Truths in Buddhism and Vedanta*, 22.

18. A. G. Arapura, "Maya and the Discourse About Brahman," in *The Problem of Two Truths in Buddhism and Vedanta*, 119.

19. Nonduality certainly has its own venerable philosophical tradition, but it has not been influential within mainstream professional philosophy.

20. Stuart Hackett, *Oriental Philosophy: A Westerner's Guide to Eastern Thought* (Madison, WI: University of Wisconsin Press, 1979), 120–21.

CHAPTER 7

1. See David Godman, *The Power of Presence: Part One* (Lithia Springs, GA: New Leaf Distributing Company, 2000).

2. See: Wallis, "Thich Nhat Hanh's Imaginary Soul" (see chap. 6, n. 14).

3. Wilber explains his "three faces of spirit" teaching as follows: Spirit in the *first person* is defined as the "great I"; spirit in the *third person* is defined as the "great It," or existence itself; and spirit in the *second person* is defined as the "great You or Thou" and as "something-that-is-always-greater-than-me," whose main purpose is described as providing a reason for personal surrender. Discussing the appropriate response to spirit in the second person, Wilber writes: "In the face of a God who is All Love, I can have only one response: to find God in this moment, I must love until it hurts, love until infinity, love until there is no me left anywhere" (*Integral Spirituality* [Boston, MA: Shambhala, 2006], 159).

4. These quotations are from Jorge Ferrer's 2011 article "Participation, Metaphysics, and Enlightenment: Reflections on Ken Wilber's Recent Work," in *Transpersonal Psychology Review* 14, no. 2 (2011), 3–24.

5. Küng, *Christianity and World Religions*, 397 (see chap. 5, n. 12).

6. Ibid, 398.

7. See Abe's response to Küng, in Christopher Ives, ed., *Divine Emptiness and Historical Fullness* (Norcross, GA: Trinity Press International, 1995), 240–41.

8. Andrew Cohen, *Evolutionary Enlightenment* (New York: Select Books, 2011), 26–27.

9. The nondual and theistic poles need not be understood as literal equals as depicted in the yin-yang symbol. Nor am I suggesting that either God or nonduality occupies the center of the other in perfect symmetry as in

the symbol. But the principle of interdependent mutual enactment, as illustrated by the symbol, is relevant nonetheless.

10. Meister Eckhart, quoted in Urban Tigner Holmes, *A History of Christian Spirituality: An Analytical Introduction* (New York: Church Publishing, Inc., 2002), 151.

11. Loy, *Nonduality*, 211 (see chap. 5, n. 2).

12. Ibid., 203.

13. See the discussion of the two truths doctrine on p. 172; see also Hans Küng's discussion in *Christianity and World Religions*, 388–89 (see chap. 5, n. 12).

14. See the discussion of the self and the evolving soul in chapter 6, pp. 174–175.

15. Blaise Pascal, quoted in *The University Record*, vol. 1 (Chicago: University of Chicago Press, 1897), 112.

16. Judith Blackstone, Dialogues on Nonduality, http://www.innerexplorations. com/ewtext/dialogue.htm, accessed August 2014.

17. See "Lai Zhide," *Wikipedia*, http://en.wikipedia.org/wiki/Lai_Zhide.

CHAPTER 8

1. In addition to my previous books, a good introduction to the evolutionary worldview can be found in Carter Phipps, *Evolutionaries* (New York: Harper Perennial, 2012). Ken Wilber's *A Theory of Everything* (Boston: Shambhala, 2000) also provides a good, if somewhat dated, introductory overview.

2. As explained in *Integral Consciousness* (p. 10), the dialectical sequence of worldview emergence orients the values of each successive worldview stage toward an alternative focus on either the individual (emphasizing the expression of the self) or the community (emphasizing the sacrifice of the self for the sake of the group). Because the emergence of the evolutionary or integral stage of development represents a dialectical return to the individualistic, or agentic, side of the dialectical spiral of development, it can be seen as a kind of higher harmonic of modernism. This understanding supports the idea that the events surrounding the emergence of modernism during the Enlightenment can help us anticipate the emergence of the evolutionary stage. See also *Evolution's Purpose*, 201–202.

3. This quote appears in many places and in a variety of versions. It is adapted from an interview of Einstein by Michael Amrine, "The Real Problem is in the Hearts of Men" (*New York Times Magazine*, June 23, 1946).

4. See *Evolution's Purpose*, 17–24 (see intro., n. 1).

5. See Paul K. Feyerabend, *Against Method: Outline of an Anarchistic Theory of Knowledge* (London: Verso, 1975).

6. Virginia Woolf, *A Room of One's Own* (New York: Harcourt Brace Jovanovich, 1929), 65.

7. See Thomas R. Rochon, *Culture Moves: Ideas, Activism, and Changing Values* (Princeton, NJ: Princeton University Press, 1998).

8. See Derek Hook, Bradley Franks, and Martin W. Bauer, eds., *The Social Psychology of Communication* (New York: Palgrave Macmillan, 2011), 88.

Selected Bibliography

Almaas, A. H. *Facets of Unity*. Boston: Shambhala, 2000.

Alston, William. *Perceiving God: The Epistemology of the Religious Experience*. Ithaca, NY: Cornell University Press, 1993.

Anthony, Lewis. *Philosophers without Gods: Meditations on Atheism and the Secular Life*. New York: Oxford University Press, 2010.

Aurobindo, Ghose. *The Future Evolution of Man: The Divine Life upon Earth*. Wheaton, IL: Quest Books, 1974.

———. *The Life Divine*. Twin Lakes, WI: Lotus Press, 1985.

Basseches, Michael. *Dialectical Thinking and Adult Development*. New York: Ablex Pub. Corp., 1984.

Bender, Courtney. *The New Metaphysicals: Spirituality and the American Religious Imagination*. Chicago: University of Chicago Press, 2010.

Bergson, Henri. *Creative Evolution*. Mineola, NY: Dover Publications, 1998.

Borg, Marcus. *The Heart of Christianity*. New York: HarperOne, 2003.

Briggs, Roger. *Journey to Civilization: The Science of How We Got Here*. Santa Margarita, CA: Collins Foundation Press, 2013.

Chopra, Deepak. *The Third Jesus*. New York: Harmony Books, 2009.

Clayton, Philip, and Steven Knapp. *The Predicament of Belief*. New York: Oxford University Press, 2011.

Clayton, Philip, ed. *Oxford Handbook of Religion and Science*. New York: Oxford University Press, 2008.

Cobb, John. *Beyond Dialogue*. Eugene, OR: Wipf and Stock Publishers, 1998.

Cohen, Andrew. *Evolutionary Enlightenment: A New Path to Spiritual Awakening*. New York: SelectBooks, 2011.

Cusa, Nicholas. *Nicholas of Cusa: Selected Spiritual Writings*. Mahwah, NJ: Paulist Press, 1997.

Cvetkovic, D., and Irena Cosic, eds. *States of Consciousness: Experimental Insights into Meditation, Waking, Sleep and Dreams*. Berlin: Springer-Verlag, 2011.

Dawkins, Richard. *The God Delusion*. New York: Mariner Books, 2008.

Deacon, Terrence. *Incomplete Nature*. New York: W. W. Norton & Sons, 2012.

Dorrien, Gary. *The Making of American Liberal Theology: Crisis, Irony, and Postmodernity: 1950–2005*. Louisville, KY: Westminster John Knox Press, 2006.

Drew, Rose. *Buddhist and Christian? An Exploration of Dual Belonging*. New York: Routledge, 2011.

Esbjorn-Hargens, Sean, and Michael Zimmerman. *Integral Ecology*. Boston: Integral Books/Shambhala, 2008.

Evans, C. Stephen. *Natural Signs and Knowledge of God*. New York: Oxford University Press, 2012.

Ferrer, Jorge. *Revisioning Transpersonal Psychology*. Albany, NY: State University of New York Press, 2002.

Forman, K. C. Robert. *Mysticism, Mind, Consciousness*. Albany, NY: State University of New York Press, 1999.

Foster, Charles. *Wired for God? The Biology of Spiritual Experience*. London: Hodder & Stoughton, 2011.

Hook, D., B. Franks, and M. Bauer, eds. *The Social Psychology of Communication*. New York: Palgrave Macmillan, 2011.

Gafni, Marc. *Your Unique Self*. Tucson, AZ: Integral Publishers, 2012.

Gardner, Howard. *Truth, Beauty, and Goodness Reframed*. New York: Basic Books, 2011.

_____. *Changing Minds*. Cambridge, MA: Harvard Business School Press, 2006.

Godman, David. *The Power of the Presence, Part One*. Lithia Springs, GA: New Leaf Distributing Company, 2000.

Goldsmith, Neal. *Psychedelic Healing*. Rochester, VT: Healing Arts Press, 2011.

Goldstein, Philip. *American Veda*. New York: Crown Archetype, 2009.

Griffin, David. *Religion and Scientific Naturalism: Overcoming the Conflicts*. Albany, NY: State University of New York Press, 2000.

Grof, Stanislav. *The Cosmic Game: Explorations at the Frontiers of Human Consciousness*. Albany, NY: State University of New York Press, 1998.

Hackett, Stewart. *Oriental Philosophy: A Westerner's Guide to Eastern Thought*. Madison WI: University of Wisconsin Press, 1979.

Harris, Sam. *The End of Faith*. New York: W. W. Norton, 2005.

Heelas, Paul. *The New Age Movement*. Cambridge, MA: Blackwell, 1996.

Heelas, Paul, and Linda Woodward. *The Spiritual Revolution*. Malden, MA: Blackwell, 2005.

Hick, John. *The New Frontier of Religion and Science*. New York: Palgrave Macmillan, 2006.

Inglehart, Ronald. *Modernization and Postmodernization: Cultural, Economic, and Political Change in 43 Societies*. Princeton, NJ: Princeton University Press, 1997.

_____. *Human Values and Social Change*. Boston: Brill Academic Publishers, 2003.

Ives, Christopher, ed. *Divine Emptiness and Historical Fullness: A Buddhist Jewish Christian Conversation with Masao Abe*. Norcross, GA: Trinity Press International, 1995.

James, William. *The Varieties of Religious Experience*. Seattle: CreateSpace Independent Publishing Platform, 2009.

Johnson, Barry. *Polarity Management*. Amherst, MA: HRD Press, 1996.

Johnston, Charles. *Necessary Wisdom: Meeting the Challenge of a New Cultural Maturity*. Berkeley: Celestial Arts, 1991.

Kapstein, Matthew T., ed. *The Presence of Light: Divine Radiance and Religious Experience*. Chicago: University of Chicago Press, 2004.

Kauffman, Stewart. *Reinventing the Sacred*. New York: Basic Books, 2010.

Küng, Hans. *Christianity and World Religions*. New York: Orbis Books, 1993.

Loy, David. *Nonduality: A Study in Comparative Philosophy*. New Haven, CT: Yale University Press, 1997.

Lynch, Gordon. *The New Spirituality*. London: I. B. Tauris, 2007.

Mackey, John, and Rajendra Sisodia. *Conscious Capitalism: Liberating the Heroic Spirit of Business*. Cambridge, MA: Harvard Business Review Press, 2012.

Maharshi, Ramana. *Talks with Ramana Maharshi*. Vista, CA: Inner Directions, 2000.

Marcel, Gabriel. *The Mystery of Being*. South Bend, IN: St. Augustine's Press, 2001.

Marshall, Paul, *Mystical Encounters with the Natural World*. New York: Oxford University Press, 2005.

Maslow, Abraham. *Motivation and Personality*. New York: HarperCollins, 1987.

McDonald, Barry, ed. *Seeing God Everywhere: Essays on Nature and the Sacred*. Bloomington IN: World Wisdom, 2003.

McGrath, Alister. *The Open Secret: A New Vision for Natural Theology*. Malden, MA: Blackwell, 2008.

McIntosh, Steve. *Integral Consciousness and the Future of Evolution: How the Integral Worldview Is Transforming Politics, Culture and Spirituality*. St. Paul, MN: Paragon House, 2007.

_____. *Evolution's Purpose: An Integral Interpretation of the Scientific Story of Our Origins*. New York: SelectBooks, 2012.

Michaelson, Jay. *Everything Is God: The Radical Path of Nondual Judaism*. Boston: Trumpeter, 2009.

Murdoch, Iris. *The Sovereignty of the Good*. New York: Routledge and Kegan Paul, 1970.

Nasr, Seyyed Hossein. *Knowledge and the Sacred*. Albany, NY: State University of New York Press, 1989.

Nhat Hanh, Thich. *Peace Is Every Step: The Path of Mindfulness in Everyday Life*. New York: Bantam Books, 1992.

Netland, Harold A. *Dissonant Voices: Religious Pluralism and the Question of Truth*. Grand Rapids, MI: William B. Erdmans Publishing, 1991.

Newberg, Andrew B., and Eugene G. D'Aquili. *Why God Won't Go Away: Brain Science and the Biology of Belief*. New York: Ballantine Books, 2002.

Otto, Rudolph. *The Idea of the Holy*. New York: Oxford University Press, 1958.

Panikkar, Raimon. *The Experience of God*. Minneapolis: Fortress Press, 2006.

Pascal, Blaise. *Pensees*. Translated by W. F. Trotter. New York: E. P. Dutton, 1958.

Phipps, Carter. *Evolutionaries: Unlocking the Spiritual and Cultural Potential of Science's Greatest Idea*. New York: Harper Perennial, 2012.

Pike, Nelson. *Mystic Union: An Essay in the Phenomenology of Mysticism*. Ithaca, NY: Cornell University Press, 1994.

Plantinga, Alvin. *Warranted Christian Belief*. New York: Oxford University Press, 2000.

Polkinghorne, John. *Science and the Trinity*. New Haven, CT: Yale University Press, 2006.

Proudfoot, Wayne. *Religious Experience*. Berkeley: University of California Press, 1987.

Ray, Paul, and Sherry Anderson. *The Cultural Creatives: How 50 Million People Are Changing the World*. New York: Harmony Books, 2000.

Reitan, Eric. *Is God a Delusion?* Malden, MA: Wiley-Blackwell, 2009.

Robinson, John. *Truth is Two-Eyed*. London: SCM Press, 1979.

Rochon, Thomas R. *Culture Moves: Ideas, Activism, and Changing Values*. Princeton, NJ: Princeton University Press, 1998.

Rolston, Holmes, III. *Science and Religion: A Critical Survey*. West Conshohocken, PA: Templeton Foundation Press, 2006.

_____. *Environmental Ethics: Duties to and Values in the Natural World*. Philadelphia: Temple University Press, 1988.

_____. *Three Big Bangs*. New York: Columbia University Press, 2011.

Rorh, Richard. *Immortal Diamond: The Search for Our True Self*. San Francisco: Jossey-Bass, 2013.

Rothberg, D., and S. Kelly, eds. *Ken Wilber in Dialogue: Conversations with Leading Transpersonal Thinkers*. Wheaton, IL: Quest Books, 1998.

Sanguine, Bruce. *The Advance of Love: Reading the Bible with an Evolutionary Heart*. Vancouver: Evans and Sanguine Publishing, 2012.

Schiller, Friedrich. *On the Aesthetic Education of Man*. Translated by Reginald Snell. Mineola, NY: Dover Publications, 2004.

Schuon, Frithjof. *The Transcendent Unity of Religions*. Wheaton, IL: Quest Books, 1984.

Schleiermacher, Friedrich. *On Religion: Speeches to its Cultured Despisers*. Edited by Richard Crouter. New York: Cambridge University Press, 1998.

Scruton, Roger. *The Soul of the World*. Princeton, NJ: Princeton University Press, 2014.

_____. *Beauty, A Very Short Introduction*. New York: Oxford University Press, 2011.

Smart, Ninian. *Buddhism and Christianity: Rivals and Allies*. Honolulu: University of Hawaii Press, 1993.

Smith, Houston, and David Griffin. *Primordial Truth and Postmodern Theology*. Albany, NY: State University of New York Press, 1989.

Smith, Houston. *Cleansing the Door of Perception*. Berkeley: Council on Spiritual Practices, 2000.

Sprung, Mervyn, ed. *The Problem of Two Truths in Buddhism and Vedanta*. Dordrecht, Holland: D. Reidel Publishing, 1973.

Taylor, Bron. *Dark Green Religion*. Gainesville, FL: University of Florida Press, 2009.

Taylor, Charles. *A Secular Age*. Cambridge, MA: The Belknap Press of Harvard University Press, 2007.

Teilhard de Chardin, Pierre. *The Phenomenon of Man*. New York: Harper & Row, 1955.

Tolle, Eckhart. *The Power of Now*. Novato, CA: New World Library, 2004.

Trungpa, Chogyam. *Training the Mind and Cultivating Loving-Kindness*. Boston: Shambhala, 2003.

Turner, Frederick. *Natural Religion*. Edison, NJ: Transaction Publishers, 2006.

Twiss, Sumner, and Walter Conser, eds. *Experience of the Sacred: Readings in the Phenomenology of Religion*. Hanover, NH: University Press of New England, 1992.

Urantia Foundation. *The Urantia Book*. Chicago: Urantia Foundation, 1955.

Wainright, William, ed. *Oxford Handbook of Philosophy and Religion*. New York: Oxford University Press, 2007.

Warren, Rick. *The Purpose Driven Life*. Grand Rapids, MI: Zondervan, 2002.

Weil, Simone. *Waiting for God*. Translated by Emma Craufurd. New York: G. P. Putnam's Sons, 1951.

Whitehead, Alfred North. *Process and Reality*. New York: Free Press, 1978.

———. *Adventures of Ideas*. New York: Free Press, 1967.

Wilber, Ken. *Sex, Ecology, Spirituality*. Boston: Shambhala, 1995.

———. *A Theory of Everything: An Integral Vision for Business, Politics, Science and Spirituality*. Boston: Shambhala, 2000.

———. *Integral Spirituality: A Startling New Role for Religion in the Modern and Postmodern World*. Boston: Integral Books/Shambhala, 2006.

Wilber, Ken, Terry Patten, Adam Leonard, and Marco Morelli. *Integral Life Practice: A 21st-Century Blueprint for Physical Health, Emotional Balance, Mental Clarity, and Spiritual Awakening*. Boston: Integral Books, 2008.

Wuthnow, Robert. *After Heaven*. Berkeley: University of California Press, 1998.

Wynn, Mark. *God and Goodness: A Natural Theological Perspective*. New York: Routledge, 1999.

INDEX

Note: Page numbers with f indicate figures.

A

Abe, Masao, 198

Absolute Being, 87, 199

Absolute Nothingness, 171, 208

Absolute Self, 128

Absolute unity, 60, 146, 158, 172

Advaita Vedanta Hinduism, 137,
140, 145, 147, 149, 155, 169,
185, 202–4. *See also* Hinduism

Adyashanti, 177

Affirmation, 168

Almaas, A. H., 148, 180

Anthropocentrism, disvalue of,
189–90

Antimodernism, 10, 32

Appeals, Habermas's three avenues
of, 242

Arapura, J. G., 182

Arguments for God, 99–100

Aristotle, 242–43

Aspirituality. *See* Secular
spirituality

Atheism, 27–30. *See also* Secular
spirituality

Atman (the self), 87, 128, 145, 176

Aurobindo, Sri, 7, 73, 196

Awareness, states of, 87, 96

B

Baba, Neem Karoli, 71

Beauty, 53–56, 53f, 71f. *See also*
Primary values

Bergson, Henri, 7, 46

Big bang, 47–48, 186

Brahman, 87, 182, 185, 202–3

Brain

    as antenna for consciousness,
97–98

    spiritual experience and, 95–98

Brain-imaging technologies, 96

Bridging polarities, 67, 68, 165

Buddhism, 8, 12

    existential spiritual polarity and,
154–55, 159–60

    love of God for nondualists and,
209–11

    merger with Hinduism, 137,
147–50, 166–67

goodness, truth, and beauty in,
53–56, 53f, 71f
integral consciousness,
64–68
in integral or evolutionary
worldview, 7–12
overview of, 63
panentheism and (from finite to
infinite), 59–63
perfecting the universe, 72–73
practice of, 63–73
progressive spirituality and,
37–39
purpose and progress and,
56–59
rise of, 5–6
spiritual leadership and,
approach to, 22
teachings of (*See* Spiritual
teachings of evolution)
toward further evolution of
spirituality, 193–220
in transcending progressive
spirituality, 172–74
value metabolism, 69–72
Evolutionary worldview
in evolutionary spirituality,
7–12, 74, 75
evolving consciousness and,
221–25, 240

integral philosophy and, 7–12,
74, 75
merger of Buddhism and
Hinduism and, 166–67
percentage of American
population in stages of, 12f
stages of cultural evolution in,
11–12
Evolution's Purpose (McIntosh), 5,
14, 44, 51, 53, 57, 224, 230
Evolving soul, 175–78
Existential form of perfection, 57
Existentialism, 27. *See also* Secular
spirituality
Existential polarity, 151–61
dialectical epistemology for
engaging, 65, 66, 160
discernment and, 153–54
in evolutionary method, 229, 236
in infinite being and finite
becoming, 107–11
nonduality and postmodernity
and, 154–56
within spiritual experience
itself, 156–61
yin-yang symbol and, 200
Experiences, introvertive and
extrovertive, 86
Experiential form of
perfection, 57

Quest Books

encourages open-minded inquiry into
world religions, philosophy, science, and the arts
in order to understand the wisdom of the ages,
respect the unity of all life, and help people explore
individual spiritual self-transformation.

Its publications are generously supported by
The Kern Foundation,
a trust committed to Theosophical education.

Quest Books is the imprint of
the Theosophical Publishing House,
a division of the Theosophical Society in America.
For information about programs, literature,
on-line study, membership benefits, and international centers,
see www.theosophical.org
or call 800-669-1571 or (outside the U.S.) 630-668-1571.

To order books or a complete Quest catalog,
call 800-669-9425 or (outside the U.S.) 630-665-0130.

McIntosh integrates the experience of nondual emptiness with the experience of a loving Creator, showing how these alternative conceptions of ultimate reality can actually serve to 'true each other up.' This book is a historically significant masterpiece that should be read by every serious spiritual practitioner."

—**Jeff Salzman**, host of the Daily Evolver online program; cofounder of Career Track Training adult education company

"Spirituality is evolving, and *The Presence of the Infinite* is proof. This book is required reading for any serious student of evolutionary spirituality. Steve McIntosh passionately and meticulously gives his well-trained and inspired intellect to his work as a philosopher, seeing philosophy's role in evolving a new worldview as an absolutely critical undertaking, with a mission to balance and integrate our rapidly evolving science and spirituality. Your understanding of your own spirituality will be challenged and clarified if you read this book with a serious heart."

—**Terry Patten**, coauthor of *Integral Life Practice*; creator and host of the online teleseminar series, Beyond Awakening

"*The Presence of the Infinite* establishes McIntosh as one of the leading intellectual authorities in progressive spiritual culture. Erudite, uplifting, and provocative, the book is written by a heart filled with love for Spirit and a razor sharp mind determined to illuminate and integrate theistic and nondual visions of the sacred. Few people have the courage or insight to ask the questions that McIntosh does and to see the evolution of culture through such a magnanimous lens. This is a book that will change the way you think about spiritual experience and the direction of our religious and secular future. Take notice—evolutionary spirituality has an eloquent and formidable new champion."

—**Carter Phipps**, author of *Evolutionaries*; cofounder of the Institute for Cultural Evolution